Social and Historical Approaches to the Bible is essential reading for students of the content and context of the Bible. Adeptly defining, unpacking, and examining several genres of biblical criticism—including chapters each for the historical-grammatical approach, source criticism, form criticism, tradition-historical criticism, redaction criticism, and social-scientific criticism—*Social and Historical Approaches to the Bible* offers clear, readable, and current information about fundamental perspectives and methods used in biblical studies. This is an indispensable handbook for the shelves of biblical students and professionals alike.

Erica Muhaisen, professor of philosophy
at the University of Colorado Denver

T0335138

SOCIAL & HISTORICAL APPROACHES TO THE BIBLE

LEXHAM METHODS SERIES

SOCIAL & HISTORICAL APPROACHES TO THE BIBLE

—

Edited by Douglas Mangum & Amy Balogh

LEXHAM PRESS

Lexham Press, 1313 Commercial St., Bellingham, WA 98225
http://www.lexhampress.com

Print ISBN 9781577996651
Digital ISBN 9781577997061

Lexham Editorial Team: Brandon Benziger, Claire Brubaker, Joel Wilcox and
     Donna Huisjen
Design: Brittany Schrock
Typesetting: ProjectLuz.com

CONTENTS

SERIES PREFACE

The Lexham Methods Series introduces a variety of approaches to biblical interpretation. Due to the field's long history, however, the coverage is necessarily selective. This series focuses on the major areas of critical biblical scholarship and their development from the nineteenth century to the early twenty-first century. While we recognize that theological approaches to interpretation have played an important role in the life of the Church, this series does not engage the wide variety of hermeneutical approaches that arise from specific theological readings of the biblical text.

The methods discussed here include the broad movements in biblical criticism that have helped define how biblical scholars today approach the text. Understanding the basics of textual criticism, source criticism, form criticism, tradition history, redaction criticism, linguistics, social-scientific criticism, canonical criticism, and contemporary literary criticism (rhetorical, structural, narrative, reader-response, post-structural) will help illuminate the assumptions and conclusions found in many scholarly commentaries and articles.

Each approach to biblical interpretation—even those that are not explicitly theological—can be defined according to a guiding presupposition that informs the method.

- **Textual criticism**: Reading the text to identify *errors in transmission* and determine the best text

- **Source criticism**: Reading the text to find the *written sources* the author(s) used

- **Form criticism**: Reading the text to find the *oral traditions* the author(s) used

- **Tradition-historical criticism**: Reconstructing the *historical development of the traditions* identified by form criticism

- **Redaction criticism**: Reading the text to understand *how it was put together* and what message the text was meant to communicate

- **Canonical criticism**: Reading the final form of the text *as Christian and Jewish Scripture*

- **Rhetorical criticism**: Analyzing the text for the *rhetorical effect of the literary devices* the writers used to communicate and persuade

- **Structural criticism**: Analyzing the text *in terms of contrast and oppositions*, recognizing that contrast is believed to be the essence of meaning within a cultural, linguistic, or literary system

- **Narrative criticism**: Reading the text *as a narrative* and paying attention to aspects including plot, theme, and characterization

- **Linguistic approach**: Analyzing the text *using* concepts and theories developed by *linguistics*

- **Social-scientific approach**: Analyzing the text *using* concepts and theories developed in the *social sciences*

The Lexham Methods Series defines these approaches to biblical interpretation, explains their development, outlines their goals and emphases, and identifies their leading proponents. Few interpreters align themselves strictly with any single approach. Contemporary Bible scholars tend to use an eclectic method that draws on the various aspects of biblical criticism outlined above. Many of these methods developed in parallel, mutually influenced each other, and share similar external influences from literary theory and philosophy. Similarly, ideas and questions arising from one approach often directly influenced the field as a whole and have become common currency in biblical studies, even though the method that generated the concepts has been radically reshaped and revised over the years.

In introducing a variety of methods, we will address each method as neutrally as possible, acknowledging both the advantages and limitations of each approach. Our discussion of a particular method or attempts to demonstrate the method should not be construed as an endorsement of that approach to the text. The Lexham Methods Series introduces you to the world of biblical scholarship.

ABBREVIATIONS

REFERENCE WORKS

AEL	*Ancient Egyptian Literature*. M. Lichtheim. 3 vols. 1971–1980.
ANET	*Ancient Near Eastern Texts Relating to the Old Testament*. J. B. Pritchard. 1954.
AYBD	*Anchor Yale Bible Dictionary* (formerly *Anchor Bible Dictionary*). D. N. Freedman. 1992.
BDAG	W. Bauer, F. W. Danker, W. F. Arndt, and F. W. Gingrich. *A Greek-English Lexicon of the New Testament and Other Early Christian Literature*. 3d ed. 1999.
BDB	*Enhanced Brown-Driver-Briggs Hebrew and English Lexicon*
BEB	*Baker Encyclopedia of the Bible*. W. A. Elwell. 2 vols. 1988.
BHRG	*A Biblical Hebrew Reference Grammar*. Christo van der Merwe, Jackie Naudé, and Jan Kroeze. 1999.
COS	*The Context of Scripture*. W. W. Hallo and K. L. Younger. 3 vols. 1997–2003.
DCH	*Dictionary of Classical Hebrew*. D. J. A. Clines. 1993.
DDD	*Dictionary of Deities and Demons in the Bible*. K. van der Toorn, B. Becking, and P. W. van der Horst. 1995.
DJG	*Dictionary of Jesus and the Gospels*. J. B. Green and S. McKnight. 1992.
DLNT	*Dictionary of the Later New Testament and Its Developments*. R. P. Martin and P. H. Davids. 1997.
DNTB	*Dictionary of New Testament Background*. S. E. Porter and C. A. Evans. 2000.

DPL	*Dictionary of Paul and His Letters.* G. F. Hawthorne and R. P. Martin. 1993.
EDB	*Eerdmans Dictionary of the Bible.* D. N. Freedman. 2000.
EDNT	*Exegetical Dictionary of the New Testament.* H. Balz and G. Schneider. 1990–1993.
GKC	*Gesenius' Hebrew Grammar.* E. Kautzsch (ed.) and A. E. Cowley (trans.). 1910.
HALOT	*The Hebrew and Aramaic Lexicon of the Old Testament.* L. Koehler, W. Baumgartner, and J. J. Stamm. 1994–1999.
IBHS	*An Introduction to Biblical Hebrew Syntax.* B. K. Waltke and M. O'Connor. 1990.
IGEL	*An Intermediate Greek-English Lexicon.* 1888.
ISBE	*International Standard Bible Encyclopedia.* Revised ed. G. W. Bromiley. 4 vols. 1979–1988.
JM	*A Grammar of Biblical Hebrew.* P. Joüon and T. Muraoka. Rev. English ed. 2006.
LBD	*Lexham Bible Dictionary.* J. D. Barry. 2012.
LEH	J. Lust, E. Eynikel, and K. Hauspie. *A Greek-English Lexicon of the Septuagint.* Revised ed. 2003.
L&N	J. P. Louw and E. A. Nida. *Greek-English Lexicon of the New Testament: Based on Semantic Domains.* 1989.
LSJ	H. G. Liddell, R. Scott, and H. S. Jones. *A Greek-English Lexicon.* 9th ed. with rev. supp. 1996.
MM	J. H. Moulton and G. Milligan. *The Vocabulary of the Greek Testament.* 1930.
NBD	*New Bible Dictionary,* 3rd ed. D. R. W. Wood. 1996.
NIDNTT	*New International Dictionary of New Testament Theology.* C. Brown. 4 vols. 1975–1985.
NIDOTTE	*New International Dictionary of Old Testament Theology and Exegesis.* W. A. VanGemeren. 5 vols. 1997.
ODCC	*The Oxford Dictionary of the Christian Church.* F. L. Cross and E. A. Livingstone. 2nd ed. 1983.
OTP	*Old Testament Pseudepigrapha.* J. H. Charlesworth. 2 vols. 1983–85.
TDNT	*Theological Dictionary of the New Testament.* G. Kittel and G. Friedrich. 10 vols. 1964–1976.

TLNT	*Theological Lexicon of the New Testament.* C. Spicq. 3 vols. 1994.
TLOT	*Theological Lexicon of the Old Testament.* E. Jenni and C. Westermann. 3 vols. 1997.
TWOT	*Theological Wordbook of the Old Testament.* R. L. Harris and G. L. Archer Jr. 2 vols. 1980.
ZEB	*The Zondervan Encyclopedia of the Bible.* Moisés Silva and M. C. Tenney. 5 vols. 2009.

COMMENTARIES

ACCS	Ancient Christian Commentary on Scripture
AYBC	Anchor Yale Bible Commentary (formerly Anchor Bible Commentary)
BCBC	Believers Church Bible Commentary
BKC	*Bible Knowledge Commentary*
BNTC	Black's New Testament Commentaries
CCS	Continental Commentary Series
FOTL	The Forms of the Old Testament Literature
IBC	Interpretation: A Bible Commentary for Teaching and Preaching
ICC	International Critical Commentary
ITC	International Theological Commentary
K&D	Keil, C. F., and F. Delitzsch. *Commentary on the Old Testament.* 1857–1878. Reprint 1996.
NAC	New American Commentary
NICNT	New International Commentary on the New Testament
NICOT	New International Commentary on the Old Testament
NIGTC	New International Greek Testament Commentary
NIVAC	The NIV Application Commentary
OTL	Old Testament Library
PNTC	The Pillar New Testament Commentary
TNTC	Tyndale New Testament Commentaries
TOTC	Tyndale Old Testament Commentaries
UBCS	Understanding the Bible Commentary Series (formerly the New International Biblical Commentary)
WBC	Word Biblical Commentary

| ZIBBCNT | Zondervan Illustrated Bible Backgrounds Commentary (New Testament) |
| ZIBBCOT | Zondervan Illustrated Bible Backgrounds Commentary (Old Testament) |

JOURNALS

ATJ	Ashland Theological Journal
BA	Biblical Archaeologist
BAR	Biblical Archaeology Review
BBR	Bulletin for Biblical Research
BSac	Bibliotheca Sacra
CBQ	Catholic Biblical Quarterly
CurBS	Currents in Research: Biblical Studies
CurTM	Currents in Theology and Mission
EQ	Evangelical Quarterly
HUCA	Hebrew Union College Annual
JAAR	Journal of the American Academy of Religion
JBL	Journal of Biblical Literature
JETS	Journal of the Evangelical Theological Society
JHS	Journal of Hebrew Scriptures
JNES	Journal of Near Eastern Studies
JNSL	Journal of Northwest Semitic Languages
JR	Journal of Religion
JSNT	Journal for the Study of the New Testament
JSOT	Journal for the Study of the Old Testament
JSSR	Journal for the Scientific Study of Religion
MSJ	The Master's Seminary Journal
NovT	Novum Testamentum
PRSt	Perspectives in Religious Studies
RBL	Review of Biblical Literature
RevExp	Review and Expositor
Them	Themelios
TS	Theological Studies
TynBul	Tyndale Bulletin
USQR	Union Seminary Quarterly Review
VT	Vetus Testamentum

WTJ	*Westminster Theological Journal*

BIBLE VERSIONS

AMP	The Amplified Bible. 1987.
ASV	American Standard Version. 1901.
BHK	*Biblia Hebraica*. R. Kittel. 1905–1973.
BHQ	*Biblia Hebraica Quinta*. A. Schenker. 2004–.
BHS	*Biblia Hebraica Stuttgartensia*. K. Elliger and W. Rudolph. 1977–1997.
CEB	Common English Bible. 2011.
CEV	Contemporary English Version. 1995.
DRB	Douay-Rheims Bible.
ESV	English Standard Version. 2001.
GNT	Good News Translation. 1992.
HCSB	Holman Christian Standard Bible. 2009.
JPS	Jewish Publication Society. 1917.
KJV	King James Version.
LEB	Lexham English Bible. 2012.
LES	Lexham English Septuagint. 2012.
LHB	Lexham Hebrew Bible. 2012.
LXX	Septuagint
MSG	*The Message.* 2005.
MT	Masoretic Text
NA27	Nestle-Aland *Novum Testamentum Graece*. 27th edition. 1993.
NA28	Nestle-Aland *Novum Testamentum Graece*. 28th edition. 2012.
NAB	New American Bible. 1970.
NASB	New American Standard Bible. 1995.
NCV	New Century Version. 2005.
NET	New English Translation. 2005.
NIV	New International Version. 2011.
NIV84	New International Version. 1984.
NJPS	*Tanakh.* Jewish Publication Society. 1985.
NKJV	New King James Version. 1982.
NLT	New Living Translation. 2007.
NRSV	New Revised Standard Version. 1989.
RSV	Revised Standard Version. 1971.

SBLGNT   Greek New Testament: SBL Edition. 2011.
TNIV   Today's New International Version. 2005.
UBS4   United Bible Societies' *Greek New Testament*. 4th edition. 1998.

1

INTRODUCING BIBLICAL CRITICISM

Amy Balogh and Douglas Mangum

Biblical criticism is a broad term that generally refers to the formal academic discipline of studying the content and context of the Bible. Under the umbrella term of "biblical criticism," we find a complicated and wide array of perspectives and methods for approaching the biblical text. These approaches typically share the common ground of critical analysis and evaluation of biblical literature.

1.1 DEFINING BIBLICAL CRITICISM

In its early years, the academic study of the Bible was divided into two main groups—higher criticism and lower criticism. "Lower criticism" was another name for what is now known as "textual criticism," an approach with the goal of confirming or recovering the best reading from the available textual witnesses (i.e., manuscript evidence). Determining the best (or most likely to be original) text logically precedes a "higher"-level analysis of the text's content. "Higher criticism" is an older label for something like what we today call "biblical criticism"—the process of making evaluative judgments about the literary content of the biblical text. Higher criticism of the Bible, however, was initially limited to the issues of authorship, date, and composition of biblical books, which consumed the attention of Bible scholars in the nineteenth and early twentieth centuries. As Norman Geisler explains, "Lower criticism has to do with the *text* of

Scripture, and higher criticism with the *source* of that text."[1] Few scholars today use these labels of higher and lower criticism, but they are common in older publications.

1.1.1 WHAT IS "CRITICISM"?

Today, the word "criticism" commonly has negative connotations, and "biblical criticism" could be easily misunderstood as "criticizing" the Bible in a negative way. Most English dictionaries list this negative sense first. For example, the first entry in *Merriam-Webster's Collegiate Dictionary* says that "criticism" is "the act of criticizing usually unfavorably."[2] In this case, "criticizing" means "finding fault." With "biblical criticism" the second entry is more relevant: criticism is "the art of evaluating or analyzing works of art or literature." *Merriam-Webster's* provides a third definition of criticism as "the scientific investigation of literary documents (as the Bible) in regard to such matters as origin, text, composition, or history."[3] This third definition reflects well the concerns of the approaches to biblical interpretation surveyed in this volume, but our working definition is that biblical criticism is the academic evaluation and analysis of the biblical text.

1.1.2 THE DISCIPLINE OF BIBLICAL CRITICISM

As "literary criticism" refers broadly to the intellectual study of literature, so "biblical criticism" refers broadly to the intellectual study of the Bible. However, this label should be understood as limited to the study of the Bible as a formal academic discipline over the last few hundred years. With such a limited scope, biblical criticism does not include ancient and medieval biblical interpretation. Likewise, not all contemporary study of the Bible qualifies as biblical criticism, since criticism implies a rationalistic perspective on the text (that is, concerned with evidence evaluated by use of reason). Many aspects of biblical research that emphasize spiritual, devotional, or emotional responses to the text do not fall under the umbrella of biblical criticism.

---

1. Norman L. Geisler, *Systematic Theology*, vol. 1, *Introduction, Bible* (Minneapolis: Fortress, 2002), 316.
2. *Merriam-Webster's Collegiate Dictionary*, 11th ed., s.v. "criticism."
3. *Merriam-Webster's Collegiate Dictionary*, 11th ed., s.v. "criticism."

According to John Barton, the term "biblical criticism" is "somewhat outmoded" as a name for the academic discipline of biblical studies.[4] He notes how "biblical criticism" as defined above covers scholarship typically labeled generically as "biblical studies," "biblical interpretation," or the "historical-critical method" (on the latter, see chapter 2 of the present volume, on "The Historical-Grammatical Approach"). While Barton is hesitant to apply "biblical criticism" in the same broad sense as "literary criticism," he acknowledges that "biblical criticism means a particular *type* of study of the Bible," not all study of the Bible.[5]

1.1.3 THE ASSUMPTIONS OF BIBLICAL CRITICISM

The "particular type" of biblical study represented by biblical criticism is defined by an evaluative, descriptive, and analytical stance toward the biblical text. Biblical criticism works on the following assumptions. First, it is focused on careful analysis of written texts that requires interpretations to be founded on textual, often grammatical or lexicographical, evidence and rational argument, not intuition, emotion, or revelation. Second, this reliance on evidence and reason requires the critic to approach the text with a certain level of openness. This perspective does not entail a level of antagonism toward the text. Rather, the reader should simply read carefully and question the apparent meaning of the text, considering the possibility that the text may have a more complex meaning than what appears at first glance. This assumption separates many critical readings from theological or ideological readings because the critic does not accept an interpretation immediately and without question. Rather, the critic works with the wording and historical context of the text in order to arrive at an interpretation.

A third assumption for biblical criticism is that texts have an inherent and objective meaning that can be discerned. According to E. D. Hirsch, "*Meaning* is that which is represented by a text; it is what the author meant by his use of a particular sign sequence; it is what the signs represent."[6]

---

4. John Barton, *The Nature of Biblical Criticism* (Louisville, KY: Westminster John Knox, 2007), 1.

5. Barton, *Biblical Criticism*, 2. Emphasis original.

6. E. D. Hirsch, Jr., *Validity in Interpretation* (New Haven, CT: Yale University Press, 1967), 8. Emphasis original.

While completely unbiased objectivity on the part of the interpreter is now recognized as an unattainable ideal, it does not negate that an author produces a text with the goal of communication, and it therefore assumes meaning is there to be discovered. Many critics have substituted the modernist assumption of their own objectivity for a postmodern self-awareness that acknowledges the theological, ideological, and philosophical presuppositions that they bring to the text and attempts to correct for those and read the text on its own terms—finding meaning in the text itself and not bringing meaning to the text.[7]

1.1.4 THE GOAL OF BIBLICAL CRITICISM

The ultimate goal of biblical criticism is simply a better understanding of the text's meaning.[8] This statement of the goal may come as a surprise, since, as mentioned above, "criticism" still has a negative connotation in some circles. Approaching the text as a "critic" has popularly been taken as an indication of an interpreter's goal to disprove and discredit the Bible. In this popular (but mistaken) caricature of biblical scholarship, the critic sets out to prove the truth claims of the Bible must be false. Individual critics inevitably approach the text with biases and presuppositions, but scholars disagree whether those biases and presuppositions are an inherent part of the method itself (see §1.2 The Need for Caution with Biblical Criticism below).[9] While it is true that some interpreters

---

7. Traditional criticism affirms the possibility of a reasonable level of objectivity and focuses on text-based meaning. Many literary approaches that still fall under the label of "biblical criticism" focus on the role of the reader and the audience in generating meaning. The debate over the locus of "meaning" in literary criticism is discussed further in Douglas Mangum and Douglas Estes, eds., *Literary Approaches to the Bible*, Lexham Methods Series 4 (Bellingham, WA: Lexham Press, 2017).

8. Peter H. Davids says, "The goal of the biblical scholar is, in the end, to understand better the meaning of the text" ("Authority, Hermeneutics, and Criticism," in *Interpreting the New Testament*, ed. David Alan Black and David S. Dockery [Nashville: Broadman & Holman, 2001], 12). Similarly, John Barton concludes, "Biblical criticism, seen positively, is a productive and mature discipline, which sets itself the task of understanding the biblical text" (*Biblical Criticism*, 7–8).

9. The extent to which people are constrained and influenced by the biases and presuppositions of their social, cultural, and historical situations is a matter of great debate across disciplines in the humanities and social sciences due largely to the questions raised by postmodernism. While not everyone has been satisfied by the answers offered by postmodern theory, A. K. M. Adam notes, "Even critics who believe that postmodernism is gravely misguided recognize that these multifarious movements have taught philosophy, theology,

throughout history have had an agenda to prove the Bible false, an honest application of the critical method requires the interpreter to avoid any a priori elimination of possible interpretive options.[10] Biblical scholar Joseph Fitzmyer states it this way:

> [The biblical texts] have to be analyzed against their proper human and historical backgrounds, in their contemporary contexts, and in their original languages. In effect, this method applies to the Bible all the critical techniques of classical philology, and in doing so it refuses a priori to exclude any critical analysis in its quest for the meaning of the text.[11]

If the goal of biblical criticism is a better understanding of the text, then the interpreter should be initially open to all the options and not arrive at the text with some conclusions already discarded. This common misunderstanding about the goal of biblical criticism—that it is about disproving the text rather than understanding the text—is at the heart of the suspicion and controversy over using academic methods to examine the Bible.

1.2 THE NEED FOR CAUTION WITH BIBLICAL CRITICISM

Biblical criticism, as defined above, is part of the larger enterprise of biblical interpretation. Complete interpretation, for a Christian interpreter, involves theological conclusions and contemporary application of the text for the benefit of believers. Biblical criticism is not inherently opposed to theology or contemporary application, but the work of the critic generally focuses on the past, leaving the present to the theologian. The complex

---

and biblical interpretation some important lessons" (*What Is Postmodern Biblical Criticism?* [Minneapolis: Fortress, 1995], xiii).

10. Much of the debate over whether biblical criticism is an appropriate approach for Christians stems from opponents of critical methodology insisting that the method is inextricably bound up with the biases and presuppositions of its early practitioners—some of whom approached the text from a strongly rational, naturalistic perspective, rejecting a priori the possibility of miracles or divine intervention in history. Many Christian scholars are willing to concede that critical tools can be utilized effectively and positively without undermining biblical authority. See Davids, "Authority," 9; Joseph A. Fitzmyer, "Historical Criticism: Its Role in Biblical Interpretation and Church Life," *Theological Studies* 50, no. 2 (1989): 244-59.

11. Fitzmyer, "Historical Criticism," 249.

issues involved with interpretation and application are addressed in many introductory texts on hermeneutics and exegesis.[12]

1.2.1 TERMINOLOGY

Discussions of method or findings in biblical interpretation often run a high risk of misunderstanding due to widespread use of shared vocabulary without widespread agreement on definitions. In other words, interpretations are likely to be misinterpreted. The most commonly used but potentially misunderstood terms are "hermeneutics," "exegesis," and "meaning."[13] Hermeneutics, in its most basic sense, refers to the methodological principles of interpretation. In practice, the term is used somewhat haphazardly to refer to anything from specific techniques of interpretation to the search for a text's contemporary relevance to the interpretive process as a whole.[14] The term "exegesis" is used to refer to both the process of interpretation and the resulting interpretation of a specific text.[15] Fitzmyer says that exegesis "seeks to draw out the meaning of the passage intended by

---

12. Recent introductory texts on biblical interpretation include the following: Stanley E. Porter and Jason C. Robinson, *Hermeneutics: An Introduction to Interpretive Theory* (Grand Rapids: Eerdmans, 2011); Anthony C. Thiselton, *Hermeneutics: An Introduction* (Grand Rapids: Eerdmans, 2009); Corrine L. Carvalho, *Primer on Biblical Methods* (Winona, MN: Anselm Academic, 2009); Jeannine K. Brown, *Scripture as Communication: Introducing Biblical Hermeneutics* (Grand Rapids: Baker Academic, 2007); Walter C. Kaiser and Moisés Silva, *Introduction to Biblical Hermeneutics: The Search for Meaning*, rev. and expanded ed. (Grand Rapids: Zondervan, 2007); Grant R. Osborne, *The Hermeneutical Spiral: A Comprehensive Introduction to Biblical Interpretation*, rev. and expanded 2nd ed. (Downers Grove, IL: InterVarsity Press, 2006); William W. Klein, Craig L. Blomberg, and Robert L. Hubbard, *Introduction to Biblical Interpretation* (Nashville: Thomas Nelson, 2003); Bruce Corley, Steve Lemke, and Grant Lovejoy, eds., *Biblical Hermeneutics: A Comprehensive Introduction to Interpreting Scripture*, 2nd ed. (Nashville, TN: Broadman & Holman, 2002); Roger Lundin, Clarence Walhout, and Anthony C. Thiselton, *The Promise of Hermeneutics* (Grand Rapids: Eerdmans, 1999); Steven L. McKenzie and Stephen R. Haynes, eds., *To Each Its Own Meaning: An Introduction to Biblical Criticisms and Their Application* (Louisville: Westminster John Knox, 1999); Moisés Silva et al., *Foundations of Contemporary Interpretation: Six Volumes in One* (Grand Rapids: Zondervan, 1996); Gerhard Maier, *Biblical Hermeneutics*, trans. Robert W. Yarbrough (Wheaton, IL: Crossway, 1994).

13. The dictionary definition of "hermeneutics" is "the study of the methodological principles of interpretation" (*Merriam-Webster's Collegiate Dictionary*, 11th ed., s.v. "hermeneutic"). "Exegesis" is defined as "an explanation or critical interpretation of a text" (*Merriam-Webster's Collegiate Dictionary*, 11th ed., s.v. "exegesis").

14. On the conflicting and confusing use of terms like "hermeneutics" and "exegesis," see Robert L. Thomas, "Current Hermeneutical Trends: Toward Explanation or Obfuscation?" *JETS* 39, no. 2 (1996): 241–56, especially 243–45.

15. Osborne, *Hermeneutical Spiral*, 21.

the inspired writer" and includes "religious and theological meaning" as part of that process.[16] Here, meaning is understood as the conclusion or takeaway of the process of exegesis—and there may often be more than one possible meaning.

1.2.2 PRESUPPOSITIONS

The critical method has been associated with presuppositions that call into question the Bible's status as sacred and authoritative Scripture, so the method itself has been pronounced guilty by association even though those presuppositions are not a necessary part of biblical criticism.[17] In defining biblical criticism here, we have been careful to emphasize that "critical" means analyzing, not attacking. That distinction has not always held true for all interpreters. The rise of biblical criticism as a methodology in the eighteenth and nineteenth centuries was accompanied by rationalist rejection of the supernatural along with intellectual skepticism about the dogmatic claims of traditional Christian theology.[18] Fitzmyer notes that with these interpreters the "fault was the presupposition with which the method was used, and not with the method itself."[19] However, the solution is not found in "presuppositionless" interpretation—the impossible ideal of a completely neutral and detached perspective on the text. The act of understanding a text at all depends on a variety of decisions made on the basis of preliminary assumptions. For example, we understand the meaning of a simple sentence, such as "She tests bears," based on prior experience of how the parts, individual words, fit into a whole—the syntax of the clause. We read "tests" as a present-tense, singular verb, not a plural noun, because it comes in the sentence at the point where we expect the verb. Changing the word order—"She bears tests"—changes the sentence because of our conventional knowledge about how the parts fit together. Now we read "bears" as the present-tense, singular verb, not a plural noun.

---

16. Fitzmyer, "Historical Criticism," 254.

17. Fitzmyer, "Historical Criticism," 252.

18. Schweitzer notes how a hatred for the "supernatural nimbus" that had come to surround the figure of Jesus motivated numerous earlier studies on the historical Jesus (Albert Schweitzer, *The Quest of the Historical Jesus: A Critical Study of Its Progress from Reimarus to Wrede*, trans. W. Montgomery, 2nd ed. [London: Adam and Charles Black, 1911], 4).

19. Fitzmyer, "Historical Criticism," 252.

A reader who made a different assumption would likely soon correct it based on context for a simple sentence such as this, but all experienced readers are undoubtedly familiar with times when they have had to reread sentences because they made the wrong assumption about how a word fit into the sentence.

Linguistic knowledge is just one area where prior understandings affect interpretation, but the influence of philosophical and theological presuppositions works along the same lines. These ideological commitments are what people generally associate with presuppositions, prejudices, or biases. Unfortunately, people are not always aware of their presuppositions. For example, Graham Stanton notes that despite a scholar's claim to have written his history of Jesus by setting aside all commitments to particular interpretations, that scholar's "own prejudices and assumptions were clearly revealed on almost every page."[20] While it is impossible to avoid all presuppositions, it is possible to minimize their influence. Postmodern philosophy brought attention to the role presuppositions and assumptions have on interpretation. Drawing attention to this role has had the positive effect of making interpreters pay more attention to explicitly articulating their own philosophical and theological commitments instead of insisting they have none.

As an example, Fitzmyer explains how he uses the historical-critical method while still holding to specific elements of faith. In his view, use of the tools provided by the critical method always consists of the method plus the interpreter's presupposition about how it should be employed. For a confessional interpreter, Fitzmyer believes that historical-critical exegesis should be combined with "elements of faith" or "faith presuppositions":

> For the plus consists of elements of faith: that the book being critically interpreted contains God's Word set forth in human words of long ago; that it has been composed under the guidance of the Spirit and has authority for the people of the Jewish-Christian heritage; that it is part of a restricted collection of sacred, authoritative writings (part of a canon); that it has been given by God to His people for

20. Graham N. Stanton, "Presuppositions in New Testament Criticism," in *New Testament Interpretation*, ed. I. Howard Marshall (Milton Keynes, UK; Waynesboro, GA: Paternoster, 1977), 65.

their edification and salvation; and that it is properly expounded only in relation to the Tradition that has grown out of it within the communal faith-life of that people.

Because the historical-critical method is per se neutral, it can be used with such faith presuppositions. Indeed, by reason of them it becomes a properly-oriented method of biblical interpretation, for none of the elements of the method is pursued in and for itself.[21]

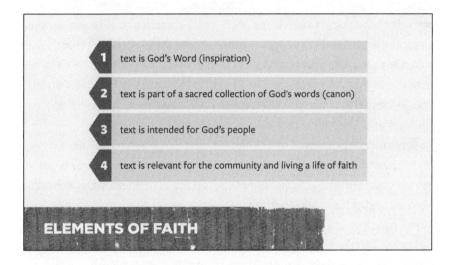

1 text is God's Word (inspiration)

2 text is part of a sacred collection of God's words (canon)

3 text is intended for God's people

4 text is relevant for the community and living a life of faith

ELEMENTS OF FAITH

Different ideological commitments will lead others to approach the text with different presuppositions—even those critical of faith. However, a negative stance toward religious belief is not an inherent part of biblical criticism.

1.2.3 BIBLICAL CRITICISM AND FAITH

Biblical criticism has great potential to challenge a person's faith. On the one hand, this potential to challenge has caused some scholars to reject biblical criticism altogether. They hold the method responsible for undermining believers' faith, especially their faith in the Bible as God's word. On the other hand, many scholars who enter the academic field of biblical studies with a faith commitment welcome the challenge biblical criticism presents and find that it actually enhances their engagement with

---

21. Fitzmyer, "Historical Criticism," 254–55.

the biblical text.[22] Despite fundamental disagreements over method, Alan Johnson urges evangelical scholars toward "unity (not uniformity) and true evangelical ecumenicity in this important area of our work."[23]

1.2.3.a Against the Use of Biblical Criticism

Scholars who stand against the use of biblical criticism in their search for the meaning of the text do so with the understanding that Christian intellectual pursuits should always be framed by and lead to a particular "orthodox" theology.[24] Such thinkers reject the challenge of engaging and wrestling with understandings of the nature of the biblical text that do not coincide with their preexisting views. This rejection has led these authors to apply to biblical criticism labels such as "negative criticism" (Geisler) and "destructive criticism" (Geisler), while sometimes characterizing its findings as a "diabolical reconstruction" of history (Harris).[25]

Arguments presented by scholars in this camp generally share three main characteristics. First, they prioritize tradition over critical inquiry, even if that tradition originates outside the Bible.[26] For example, Robert L. Thomas begins his essay "Historical Criticism and the Evangelical: Another View" by appealing to a church tradition that assumes that the Synoptic Gospels—Matthew, Mark, and Luke—were all written independently of one another.[27] He then spends the remainder of the article (in addition to

---

22. The debate over whether critical methods are appropriate for evangelical Christian scholars has gone on for decades. The issue came to the forefront of evangelical scholarship in the 1970s and 1980s with many articles appearing in the *Journal of the Evangelical Theological Society* (*JETS*) arguing for or against the adoption of critical methods. For a balanced introduction to the issues at stake, see Alan F. Johnson, "The Historical-Critical Method: Egyptian Gold or Pagan Precipice?" *JETS* 26 (1983): 3–15. For another survey of the debate, see Grant R. Osborne, "Round Four: The Redaction Debate Continues," *JETS* 28 (1985): 399–410.

23. Johnson, "Historical-Critical Method," 15.

24. Many of these scholars apply the adjective "orthodox" to faith and doctrine, but do not explain what exactly these beliefs ought to entail.

25. Norman L. Geisler, "Beware of Philosophy: A Warning to Biblical Scholars," *JETS* 42, no. 1 (1999): 3–19; Geisler, "The History of Destructive Biblical Criticism" in *Systematic Theology* (Minneapolis: Fortress, 2002), 1:315–49; R. Laird Harris, *Exploring the Basics of the Bible* (Wheaton, IL: Crossway, 2002), 79.

26. This tendency is also noted and critiqued in Christopher M. Hays, "Towards a Faithful Criticism," in *Evangelical Faith and the Challenge of Historical Criticism*, ed. Christopher M. Hays and Christopher B. Ansberry (London: SPCK, 2013), 1–23.

27. Robert L. Thomas, "Historical Criticism and the Evangelical: Another View," *JETS* 43 (2000): 97–111. Osborne points out the flaws of this approach in Grant R. Osborne, "Historical

other pieces he has written) rejecting the working theories and assumptions held by the majority of New Testament scholars, who believe that the texts of the Synoptic Gospels share some sort of literary dependence, either on one another or on common sources. Some have even gone so far as to talk about "two Bibles," one that is the result of biblical criticism and another that is the scriptural word of God for believers.[28]

Second, arguments against the coexistence of faith and criticism are usually on the offensive, pushing against biblical criticism rather than offering an apologetic defense of orthodoxy itself. For example, in his presidential address to the Evangelical Theological Society in 1998, titled "Beware of Philosophy: A Warning to Biblical Scholars" (later published in *JETS*), Norman Geisler systematically lists each major philosophical movement since the Enlightenment and explains the specific danger he believes each poses to an evangelical Christian worldview.[29] Geisler includes historical criticism of the Bible at the end of this list and goes on to offer advice as to how to guard against philosophy in general, lest the scholar "fall prey to its subtle influences on his theology."[30] He then concludes by stating that "preserving orthodoxy ... is spiritual warfare," and therefore one ought to know the enemy so as to best defend against it.[31]

Finally, arguments against biblical criticism often set it up as a "straw man" by overstating its conclusions and providing caricatures of it supporters. For example, references to critics as "the unbelieving type" who claim that "the Bible is a mass of falsehood (as the liberal critics teach)" or compare modern biblical scholars to "those who are unstable and distort the Scripture to their own destruction" (2 Pet 3:16) are harsh at best and misrepresentative at worst.[32] While there are examples of scholars who are not "believers" or who suggest that the Bible is not "true," there is a whole spectrum of positions between the extremes of "orthodox" and "liberal" that argue that critical inquiry and faith go hand in hand.

Criticism: A Brief Response to Robert Thomas's 'Other View,' " *JETS* 43 (2000): 113–17.

28. Robert W. Yarbrough, "Should Evangelicals Embrace Historical Criticism? The Hays-Ansberry Proposal," *Them* 39, no. 1 (2014): 49.

29. Geisler, "Beware of Philosophy."

30. Geisler, "Beware of Philosophy," 14.

31. Geisler, "Beware of Philosophy," 18.

32. These examples are drawn from Harris, *Exploring the Basics of the Bible*, 77–78.

1.2.3.b For the Use of Biblical Criticism

Scholars who argue for a positive relationship between faith and biblical criticism often pair their specific arguments with a general call for caution in the application of critical methods and in the process of drawing conclusions. Grant Osborne insists that he and other evangelicals who endorse the use of biblical criticism have always urged "a cautious use" of such critical tools.[33] Donald Hagner also advocates "a reasonable and cautious Biblical criticism."[34]

Biblical criticism does not necessarily lead to radical denial of the historicity of the figures and events described in the biblical text, nor does it force theology out the window; the determining factors are the spirit in which a person performs biblical criticism (e.g., skepticism, optimism) and their ability to bring into dialogue preexisting commitments and new analytical findings.[35] In other words, the assumptions and presuppositions of the interpreter, as discussed above, affect how critical approaches are used. Evangelical scholars such as Osborne and Hagner believe that critical methods can be applied without accepting assumptions that are antithetical to faith, such as the a priori rejection of the possibility of miracles or other supernatural occurrences.[36]

Theologians such as Carl F. H. Henry and Millard Erickson also express the view that biblical criticism can be used constructively, even while they warn strongly against its potential misuse.[37] Henry writes:

---

33. Osborne, "Round Four," 400.

34. Donald A. Hagner, "Interpreting the Gospels: The Landscape and the Quest," *JETS* 24 (1981): 37.

35. For an example of this kind of scholarship, see Grant R. Osborne, "Historical Criticism and the Evangelical," *JETS* 42, no. 2 (1999): 193–210. This article and Osborne's later piece, "Historical Criticism: A Brief Response," are both in dialogue with the volume *The Jesus Crisis: The Inroads of Historical Criticism into Evangelical Scholarship*, ed. Robert L. Thomas and F. David Farnell (Grand Rapids: Kregel, 1998), and Thomas' follow-up article, "Historical Criticism and the Evangelical: Another View."

36. Hagner argues that even though evangelicals "cannot accept the vitiating and unsubstantiated presuppositions of modern scholarship," they should still be ready to "reach out and affirm the truth that is there, thus showing that the truth of scholarship is not necessarily inimical to the faith of orthodox Christianity" ("Interpreting the Gospels," 37).

37. Carl F. H. Henry, "The Uses and Abuses of Historical Criticism," in *God, Revelation and Authority* (Wheaton, IL: Crossway Books, 1999), 4:385–404; Millard J. Erickson, "Theology and Critical Study of the Bible," in *Christian Theology*, 2nd ed. (Grand Rapids: Baker Academic, 1998), 85–114.

Freed from the arbitrary assumptions of critics who manipulate it in a partisan way, the method is neither destructive of biblical truth nor useless to Christian faith; even though its proper role is a limited one, it is highly serviceable as a disciplined investigative approach to past historical events.[38]

Similarly, Erickson emphasizes that the assumptions with which critical methods are employed make the difference, since they can be "based on assumptions that are consistent with the full authority of the Bible."[39] Henry and Erickson both also provide guidelines for using biblical criticism responsibly. Their guidelines promote the cautious use of critical methodologies endorsed by Hagner, Osborne, and others.

The divisive rhetoric of those opposed to biblical criticism contrasts with Johnson's call for unity. Johnson recognizes the importance of "those who would rightly warn us against the danger of unbelief expressed in our methods," but he supports a patient, thoughtful, and civil attitude toward evangelical scholars who use critical methods in their "believing interpretation" of the Bible because they all share the same goal of "deeper appreciation of sacred Scripture and its full appropriation to our lives and to the mission of the Church in our age."[40]

1.3 DEVELOPMENT OF SOCIAL & HISTORICAL APPROACHES

Many books and articles on biblical interpretation refer or allude to three interrelated areas of critical investigation: the world *behind* the text, the world *of* the text, and the world the text *creates*.[41] This volume deals with the main tools scholars use to understand the world *behind* the text (the social, cultural, and historical world of the Bible) and the world *of* the text (the actions, events, and ideas described by the text). These approaches look into where and how the text originated, with whom, and to what end. Generally speaking, understanding the worlds *behind* and *of* the text

---

38. Henry, *God, Revelation, and Authority*, 401.
39. Erickson, *Christian Theology*, 114.
40. Johnson, "Historical-Critical Method," 14–15.
41. For example, see Carvalho, *Primer on Biblical Methods*.

means working to understand the authors' language, the literary and oral sources they may have used, their techniques of composition and compilation, and the ideological goals that informed their decision-making. Literary criticism and social, historical criticism share an interest in the world *of* the text, but contemporary literary criticism tends to focus on the world the text *creates*.[42]

The historical-grammatical approach (chapter 2) is a tool used whenever an interpreter seeks to understand a particular word or phrase in the original language of the passage at hand (e.g., Hebrew, Aramaic, Greek). This type of analysis involves looking up the range of meanings a word or combination of words may have had in antiquity; this sometimes also involves looking up cognate terms from related languages and cultures. Most forms of biblical criticism begin here, as a first step toward understanding broader issues, but there have been and continue to be scholars dedicated to this approach alone. These are the scholars who create the tools, such as lexicons and grammars, that other scholars use in their research.

The next four approaches covered in this volume—source, form, tradition-historical, and redaction criticisms—are intimately related. All of these methods are defined and described in more detail in their respective chapters, but we offer a concise definition of each here to highlight the primary distinctions among the methods.

- Source criticism (chapter 3) looks for evidence that the biblical text was compiled from earlier, written sources. Source criticism is often associated with research on the Pentateuch and the Synoptic Gospels. The "Documentary Hypothesis," which describes the Pentateuch as a combination of four earlier sources, is an example of source criticism.

- Form criticism (chapter 4) considers whether the Bible was composed from oral, rather than written, sources. Form critics look for the social and historical setting behind these oral traditions, but they also classify biblical texts according to genre and list typical features that should be associated with certain genres. The categorization of psalms according to typical

---

42. For more on literary criticism, see Mangum and Estes, *Literary Approaches to the Bible*.

patterns—such as complaint psalm, thanksgiving psalm, or royal psalm—is an example of form criticism.

- Tradition-historical criticism (chapter 5) looks for evidence of the development of biblical traditions and attempts to explain how those traditions developed from their early forms into the written form found in the biblical text. One example is the idea that the Pentateuch grew around an ancient Israelite confession of faith (identified with Deuteronomy 26:5–9) that gave the people a common religious identity.[43]

- Redaction criticism (chapter 6) looks for evidence indicating how the Bible was compiled and edited (or redacted) into longer, literary texts. The method often builds on aspects of source and form criticism, but redaction criticism is concerned with how the text came to be in its final, biblical form. Redaction critics attempt to explain what motivated the editors to shape the biblical text in a particular direction. For example, while source critics separate the flood narrative of Genesis 6–9 into two sources, redaction critics look into how, why, and to what effect the two sources may have been combined.

Without such summarizing statements, it can be easy to lose sight of where one of these criticisms begins and another ends, especially once they are put into practice. It is important to keep in mind that all of these criticisms are tools in a toolbox; most scholars begin with a project or problem and only later decide which critical tools they will use to perform their analysis. In most modern scholarship, the interpreter declares their method at the outset, which allows them to then move freely between approaches throughout their work. Rarely do scholars pause and declare that they are now putting down one criticism to pick up another.

Finally, we end this volume with a chapter dedicated to social-scientific criticism (chapter 7). The social-scientific approach is, in many ways, a

---

43. Gerhard von Rad developed a theory of the growth of Israelite religion and the composition of the Pentateuch that began with the idea that Deuteronomy 26:5–9 reflected the earliest, oral stage of Israel's confession of faith. For further discussion, see chapter 5, §5.2.1.

culmination of the methods that precede it, as it emerged in the latter half of the twentieth century as biblical critics recognized that the social sciences—including anthropology, sociology, psychology, history, and linguistics—had developed theories and concepts that could help explain the social, cultural, and historical world of the Bible. With the perspective that the biblical texts are both reflections of and responses to the ancient worlds that its authors and audiences inhabited, social-scientific criticism seeks to understand the historical occasions and circumstances that inspired the biblical writings.

APPROACH	FOCUS
Historical-grammatical criticism	Meaning of a word or group of words
Source criticism	Preexisting textual sources and their historical setting
Form criticism	Oral traditions and their social and historical setting
Tradition-historical criticism	Development of older oral or written traditions into their biblical form.
Redaction criticism	The method and ideology of the compilers of the material
Social-scientific criticism	Social and historical contexts relevant for understanding the biblical text.

APPROACHES COVERED

The methods discussed in chapters 2 through 6 are all part of the social-scientific critic's toolbox, but the other tools in the interpreter's kit vary widely. The precise identification of these tools depends on which of the social sciences the interpreter brings to bear on the biblical text. This is perhaps the most fruitful approach to understanding the "world *behind* the text" yet, as it encourages the interpreter to analyze the Bible from multiple angles, to use the bodies of knowledge made available through different disciplines, and to draw from a variety of skill sets and methods that have been tried and tested throughout the academy.

1.4 CONCLUSION

Most biblical scholars are willing to admit that the various methods used in biblical criticism (those discussed in this volume and others) are just as open to critique as the texts they are designed to analyze.[44] This is why it is helpful to think of the various forms of biblical criticism—historical-grammatical, source, form, tradition-historical, redaction, social-scientific, and so on—as tools in a toolbox. Each one has a specific function, and the result of its application is highly dependent on the skill with which a person uses it. Just because a hammer can be used to smash something does not mean its only function is destruction; it means that one must receive training in how to use it constructively. In fact, boycotting critical methods does not shield people from its findings; "it simply deprives them of guidance and wisdom in engaging with those ideas."[45]

Furthermore, a specific job may require a number of tools at different stages of the project. Just as not every job can or should be performed with a hammer, so there is no one method that does everything a biblical interpreter may set out to do. In this way, biblical criticism is a craft that entails command of a variety of approaches and knowledge of which approach is most appropriate for which task. Biblical criticism is not the only way of engaging the biblical text; it may also be engaged theologically, which many hold to be a separate, though related, project.[46]

The toolbox approach to biblical criticism, in addition to the ability to apply its methods, frees the scholar to make an informed and mindful decision about their scholarship. If the scholar wants to know more about the underlying forms of the biblical text, they may choose to begin with form criticism; if their questions are of a social nature, they may begin with tradition-historical criticism and move into social-scientific. Of course, the toolbox approach also requires that the scholar be aware of their own role, voice, and goals—whether scholarly, confessional, personal, or otherwise—in advance of performing their analysis. Hays and Ansberry refer to this as having "faithful criticism and a critical faith," meaning that scholars who are also people of faith ought to engage the Bible with both academic, intellectual honesty and a faith-based eagerness to challenge

---

44. John Piper, "Historical Criticism in the Dock: Recent Developments in Germany," *JETS* 23, no. 4 (1980): 331.

45. Christopher B. Ansberry and Christopher M. Hays, "Faithful Criticism and a Critical Faith," in *Evangelical Faith and the Challenge of Historical Criticism*, 205–6. See also Yarbrough, "Should Evangelicals Embrace Historical Criticism?"

46. By contrast, Ansberry and Hays argue for accepting the "mutual influence of historical-critical and theological approaches" ("Faithful Criticism and a Critical Faith," 207–9).

one's assumptions for a better understanding of the text. This emphasizes the notion that biblical criticism is, in and of itself, a lifestyle of faith.[47]

Edgar Krentz adopts a similar argument with the declaration, "Criticism is *confessionally* responsible exegesis today."[48] From the perspective of Krentz and others, critical tools are not only useful in the search for the biblical text's meaning but are indeed *necessary* for responsible interpretation. Critical perspectives are necessary because they force the interpreter to base their conclusions on the text alone. Contrary to the notion that biblical criticism denigrates the biblical text, biblical criticism elevates the text and places it at the absolute center. In so doing, biblical criticism more often than not decenters whatever assumptions and presuppositions about the Bible that a person has brought with them.

However, whether evangelical biblical criticism actually prioritizes the text itself has been challenged. In his review of the book *Evangelical Faith and the Challenge of Historical Criticism*, edited by Christopher M. Hays and Christopher B. Ansberry, Christopher Rollston critiques the way Hays and Ansberry handle the challenges biblical criticism presents to Christian theology, noting that since they "have predetermined that some religious dogmas are nonnegotiable," they have effectively prioritized doctrine over the text itself—"the actual biblical text, therefore, is placed in bondage to religious dogma."[49] In other words, if the interpreter is still restricted by certain theological commitments, then the content of the text itself is not the main determining factor for interpretation. This is where the intention of the interpreter comes into play—are we willing to let the Bible challenge, and even change, our thoughts and beliefs about what we assume or have been taught about what the Bible says?

Evaluating the conclusions of biblical criticism by whether they undermine particular Christian doctrines is problematic because there are many instances in which biblical interpretations present strong challenges to different theological positions. Many theological disagreements also involve

---

47. Ansberry and Hays, "Faithful Criticism and a Critical Faith," 207–13.

48. Edgar Krentz, "Historical Criticism and Confessional Commitment," *CurTM* 15, no. 1 (1988): 131. Emphasis original.

49. Christopher A. Rollston, review of Christopher M. Hays and Christopher B. Ansberry, eds., *Evangelical Faith and the Challenge of Historical Criticism* (London: SPCK, 2013), *RBL* (2016), www.bookreviews.org/bookdetail.asp?TitleId=10145&CodePage=930,10145,7601,8651,3944.

disagreement over the interpretation of relevant biblical texts, regardless of how the competing interpretations came to be. This is where the individual or collective interpreter(s) have to make a decision. One can either reject the findings of biblical criticism, reject the doctrine or dogma in question, or find a compromise between the two. This requires discernment and a full weighing of the competing positions.

Regardless of one's initial (or final) position on the biblical text, the act of placing it at the center of discussions of its own meaning and history calls into question the notion that a person may fully understand the Bible by simply reading it. The need for help in the form of analytical tools becomes apparent, if not in Genesis or Exodus, then certainly within a few verses of Leviticus. In the following chapters, the contributors introduce various approaches that biblical scholars use to interpret the Bible. Each approach can be used as a tool for discovering greater insight in the biblical text.

1.5 RESOURCES FOR FURTHER STUDY

Barton, John. *The Nature of Biblical Criticism.* Louisville, KY: Westminster John Knox, 2007.

Barton's book offers a good overview of how the methodologies of biblical studies developed and how they relate to other approaches to the Bible. In the chapter "Biblical Criticism and Religious Belief," he surveys the uneasy relationship between believing communities and critical approaches to the Bible, concluding that biblical criticism is not inherently hostile to faith.

Davids, Peter H. "Authority, Hermeneutics, and Criticism." In *Interpreting the New Testament: Essays on Methods and Issues*, 2–17. Nashville, TN: Broadman & Holman, 2001.

Davids' essay lays out the complicated relationship between interpreting the Bible critically and accepting its authority theologically. He also points out that the critical methodology itself needs to be considered separately "from the skeptical presuppositions of some of its practitioners" (9). Holding those same assumptions or presuppositions is not required for making use of the methods.

Erickson, Millard J. *Christian Theology*. 2nd ed. Grand Rapids: Baker
Academic, 1998.

In his section "Theology and Critical Study of the Bible," Erickson
admits that biblical criticism can be useful when it is "based
on assumptions that are consistent with the full authority of
the Bible" (114). He surveys and evaluates form criticism and
redaction criticism, acknowledging both positive and negative
aspects of the methods. Erickson offers six guidelines for using
critical methodologies appropriately within the framework of
Christian theology.

Geisler, Norman L. *Systematic Theology*. Vol. 1, *Introduction, Bible*.
Minneapolis: Bethany House, 2002.

Geisler begins his discussion of biblical criticism by noting there
are positive and negative forms and that evangelicals only oppose
the negative, destructive kind because of its anti-supernatural,
anti-Bible presuppositions. Rather than discuss how the positive
form could be applied constructively, as Erickson does, Geisler
devotes a lengthy chapter, titled "The History of Destructive
Biblical Criticism," to surveying the philosophical and religious
background that encouraged the development of biblical
criticism. Since he also criticizes evangelical scholars who have
appropriated critical methods and never offers an example of the
positive, constructive form of "higher criticism," readers are left
with the impression that biblical criticism is inherently hostile to
Christian belief.

Kaiser, Walter C., Jr., and Moisés Silva. *Introduction to Biblical
Hermeneutics: The Search for Meaning*. Rev. and exp. ed. Grand
Rapids: Zondervan, 2007.

Silva's chapter "Contemporary Approaches to Biblical
Interpretation" includes a brief but clear explanation of the
concerns associated with applying critical methodologies to the
study of the Bible. He notes the problems with terminology, the
negative connotations of "criticism," and the way assumptions
have influenced the application of critical methods.

2

THE HISTORICAL-GRAMMATICAL APPROACH

Judith Odor

The historical-grammatical approach (also known as the grammatical-historical or grammatico-historical method) is a method of biblical interpretation that uses the tools of historical and grammatical research to discover the meaning of a biblical text. This method of interpreting the Bible is the culmination of several centuries of debate and development. The term "historical-grammatical" itself refers to the roles that historical and grammatical knowledge play in both guiding and limiting interpretation. In other words, in historical-grammatical interpretation, a thorough understanding of language leads the reader toward certain interpretations that fit the use of the original language, while simultaneously discouraging interpretations that conflict with a straightforward reading of the words themselves. In the same way, understanding the original historical context of the passage prevents the modern reader from drawing purely modern conclusions regarding its interpretation, while at the same time opening up new ideas and ways of thinking that shed light on what the text may have meant to its original audience.

The significance of the historical-grammatical approach to interpretation should not be underestimated, nor should the influence of this method on other approaches to the Bible be overlooked. The influence of the historical-grammatical method on later critical approaches, such as source criticism, form criticism, and redaction criticism, may be easily traced.

On the other hand, many postmodern approaches deliberately flaunt the traditional boundaries of historical criticism; similarly, certain reader-oriented hermeneutics ignore the historical-grammatical approach in favor of an individual-centered interpretation.

2.1 DEFINITION AND GOAL OF THE METHOD

2.1.1 DEFINITION

A complete definition of the historical-grammatical approach must include this method's basic elements and the various roles they play, but also its purpose, assumptions, and the key aspects of its development. The historical-grammatical approach is a two-pronged approach, bringing together the study of language and history to identify meaning in the text. A grammatical understanding of the text presumes that it is most clearly interpreted in its original language and that the original meaning of the text is the preferred reading. Setting the text within its historical context means relating it to pertinent archaeological and historical discoveries, thus bringing both material witnesses and sociocultural data to bear on the situation and words of the text. Further interpretation occurs within the bounds of historical contextualization and more in-depth grammatical analysis.

2.1.2 GOAL OF THE METHOD

The goal of historical-grammatical analysis is to understand the biblical text as it would have been understood by its original, historical audience. Thus, both the linguistic and historical contexts of that audience are key factors in illuminating the text. The popularity of this approach soared in the nineteenth century, reflecting concurrent developments in both archaeology and philology that gave interpreters new understandings and new tools to apply to study of the Bible.

2.1.3 UNDERLYING ASSUMPTIONS

The assumptions undergirding historical-grammatical analysis reflect concerns and developments of the past two centuries, and especially of the nineteenth century. First, and most fundamental, is the concept that the Bible is historical in nature: it is a text written in a particular time and place with a particular historical audience in mind. This perspective on the Bible may be found throughout the history of the church (see below), but for centuries it was overshadowed by the doctrine of inspiration, which dehistoricized the text of the Bible so that it may transcend the boundaries of history and communicate anew to each generation. Within this frame of reference, allegories and spiritual/mystical interpretations abounded. The Pietistic movement freed the text from the strictures of history, scholasticism, and traditional dogma, creating a model in which the biblical text contained a spiritual message for each reader; this resulted in the invention and acquisition of creative interpretations that conflicted dramatically with each other and with a straightforward reading of the text.[1] The historical-grammatical method offered the corrective response many sought as an alternative to both Pietism and liberal historical criticism, which many nineteenth-century conservative Christian scholars considered to have abandoned entirely the theological tenet of inspiration.[2]

In addition, the historical-grammatical approach reflects then-current theories of meaning, with an emphasis on three basic tenets: (1) words point directly to a single reality or referent; (2) this referent is equivalent to the word's meaning; and (3) the meanings of words can be identified without hesitation and do not change substantially based on context. As Terry states, "[a] fundamental principle in grammatico-historical exposition is that words and sentences can have but one signification in one and the same connection. The moment we neglect this principle we drift out upon a sea of uncertainty and conjecture."[3] Symbolic and typological readings were discouraged because they did not reflect the plain, established meanings of the words in the text. With linguistic developments in the twentieth century, a distinction was made between the referent of a word and that which the word signified or symbolized. This distinction

---

1. John H. Sailhamer, *Introduction to Old Testament Theology: A Canonical Approach* (Grand Rapids: Zondervan, 1999), 122–23.

2. David E. Aune, "Historical Criticism," *The Blackwell Companion to the New Testament*, ed. David E. Aune (Malden, MA: Wiley-Blackwell, 2010), 104–105.

3. Milton S. Terry, *Biblical Hermeneutics: A Treatise on the Interpretation of the Old and New Testaments* (New York: Phillips & Hunt, 1883), 205.

allows the interpreter to take more seriously polysemy, symbolic language, and typological readings.[4]

2.1.4 KEY CONCEPTS

The essential idea that guides the use of the historical-grammatical approach is that the original author of any given text had only one idea in mind as to its meaning. As a foundational concept, the idea of a single, intended meaning provides the rationale for valuing the minutiae of the biblical text. Words communicate meaning—whether literally or symbolically—and thus language must be the first step toward illuminating the message of the text. For those who hold to the doctrine of inspiration, this adds yet another level of importance to the task of historical-grammatical analysis.

2.2 DEVELOPMENT OF THE HISTORICAL-GRAMMATICAL APPROACH

While the historical-grammatical approach achieved popularity in the nineteenth and twentieth centuries, its roots may be traced back far earlier. This is especially true for the philological or grammatical side of the method. In fact, the advancements that sparked the development of grammatical analysis emerged in the medieval era, among rabbinical communities, and continued to influence the study of biblical languages for centuries before the historical-grammatical approach was fully developed.

2.2.1 THE GRAMMATICAL APPROACH

2.2.1.a Biblical Hebrew, Aramaic, and Greek

Grammatical analysis means analyzing the languages in which the Bible was originally written—or at least the languages of the earliest extant manuscripts—Hebrew, Aramaic, and Greek. Each of these languages poses its own unique challenges, and no language is static over time; instead, it changes to meet the unique needs and demands of each generation, region,

---

4. E. D. Hirsch, *Validity in Interpretation* (New Haven: Yale University Press, 1967); Paul Ricoeur, *Interpretation Theory: Discourse and the Surplus of Meaning* (Fort Worth: Texas Christian University Press, 1976), 6.

or historical context. Thus, biblical Hebrew represents various periods of the Hebrew language, extending over hundreds of years, and different biblical texts reflect these changes in the written language.[5] In the same way, those portions written in Aramaic (e.g., Ezra 4:6—6:18; 7:12–26; Dan 2:4—7:28) reflect the Aramaic of a variety of time periods.[6] Greek is also dynamic and exists in multiple dialects, moving from Attic Greek and into Koine Greek during the Second Temple period. Such changes are demonstrated by shifts in grammar, vocabulary, pronunciation, and spelling, just to give a few examples.[7]

2.2.1.b Related Languages

In addition to the traditional triad of Hebrew, Aramaic, and Greek, the study of related languages has proven helpful in interpreting the biblical text. Ancient Semitic languages, such as Ugaritic and Akkadian, inform current understandings of both ancient Hebrew and ancient Near Eastern cultures more broadly, through the study of their respective texts. In much the same way, Latin sources add significant information that sheds light on the earliest reception of the biblical text and on later church history and interpretation. However, since the biblical text is itself limited to Hebrew, Aramaic, and Greek, the following investigation of developments within the study of biblical languages is limited to these three.

2.2.1.c Early Research on Biblical Languages

2.2.1.c.1 Medieval Jewish Philologists

The historical-grammatical approach to interpreting the Bible finds its roots in an exegetical method known as *peshat*, "straight," that developed within rabbinical circles in Europe in the medieval era. The *peshat* method was a more literal way of interpreting the text, as opposed to *derash*, "inquire," which was more allusive and symbolic.

---

5. Edward Horowitz, *How the Hebrew Language Grew* (New York: Jewish Education Committee Press, 1960).

6. See Franz Rosenthal, *A Grammar of Biblical Aramaic: With an Index of Biblical Citations*, 7th exp. ed. (Wiesbaden: Harrassowitz, 2006).

7. See Chrys Caragounis, *The Development of Greek and the New Testament: Morphology, Syntax, Phonology, and Textual Transmission* (Grand Rapids: Baker Academic, 2006).

2.2.1.C.1.A SAADIA GAON (D. 942). Saadia Gaon, or Saadia ben Joseph, (882–942) is known as "the father of *peshat*-exegesis."[8] As leader of the academy of Sura in Babylonia, where the official language was Arabic, Saadia "dreamed of providing his people with a proper translation of the Torah, conforming to the tenets of both traditional Judaism and contemporary philosophy—not to mention the canons of—Arabic grammar and style."[9]

The translations available to Saadia's contemporaries were literal to the point of being incomprehensible, not only to the average Jew but also to the Muslim elite, who thus viewed Judaism as intellectually backward. Much of Saadia's philosophy of interpretation—his hermeneutic—was developed in the process of creating a translation of the Hebrew Bible that reflected the original text without falling prey to a style that would make understanding the text difficult or prohibitive for an intellectual audience.

The method Saadia developed was based on three principles: (1) Biblical texts should be understood according to the meanings the words convey. (2) Such meaning ought to be tempered by only human reason and tradition. (3) If the literal meaning of a verse yields an illogical or nonsensical interpretation, then a metaphorical understanding is preferred.[10]

Thus the meaning of the text is understood primarily through knowledge of Hebrew grammar and, secondarily, through common sense and tradition. These three principles were adopted by commentators, both Jewish and Christian, and formed the foundational assumptions for commentaries written throughout Europe for the next several centuries.[11]

2.2.1.C.1.B IBN JANAH (C. 1030). Following close on the heels of Saadia Gaon came Jonah ibn Janah from Spain, who created the first comprehensive Hebrew dictionary and grammar. Unlike Saadia, Ibn Janah did not write commentaries; however, "his grammar and dictionary include

---

8. Richard C. Steiner, *A Biblical Translation in the Making: The Evolution and Impact of Saadia Gaon's Tafsīr* (Cambridge, MA: Harvard University Press, 2010), 156.

9. Steiner, *Biblical Translation in the Making*, 154.

10. Adapted from p. 142 of Robert A. Harris, "Medieval Jewish Biblical Exegesis," in *A History of Biblical Interpretation: The Medieval through the Reformation Periods*, eds. Alan J. Hauser and Duane F. Watson (Grand Rapids: Eerdmans, 2009), 141–71.

11. Sailhamer, *Introduction to Old Testament Theology*, 134.

many explanations of verses and even broader biblical contexts ... and so essentially provided a philological gateway to the Bible for any interested student."[12]

2.2.1.C.1.C RASHI (RABBI SOLOMON BEN ISAAC, 1040–1105). The interest in Hebrew grammar and its impact on interpretation continued its northern trajectory into France as Rabbi Solomon ben Isaac—better known as Rashi—continued to develop *peshat* as an exegetical method. Though Rashi still demonstrated some midrashic ("inquiring"; from *derash*) tendencies in his commentaries, he considered *peshat* to illuminate "the true meaning of the Hebrew Bible."[13] His method was based primarily on grammar and philology, though he also emphasized the use of immediate textual context to guide linguistic understanding.[14] Rashi's emphasis on *peshat* as the plain meaning of the text functioned, in part, as an apology against christological readings of the OT, arguing that the true meaning of the Hebrew Bible was the *peshat* reading that paid attention to the basic meanings of words and to their historical context, not one that imposed later, ahistorical readings onto the text. Rashi's influence was such that, centuries later, the Reformers concluded that a literal reading of the OT "could no longer be linked to Christ."[15]

2.2.1.C.1.D IBN EZRA (D. 1167). From Andalusia, Spain, Rabbi Abraham ibn Ezra consolidated all the advances made in the past century in Spain (Ibn Janah), Babylonia (Saadia Gaon), and France (Rashi). Ibn Ezra's thinking was shaped by both the Jewish exegetical tradition and its Muslim milieu; as such, he came to view grammar, philology, poetics, science, and philosophy as the keys to biblical interpretation.[16]

Ibn Ezra continued in the path his predecessors forged: he adopted grammar, philosophy, and tradition as the principles that guided his

---

12. Harris, "Medieval Jewish Biblical Exegesis," 143.

13. Sailhamer, *Introduction to Old Testament Theology*, 135; see also Harris, "Medieval Jewish Biblical Exegesis," 145.

14. Mordechai Z. Cohen, *Three Approaches to Biblical Metaphor: From Abraham ibn Ezra and Maimonides to David Kimhi* (Leiden: Brill, 2003), 33; see also Harris, "Medieval Jewish Biblical Exegesis," 144.

15. Sailhamer, *Introduction to Old Testament Theology*, 136.

16. Cohen, *Three Approaches to Biblical Metaphor*, 33.

methodology.[17] In contrast to his predecessors, however, Ibn Ezra placed heavy emphasis on the role of grammar in establishing the bounds of interpretation. Thus the plain meaning of the text—its content—took shape based on its grammatical form; therefore, in order to grasp the content, the forms of the language must be mastered. In this way Ibn Ezra sought to avoid speculation, especially concerning metaphoric or figurative language, which was common among his contemporaries.[18]

In keeping with this reductionist view of language, Ibn Ezra's approach was guided by "the ideal of an exegetical economy" in which "a *peshat* reader limits himself to the most modest assumptions necessary for filling gaps and resolving exegetical difficulties in the biblical text ... [which] insures that his readings go no further than the biblical data can support."[19] These "modest assumptions" were—in Ibn Ezra's methodology—almost entirely determined by the rules of Hebrew grammar and philology. Restricting the reader to the strictest adherence to the rules of the Hebrew language protected the reader from speculation and unfounded mysticism.[20]

Paying close attention to the Hebrew of the text also included taking its literary context into account, much as Rashi taught. However, Ibn Ezra's idea of exegetical economy prompted him to reject many midrashic readings due to their failure to make sense of the text's context.[21] In this way he used context to help determine the boundaries of interpretation, much as he also used grammar to determine the boundaries of meaning. For Ibn Ezra, these concepts elevated *peshat* as not only the best way to determine the literal or true meaning of the text, but also as the best way to uncover its "original *intended* meaning."[22]

2.2.1.C.1.E KIMHI (D. 1235). From Provençal, France, Rabbi David Kimhi (1160–1235)—also known as Radak—synthesized the differing approaches to *peshat*. He integrated the Spanish school, represented by Ibn Ezra's

---

17. Irene Lancaster, *Deconstructing the Bible: Abraham ibn Ezra's Introduction to the Torah* (London: Routledge, 2002), 178; see also Harris, "Medieval Jewish Biblical Exegesis," 152–54.

18. Cohen, *Three Approaches to Biblical Metaphor*, 235–41.

19. Cohen, *Three Approaches to Biblical Metaphor*, 235–36.

20. Cohen, *Three Approaches to Biblical Metaphor*, 241.

21. Cohen, *Three Approaches to Biblical Metaphor*, 253.

22. Lancaster, *Deconstructing the Bible*, 53; italics added.

emphasis on pure philology, and the French literary school, developed by Rashi, creating a method of interpretation that was grounded on the rules of grammar without abandoning centuries of tradition and rabbinical wisdom.[23] Radak is well known for his treatment of difficult texts and allusions in the Hebrew Bible, offering clear explanations that also serve to demonstrate this integrated form of *peshat*. In addition, Radak wrote lexical works that provide insight into Hebrew verbal roots and forms.

2.2.1.c.2 Renaissance

With the fall of Constantinople in 1453, Europe received a wave of scholars trained in the dialect of Greek that was native to the eastern Roman Empire. These scholars brought with them entire libraries of classical—that is, ancient Greek—literature, including poetry, essays, historical works, and philosophical and scientific treatises. This inundation of classical intellectualism and sudden access to its resources arrived in Europe at the precise point when interest in ancient history, language, and ideas was on the rise.

2.2.1.C.2.A REVIVAL OF GREEK. The roots of the movement to revive Greek began well before the Renaissance in Europe, before the decisive victory of the Ottoman Empire over Constantinople in 1453. Paving the way for this new interest in classical values and education, Manuel Chrysoloras (1350–1415) was invited to Florence from Constantinople to tutor the intellectual and political elite in southern Italy. Chrysoloras trained an entire generation of scholars in Greek language and literature, thus changing the face of scholarship in Italy and, by extension, Europe.[24] When Constantinople fell, Europe was ready to receive its scholars with open arms.

One scholar affected by this influx of classicism was Desiderius Erasmus (1469–1536). Much as Saadia Gaon had centuries earlier, Erasmus desired to produce a translation of the Bible that reflected the language of the original text without sacrificing readability and understanding. As Saadia had discovered regarding the Hebrew Bible in his generation, translations of

---

23. Harris, "Medieval Jewish Biblical Exegesis," 156.

24. Kenneth R. Bartlett, *A Short History of the Italian Renaissance* (Toronto: University of Toronto Press, 2013), 8.

the NT available to Erasmus were "so literal as to be obscure."[25] Erasmus' interest in translation eventually developed into a lifelong labor to decide which among the many manuscripts and variants circulating in the libraries of Europe was the original text.

Coming on the heels of the advances made by preceding rabbis and inundated by the sudden availability of Greek resources, Erasmus made philology the foundation of his work, with the conviction that understanding the language of the Greek NT would be the first step toward proper interpretation.[26] In Erasmus' hermeneutic, grammar became the "handmaiden" of theology, and failure to master NT Greek would result in an inability to probe the mysteries of the text, let alone build a sound theology that maintained integrity.[27]

After years of intensive labor, in 1516 Erasmus finally published the *Novum Instrumentum Omne*. It was the first Greek NT ever to be printed and bore the marks of Erasmus' painstaking philological work in making sense of the various manuscripts and variants. The Greek text he published was eventually also used to create the first English New Testament (1526), the Geneva Bible (1557 NT, 1560 OT), and eventually the King James Version (1611).[28]

2.2.1.C.2.B REVIVAL OF HEBREW. Although the Renaissance did not prompt the same level of interest in the Hebrew language as it did in Greek, philological developments continued based on the previous work of the earlier rabbis. However, the atmosphere of the Renaissance, with its interest in ancient ideas and languages, merged neatly with general advances in philology and philosophy of language. Of the Renaissance scholars who studied, taught, and published works on Hebrew, the work of Johannes Reuchlin was perhaps the most important.

The foundation on which Reuchlin built his philosophy of language and his hermeneutic was the Johannine concept of the Word of God as

---

25. Erika Rummel, *Erasmus as a Translator of the Classics* (Toronto: University of Toronto Press, 1985), 17.

26. Rummel, *Erasmus*, 4.

27. Rummel, *Erasmus*, 18.

28. Herbert W. Bateman IV, *Interpreting the General Letters: An Exegetical Handbook* (Grand Rapids: Kregel Academic, 2013), 135.

the intermediary between God and humanity (John 1). For Reuchlin, this divine Word, as explained in the opening of John's Gospel, was both Christ and a literal text. In Reuchlin's philosophy, the Bible is the textual form of the divine Word, which serves as God's intermediary. This theology guided Reuchlin's prioritization of language and provided boundaries for interpretation.[29] Reuchlin's lexicon followed Kimhi's (Radak's) approach, creating not only a reference but a tool for learning that made his work accessible, regardless of whether one had access to tutors.[30] In the same way, his *De rudimentis Hebraicis* (1506) became the standard Hebrew grammar among biblical scholars for the next three hundred years.[31]

2.2.1.c.3 A Methodological Synthesis

It is essential to recognize that a definite trajectory in both method and philosophy of interpretation was developed in and emerged out of the Renaissance, contributing to the rise of the Enlightenment. The primacy of grammar in the task of exegesis and interpretation had been established not only by the medieval rabbis but also by their Jewish and Christian intellectual heirs of the Renaissance. What remained was the task of synthesis, the integration of various positions and perspectives into one whole, creating a method that both reflected the advances made in prior centuries and provided a path forward for practical exegesis and interpretation.

The man many regard as the founder of the historical-grammatical method in its modern form is Johann August Ernesti (1707–1781). In his *Institutio Interpretis Novi Testamenti* (1761), Ernesti outlined a formal methodology for the historical-grammatical approach.[32] This was the first work dedicated solely to explaining and demonstrating a particular hermeneutical method. Ernesti's keen integration of the interpretive methods and approaches discussed thus far made *Institutio* not only unique but also the premier reference work of its kind for the next several generations.

---

29. Sophie Kessler Mesguich, "Early Christian Hebraists," in *Hebrew Bible/Old Testament: The History of Its Interpretation: Volume II: From the Renaissance to the Enlightenment*, ed. Magne Sæbø (Göttingen: Vandenhoeck & Ruprecht, 2008), 258.

30. Mesguich, "Early Christian Hebraists," 259.

31. Sailhamer, *Introduction to Old Testament Theology*, 123.

32. Robert Moore-Jumonville, *The Hermeneutics of Historical Distance: Mapping the Terrain of America* (Lanham, MD: University Press of America, 2002), 104.

Ernesti's core focus was on elucidating "the plain meaning of words in their literary and historical contexts," a plain meaning that overcame, as much as possible, the reader's own subjective biases and anchored the reading on objective grounds.[33] The inclusion of literary and historical context is significant, as these factors provide further guidance in interpretation and discourage speculative readings. Ernesti described his synthesis of linguistic and historical concerns as firmly founded on linguistic knowledge and the application of "grammatico-historical" analysis. In the following two centuries his method achieved great popularity.

2.2.1.d Nineteenth-Century Philology

Interest in philology continued through the Enlightenment and into the Industrial Age, yet the developments that most affected the historical-grammatical method as it is recognized today occurred in the nineteenth century. The research and publications of this century laid the foundation for most grammatical work on biblical languages until the mid-twentieth century.

AUTHOR	TITLE	YEAR
Wilhelm Gesenius	*Gesenius' Hebrew Grammar*	1813
Heinrich August Ewald	*A Grammar of the Hebrew Language*	1828
Georg Curtius	*A Grammar of the Greek Language*	1872
A. T. Robertson	*A Grammar of the Greek New Testament in Light of Historical Research*	1914

SIGNIFICANT GRAMMARS OF THE 19TH AND EARLY 20TH CENTURIES

2.2.1.d.1 Biblical Hebrew

In the realm of biblical Hebrew, the works of Wilhelm Gesenius (German, 1786–1842) and Georg Heinrich August Ewald (German, 1803–1875) have

---

33. Moore-Jumonville, *Hermeneutics of Historical Distance*, x.

proven to be the most influential. In 1813 Gesenius published the first edition of his Hebrew grammar, which has not been out of print since.[34] Gesenius' grammar continues to serve as an invaluable resource for Hebrew scholars today.[35] Gesenius produced a number of works on Hebrew lexicography from 1810 until his death in 1842.[36] His lexicon of biblical Hebrew and Aramaic published in 1833 provided the basis for the well-known Brown-Driver-Briggs Hebrew lexicon.[37]

Gesenius' contemporary Georg Ewald taught at Göttingen from 1824–1866 (except for a hiatus from 1833–1847) as professor of OT exegesis and theology. Ewald's *Grammatik der hebräischen Sprache* (1828) became the standard grammar of Hebrew for several generations and shaped the way most grammars were written thereafter.[38]

2.2.1.d.2 New Testament Greek

Of nineteenth-century Greek scholars, the grammars of Georg Curtius and A. T. Robertson most definitively changed the face of the study of NT (Koine) Greek.[39] Curtius' grammar provided students of Greek with much the same approach and service that Ewald's grammar did for Hebrew

---

34. Gesenius' grammar is most widely used in editions based on the 2nd English edition published in 1910: Wilhelm Gesenius, *Gesenius' Hebrew Grammar*, ed. E. Kautzsch and A. E. Cowley, 2nd English ed. (Oxford: Clarendon Press, 1910).

35. See Edward Frederick Miller, *The Influence of Gesenius on Hebrew Lexicography* (1927; repr., Piscataway, NJ: Gorgias, 2009); Miller's book is also reprinted in the Gorgias Press edition of *Gesenius' Hebrew Grammar*: E. Kautzsch, *Gesenius' Hebrew Grammar and the Influence of Gesenius* (1910; repr., Piscataway, NJ: Gorgias, 2008).

36. In the preface to his translation of Gesenius' lexicon, Tregelles lists Gesenius' various publications on Hebrew lexicography (*Gesenius' Hebrew-Chaldee Lexicon to the Old Testament Scriptures*, trans. Samuel Prideaux Tregelles [London: Samuel Bagster and Sons, 1857], iii–iv.)

37. Wilhelm Gesenius, *Lexicon Manuale Hebraicum et Chaldaicum in Veteris Testamenti Libros* (Leipzig, 1833); Francis Brown, Samuel R. Driver, and Charles A. Briggs, eds., *A Hebrew and English Lexicon of the Old Testament, with an Appendix Containing the Biblical Aramaic* (Oxford: Oxford University Press, 1906).

38. Walter Gross, "Is There Really a Compound Nominal Clause in Biblical Hebrew?" *The Verbless Clause in Biblical Hebrew: Linguistic Approaches*, ed. Cynthia L. Miller (Winona Lake, IN: Eisenbrauns, 1999), 21.

39. Georg Curtius, *A Grammar of the Greek Language*, ed. William Smith (New York: Harper & Bros., 1872); A. T. Robertson, *A Grammar of the Greek New Testament in the Light of Historical Research* (New York: George H. Doran Co., 1914).

scholars. However, it was his insight into the Greek verbal system and its means of indicating relationship to time that truly changed Greek studies.[40]

A. T. Robertson's Greek grammar is not pedagogical, but instead offers a comprehensive description of the language itself. His *A Grammar of the Greek New Testament in Light of Historical Research* (1914) is an exhaustive work, providing more detail in its fourteen hundred pages than had any other grammar. Robertson's grammar clearly demonstrates the priority of language and grammatical knowledge in his hermeneutic, as well as the roles that history and philology play in this process, but the best (and most approachable) description of his method of interpretation is found in *The Minister and His Greek New Testament* (1923).[41] In this slim volume Robertson strongly encourages those in pastoral ministry to learn Koine Greek; in his view, knowledge of the original language provides insights into the text that translations alone cannot achieve.[42] In addition, Robertson notes the depth of interaction with the text that working with another language demands; such depth of thought and interaction invariably produces better exegesis and deeper interpretation.[43]

2.2.2 DEVELOPMENT OF THE HISTORICAL APPROACH

Unlike the grammatical side of the historical-grammatical method, the historical approach did not develop slowly and steadily over a period of several centuries. Instead, history was, as noted above, considered only within the realm of philological developments; a historical understanding of language meant understanding how it was used in a particular time and place in history. The fascination of the Renaissance with classicism and humanism was limited to an understanding of history based solely on its surviving literature. It was not until the nineteenth century and the dawn of archaeology that significant strides were made toward understanding the historical backdrop of the biblical text.

---

40. Constantine R. Campbell, *Basics of Verbal Aspect in Biblical Greek* (Grand Rapids: Zondervan, 2008), 27.

41. A. T. Robertson, *The Minister and His Greek New Testament* (New York: George H. Doran Co., 1923).

42. Robertson, *Minister and His Greek New Testament*, 18–19.

43. Robertson, *Minister and His Greek New Testament*, 21.

2.2.2.a The World of the Text

The long-standing identification of the Bible as a historical text—one written in a particular time period to a particular audience—paved the way for the insights of the nineteenth century. Reconstructing the world of the text was thus a direct result of that century's work in reconsidering the definition of "historical" with respect to a text.

Throughout the nineteenth century, an awareness grew that a historical context is greater than the sum of its literature. More than language, the world of the text was composed of events, people, places, cultures, and artifacts. Together, these created a fully faceted world that, appropriately built, could inform and illuminate one's interpretation of that context's text(s).

2.2.2.a.1 Ancient History

As noted above, knowledge of ancient history was, until the nineteenth century, primarily based on extant literary records. In this case, the Greek and Latin classics provided insight into the culture, society, leadership, and major events of the first century. Scholars used these classics to help reconstruct the historical context of various texts, including the NT. As for the OT, little to no textual sources were available from the relevant time periods; most of what scholars knew about the ancient Near East, including Egypt, came through the biblical text or classical histories, like those of Herodotus or Josephus, written long after the events they described.

However, growing international politics and advances in transportation technology made access to the artifacts and texts of these eras possible for the enterprising scholar and even adventurer.[44] For example, the library of the Assyrian king Ashurbanipal (r. 668–627 BC) was discovered in the ruins of ancient Nineveh in the mid-nineteenth century. The texts preserved there provided significant information about the history of the ancient Near East, once scholars had deciphered Akkadian. At the same time, comparable discoveries were made in Italy, Greece, Turkey, Egypt, and elsewhere in the Middle East. Scholars now had easier access to primary resources—statuary, coins, architecture, and manuscripts—from places all over the ancient Mediterranean and ancient Near East, bringing history alive through their physical presence. Acquisition of these

---

44. See Dorothy King, *The Elgin Marbles* (London: Hutchinson, 2006).

treasures created a desire for more and an impetus to fund teams of explorers who would seek out physical evidence of ancient history. Thus, the field of archaeology was born.

2.2.2.a.2 Archaeology

The early teams of explorers were, of course, the forerunners of modern archaeologists. Their methods were crude, and they often destroyed valuable historical evidence as they searched for lucrative artifacts.[45] However, serious scholars also set out to find historical evidence of myth and legend. Heinrich Schliemann (1822–1890) was one such archaeologist.

Schliemann focused his efforts on finding ancient Troy, famous because of the works of Homer. In 1871 he began excavating Hissarlik in Turkey, trying to reach the lower levels of the site—levels he assumed would match ancient Troy. In his haste, Schliemann destroyed thousands of years of historical evidence and, as a result, decades of debate ensued regarding proper methodology in archaeological excavation.[46] However, two of Schliemann's contributions proved to be tremendous advances in the field: his identification of "tells," or huge mounds of earth, as possible locations for historical sites and his concept of stratigraphy, the idea that different periods of human occupation would collect in different and consecutive layers of dirt at the site.[47]

William Flinders Petrie (1853–1942) was the first to apply science to stratigraphy, using ceramic pottery in concert with the layers of the site to identify rough dates for the periods evidenced.[48] Kathleen Kenyon (1906–1978) then transformed Petrie's basic method into a strict and detailed scientific process that has shaped the way archaeology is done today, especially in the areas of stratigraphic detailing and ceramic dating.[49]

---

45. See Susan Heuck Allen, *Finding the Walls of Troy: Frank Calvert and Heinrich Schliemann at Hisarlik* (Berkeley: University of California Press, 1999), 167, 365.

46. Allen, *Finding the Walls of Troy*, 4.

47. Archaeologists came to discover that these mounds in the Middle East, called tells, had typically been the sites of ancient cities. The mound developed as successive generations rebuilt the city on the same spot. The different levels of occupation of a mound could be determined by stratigraphy—the careful identification of the successive layers.—Eds.

48. Joseph A. Callaway, "Sir Flinders Petrie, Father of Palestinian Archaeology," *BAR* 6, no. 6 (1980): 44–55.

49. Larry G. Herr, "W. F. Albright and the History of Pottery in Palestine," *Near Eastern Archaeology* 65, no. 1 (2002): 53.

The final result, then, was a highly detailed depiction of the world and history of a site, a depiction built not from literature, which interprets the culture it relates, but of artifacts that provide bare testimony to the way of life in a given place at a given time. Granted, the interpretation of those artifacts is only an interpretation, yet the physical realities themselves bear witness in a way that grounds and provides boundaries for that interpretation. The historical world was suddenly a much richer, more complex reality to biblical scholars than it had been a mere century before.

2.2.2.a.3 Reading Historically

A. H. Sayce offers the best demonstration of precisely how these tremendous changes in the modern concept of the historical world affected biblical scholars. In *The "Higher Criticism" and the Verdict of the Monuments*, Sayce outlines what he considers the appropriate critical approach to the Bible in light of the archaeological discoveries.

Yet Sayce does not consider the ideal critic to be limited to historical considerations: quite the contrary, he asserts that language is the foundation of the critic's reading process.[50] Philological or grammatical analysis is to be followed by literary analysis, and it is only after this point that historical considerations come into play.[51] Once the critic stands firmly on this foundation, historical knowledge may inform and shape the interpretation.

It is to this effort that Sayce devotes the remainder of his work. He draws from the findings of Schliemann in Greece and Petrie in Egypt (among others) in order to demonstrate ways in which new historical evidence may inform one's reading of the text. Sayce reflects the assumptions of his time in that archaeology may recreate history without agenda, thereby providing certain, objective, and safe boundaries that may guide interpretation.

This method and set of assumptions holds that absolute certainty may be reached by means of grammatical skill and historical knowledge. All of Sayce's examples affirm the biblical text, without going into the issue of inspiration. Sayce's work carefully avoids theology—a separation that

---

50. A. H. Sayce, *The "Higher Criticism" and the Verdict of the Monuments* (London: SPCK, 1894), 4–5, 8.

51. Sayce, *"Higher Criticism" and the Verdict of the Monuments*, 9–10.

some schools of thought within the historical-grammatical method later sought to rectify.

2.2.2.b The History of the Text

One final implication of reading the Bible as a historical text must be addressed before examining the final synthesis and development of the historical-grammatical method as it is known today. Thus far, discussion of the Bible as a historical text has focused rather broadly on the ancient world in which the text was originally written. However, the historical nature of the text implies two issues. First—and more closely related to the discussions thus far—the text has a specific historical context that includes when it was written, by whom, to whom, and for what purposes. Second, the text itself has a history, beginning with its origin and ending with the modern era.

2.2.2.b.1 Textual Transmission

The history of the text itself is usually described as the history of the text's transmission. In other words, this view of the text considers all of the ways in which the text has been handed down through the centuries and looks specifically at various manuscripts of the text.[52] These manuscripts are not all identical in material, format, or in word-for-word content. Some manuscripts are papyrus, while others are made of leather; some are scrolls, while others are codices (early books). Most of the variations between manuscripts are relatively minor, noticeable only to the trained eye.

Manuscript evidence may be grouped according to texts that follow roughly the same traditions in wording. Tracing the small changes in wording or even in lettering allows textual critics to determine the most likely original reading of the text. This work is foundational to all textual analysis, as the most likely original wording must be determined before proceeding to analyze the grammar of the passage. In fact, many of those who made significant philological advances in the past did so while engaging in this first step of textual criticism. Erasmus is perhaps the best example

---

52. Textual criticism is the study of the development of a text through comparison of all the available evidence to determine the best or original text. For more on textual criticism, see Wendy Widder, *Textual Criticism of the Bible*, ed. Douglas Mangum, Lexham Methods Series 1 (Bellingham, WA: Lexham Press, 2013).

of this, as he sought to create a more readable translation; in the process of determining which text ought to be translated, he published the first critical edition of the Greek NT.

The nineteenth-century focus on uncovering the history of and behind the biblical text inspired numerous critical editions of the Bible. Scholars such as Constantin von Tischendorf not only created a new critical edition of the NT with manuscript notes, but also described the scientific process by which a text and its variants should be analyzed.[53] Brooke Foss Westcott (1825–1901) and John Anthony Hort (1828–1892) collaborated on yet another critical edition, *The New Testament in the Original Greek* (1881).[54] One of their major contributions was the organization of the various manuscripts into families that demonstrated the same trends of variants.

The *Novum Testamentum Graece*, produced by a team of critical scholars led by Eberhard Nestle, his son Erwin Nestle, Kurt Aland, Barbara Aland, and others, has become the standard critical edition for today's biblical scholars.[55] The Nestle-Aland NT is the product of decades of analysis, revision, and continual incorporation of newly discovered manuscripts. In *The Text of the New Testament: An Introduction to the Critical Editions and to the Theory and Practice of Modern Textual Criticism*, Kurt Aland and Barbara Aland outline the process of textual transmission and the current methodology of NT textual criticism, the work of determining the most likely original reading.[56]

---

53. Tischendorf published many editions of his Greek New Testament. The eighth edition was an important one because of the addition of many new manuscripts. Constantin von Tischendorf, ed., *Novum Testamentum Graece,* editio octava critica maior, 2 vols. (Leipzig: Giesecke & Devrient, 1869, 1872); see also Armin J. Panning, "Tischendorf and the History of the Greek New Testament Text," *Wisconsin Lutheran Quarterly* 69, no. 1 (1971): 12–25.

54. Brooke Foss Westcott and Fenton John Anthony Hort, eds., *The New Testament in the Original Greek* (Cambridge: Macmillan, 1881).

55. Eberhard Nestle et al., eds., *Novum Testamentum Graece,* 28th rev. ed. (Stuttgart: Deutsche Bibelgesellschaft, 2012).

56. Kurt Aland and Barbara Aland, *The Text of the New Testament: An Introduction to the Critical Editions and to the Theory and Practice of Modern Textual Criticism,* 2nd ed. (Grand Rapids: Eerdmans, 1995). For an introductory-level description of NT textual criticism, see J. Harold Greenlee, *Introduction to New Testament Textual Criticism* rev. ed. (Peabody, MA: Hendrickson, 1995); or David Alan Black, *New Testament Textual Criticism: A Concise Guide* (Grand Rapids: Baker, 1994).

AUTHOR	TITLE	YEAR
Tischendorf	*Novum Testamentum Graece*	1849
Westcott and Hort	*The New Testament in the Original Greek*	1881
Nestle	*Novum Testamentum Graece*	1898

SIGNIFICANT 19TH-CENTURY CRITICAL EDITIONS OF THE NEW TESTAMENT

2.2.2.b.2 Date of Composition

Ascertaining the date of a text's composition is often challenging. It involves dating the manuscript evidence (the external evidence) to determine the earliest extant witness to the text, which gives the latest possible date. The content of the text (the internal evidence) should also be considered: cultural and historical details provide insight into the possible date of writing, especially when these details are incidental and could be considered unknown to anyone but the text's author.

2.2.2.b.3 Authorship

When a NT text identifies its own author (e.g., Rom 1:1), the scholar using a historical-grammatical approach typically gives the text the benefit of the doubt unless the identification is nonspecific or the content of the text does not seem to conform to other texts known to have been written by the same author. For example, debate continues regarding the identification of the elder John in the Johannine Letters.

When the text identifies no author at all, church tradition may provide an answer. Church father Eusebius (c. 260–339) identifies many such traditions, providing modern scholars with an ancient witness to the question of biblical authorship (Eusebius, *Ecclesiastical History*). Where Eusebius' identification fits the content, style, and concerns of the text, his witness may be accepted as authoritative.

Other processes involved in identifying an anonymous author include comparing the content of the text at hand to other texts whose author is known. The ongoing comparison of the Gospel of John to the Johannine Letters offers a more complex view of this issue: the disciple John, brother of James, is traditionally named the author of these books, yet the Gospel is technically anonymous. However, it shares theological concerns with the Johannine Letters, which self-identify their author as John the elder. Scholars continue to debate whether John the elder is the same as John the disciple.[57]

2.2.2.b.4 Audience

Finally, the target audience of the text must be identified. Knowing for whom the epistle or narrative was meant provides the modern reader with a helpful direction and boundaries for determining the intended meaning of the text. The social, political, and linguistic situations of the audience affect how the text was written and how the audience might have interpreted it. For example, Romans 13:1–7 would have affected a Palestinian audience on the verge of war with Rome very differently from how it would have an audience in Rome or even Asia Minor. Understanding the concerns and situations of the audience changes how the modern reader interprets the ancient text.

2.2.3 THE HISTORICAL-GRAMMATICAL APPROACH: A METHODOLOGICAL SYNTHESIS

Thus far, discussion of the historical-grammatical method has proceeded along two, mostly distinct, pathways. Although the general thrust of the approach may be apparent, it is essential to consider how the two factors—grammar and history—become intertwined and develop into a single method, a unified whole. Both the historical development and modern expression of the historical-grammatical method must be taken into account in order to create a fully realized portrait of this method.

---

57. Raymond E. Brown, *An Introduction to the Gospel of John* (New Haven, CT: Yale University Press, 2003), 189–99.

2.2.3.a Adoption and Definition in the Nineteenth Century

The emphasis of the nineteenth century on understanding the text through understanding the world of the text led a significant number of scholars to begin to read the Bible as historical literature, applying the same boundaries and freedoms that they would to classical literature. Both scholars and church leaders in America watched the development of historical criticism—this type of historical reading—in the nineteenth century with a blend of approbation and concern. The emphasis on reading the text as a historical text and interpreting it within the world in which it was written were cause for celebration in that a historical reading of a text offered some boundaries to protect against speculative or harmful interpretations.

However, the boundaries many of these scholars applied to historical literature reflected the convictions and assumptions of their own generation. Of these, the overwhelming popularity of David Hume's arguments against supernatural events most strongly affected the way in which these scholars read biblical literature.[58] Thus, for some, historical criticism explicitly refused to accept as real or true any supernatural claims contained within the Bible, especially the NT.

Scholars holding to the doctrine of the inspiration of Scripture, then, were faced with a decision: either accept the anti-supernatural bias of historical criticism or develop an alternative perspective on the issue that allows for the supernatural or miraculous stories contained within the Bible. Additionally, historical-grammatical methods seemed to offer certainty to both scholars and ministers—an attractive quality for those who sought solid ground for students and lay members alike.

The nineteenth century was a time of seeking absolute truths, things that could be known as real and true beyond any doubt, and was full of optimism regarding this search. The certainty that one could find absolute truths spilled over into language and history. While the evidence provided by archaeology seemed to promise absolute truths regarding the realities of history, theories of language during that same period reflected the same certainty: that words always mean the same thing, always pointing to the same reality each time they are used.

---

58. Craig Keener, *Miracles: The Credibility of the New Testament Accounts* (Grand Rapids: Baker Academic, 2011), 107–208.

In 1883 two books were published that together catapulted the histori-cal-grammatical method into popularity, especially within the American evangelical movement: *Biblical Hermeneutics* by Milton Terry and *Biblical Study: Its Principles, Methods and History* by Charles Augustus Briggs. Terry's *Biblical Hermeneutics* was especially influential, providing a detailed description of the historical-grammatical method, as well as a philosophi-cal and theological apology for the method's use. Terry captures the attitude and linguistic positivism of his generation: "A fundamental principle in grammatico-historical exposition is that words and sentences can have but one signification in one and the same connection. The moment we neglect this principle we drift out upon a sea of uncertainty and conjecture."[59]

This promise of certainty and understanding would, it was hoped, make the Bible less distant and more approachable to the average person.[60] All that was required was an understanding of the grammar and historical context of any given text. Terry emphasized the approachability of the biblical text again and again, noting that the method "focused both on the grammatical connections within the text as ordinary human language" and that "biblical language is the language of everyday human communication."[61]

Further, Terry described the historical factor in equally approach-able language, observing that "the authors wrote in an historical setting, addressing particular situations and limited by certain historical circum-stances. This means that biblical literature can and must be studied *as any other book* would be studied."[62]

The desire to lessen the distance between the modern reader and the biblical text resulted in an emphasis on the features that the biblical text shared with other purely historical texts. Such an emphasis brought histor-ical-grammatical methods further in line with historical criticism, a move that spurred later theologians and biblical scholars to reconsider both how broadly they wished to define historical-grammatical methods and how these methods fit with theological inquiry and the doctrine of inspiration. Modern expressions of this approach demonstrate the shift and redefinition

---

59. Terry, *Biblical Hermeneutics*, 205.
60. Moore-Jumonville, *Hermeneutics of Historical Distance*, x.
61. Moore-Jumonville, *Hermeneutics of Historical Distance*, 105.
62. Moore-Jumonville, *Hermeneutics of Historical Distance*, 105.

that took place in the generations following the emergence of historical criticism and the contributions of those like Sayce, Terry, and Briggs.

2.2.3.b Modern Historical-Grammatical Method

The broadest definition of the historical-grammatical method continues to identify language as the solid foundation of interpretation. This process of interpretation is, in turn, informed and guided further by the text's historical context: "it seeks to understand the language of the text (grammar) in the light of the situation in which it was first written or spoken (history)."[63] However, within some specific theological traditions, one finds more specific definitions of and limitations on the historical-grammatical approach.

William Tolar, an evangelical Baptist, emphasizes the grammatical analysis involved in the historical-grammatical method: "we must concern ourselves not only with knowing the meaning of individual words but also with understanding their relationships in sentences, in paragraphs, and in their genre."[64] The result of such analysis, combined with the requisite historical contextualization, results in "a correct interpretation," or one that reveals "the meaning placed there by the original author."[65] Tolar's focus, then, is on the role grammar plays in the hermeneutical process, and he is confident in the ability of the method to reveal the original author's intended meaning.

This confidence is taken a step further by Robert Thomas (1928–). Thomas echoes the certainty of Milton Terry concerning the potential of historical-grammatical methods to provide "an objective awareness of what biblical writers intended when they penned the words of Scripture."[66] The same emphasis may thus be seen in both Tolar and Thomas: the goal of historical-grammatical methods is to reveal the originally intended meaning of the text. However, Thomas adds to this goal that of scientific objectivity:

---

63. John Bright, *The Authority of the Old Testament* (London: SCM Press, 1967), 169; cited in Graeme Goldsworthy, *Gospel-Centered Hermeneutics: Foundations and Principles of Evangelical Biblical Interpretation* (Downers Grove, IL: IVP Academic, 2006), 204.

64. William B. Tolar, "The Grammatical-Historical Method," in *Biblical Hermeneutics: A Comprehensive Introduction to Interpreting Scripture*, ed. Bruce Corley, Steve W. Lemke, and Grant I. Lovejoy (Nashville, TN: Broadman & Holman, 1996), 22.

65. Tolar, "Grammatical-Historical Method," 21.

66. Robert L. Thomas, *Evangelical Hermeneutics: The New versus the Old* (Grand Rapids: Kregel, 2002), 48.

The method consciously seeks to rule out any personal biases or predispositions in order to let the rules of grammar and the facts of history of each text speak for themselves. That quest for objectivity has allowed the Bible to yield propositional truths that constitute a sure foundation for evangelical Christianity.[67]

Thomas sets forth a view of the historical-grammatical approach that assumes a high level of objectivity, that "an interpreter can analyze passages involving obscure biblical customs or figures of speech and explain them accurately without allowing his own culture or circumstances to influence his conclusions."[68] Thus the final product Thomas envisions is "the one meaning that is correct," which the objective interpreter is able to settle on "with conviction and certainty."[69]

Thomas' goal of objectivity is related to his assertion that each text holds only one meaning and that the literal interpretation of the text is both the correct interpretation and the goal of the historical-grammatical approach.[70] Thus, Thomas maintains a position very close to that held by Terry in the nineteenth century, affirming objectivity, the notion of one meaning per text, and a literal reading all as part of the process of grammatical and historical analysis.

Finally, Graeme Goldsworthy (1934–) offers a Reformed perspective on the historical-grammatical approach. He, too, affirms the goal of the method to be "the meaning of a text as it was originally intended."[71] Unlike Thomas, however, Goldsworthy does not claim objectivity as a goal for the interpreter, nor does he explicitly argue for a single meaning per text. Instead, he argues that Reformed scholars need to develop "a truly historical-critical method that acknowledges the Lord of all history," thus moving the methodology away from dependence on the competency or objectivity of the reader and toward a deliberate engagement with the divine as part of the interpretive process.[72]

---

67. Thomas, *Evangelical Hermeneutics*, 48.
68. Thomas, *Evangelical Hermeneutics*, 432–33.
69. Thomas, *Evangelical Hermeneutics*, 127.
70. Thomas, *Evangelical Hermeneutics*, 283, 353.
71. Goldsworthy, *Gospel-Centered Hermeneutics*, 205.
72. Goldsworthy, *Gospel-Centered Hermeneutics*, 196.

These brief overviews of distinct perspectives on the historical-grammatical approach demonstrate that the historical core of the method—grammatical analysis informed and bounded by historical contextualization—remains foundational to the method today. Yet the very simplicity of this description demonstrates that it also allows for further definition and shaping based on the theological and philosophical convictions of the reader.

2.3 APPLICATIONS OF THE HISTORICAL-GRAMMATICAL APPROACH

The following examples of the historical-grammatical approach engage the core of the critical process. In other words, these brief examples will demonstrate ways in which knowledge of Koine Greek and of the world of the NT text may inform and illuminate the text in unexpected and often profound ways.

2.3.1 SEA VOYAGES: ACTS 27:1–44; 28:1–11

The Mediterranean voyages of Paul are easily overlooked by the average reader. In fact, their contribution to the overall narrative of Acts does not seem immediately apparent. However, they do provide a wealth of information affirming not only the historical nature of Acts but also the particular interests of Luke.[73]

For example, Luke's narrative consistently points to the innocence of Paul in the midst of false accusation. In light of this theme, the account of the snakebite on the island of Malta (Acts 28:3–6) becomes far more than a near-tragedy. Hemer observes that the "fear and superstition" attached to snakes in general had developed in ancient times into a belief that snakes serve as "the agent of vengeance," biting and killing those who escape the law.[74] That Paul survived the snakebite would have suggested to the Maltese that he not only had some sort of supernatural power but also that nature itself proved his innocence even as he was on his way to be tried in Rome.

---

73. Colin J. Hemer, *The Book of Acts in the Setting of Hellenistic History*, ed. Conrad H. Gempf (Tübingen: J. C. B. Mohr, 1989; repr., Winona Lake, IN: Eisenbrauns, 1990), 132–54.

74. Hemer, *Book of Acts*, 153.

The accounts of Acts also frequently argue for the superiority of God's plan and God's rule over that of the Roman Empire. In keeping with this theme, then, Paul's voyage to Rome contains other details that cast the entire enterprise in an ironic light. Luke observes that the ship Paul embarked on after the Maltese adventure had as a figurehead a representation of twins. These would be the twins Castor and Pollux, who "also became closely associated with the imperial family and imperial cult. The shield, spear, armor, and horse employed by Castor and Pollux became symbols of the dominance of Roman imperial power."[75] Thus when Paul finally arrived in Rome—actually in Puteoli, a harbor town near Rome— he arrived under the figurehead of the Roman Empire; yet Luke's account clearly emphasizes the plan of God at work in events: though secular powers appeared to be controlling events, God's plan continued to direct and use those events to grow the kingdom of God (Acts 28:30–31).

Both of the above examples engage in historical criticism. Understanding the historical world of the text enables the reader to appreciate cultural and symbolic overtones that add depth and significance to otherwise easily overlooked passages.

2.3.2 THE WORD WAS GOD: JOHN 1:1

The question of the correct interpretation of John 1:1 is, at heart, one of linguistic skill and grammatical knowledge. The second phrase, "and the Word was God," has also been translated "and the Word was a god," reflecting the lack of a definite article before *theos* ("God") in the Greek text. Responses to this translation have frequently appealed to a rule of Greek grammar known as Colwell's rule. Colwell based his rule on a careful and detailed examination of all such noun constructions in the NT. This principle states that, in Greek, a definite noun in the predicate of the sentence will usually lack the article, and a noun without an article in the predicate of the sentence is normally qualitative (that is, describing the quality of something in size, appearance, value, etc.), sometimes definite, and rarely indefinite.[76] (In English, we give a definite noun the article "the"—e.g.,

---

75. Lynn Allan Kauppi, *Foreign but Familiar Gods: Greco-Romans Read Religion in Acts* (New York: T&T Clark, 2006), 113–14.

76. Daniel B. Wallace, *Greek Grammar beyond the Basics: An Exegetical Syntax of the New Testament* (Grand Rapids: Zondervan, 1996), 267–68.

"the book"—while an indefinite noun has "a" or "an" preceding it—e.g., "a book.") In other words, according to this rule, the lack of a definite article in the second phrase of John 1:1 makes it likely that it should be understood as "the God" rather than "a God." Many scholars point to the rule and immediately conclude that an anarthrous (that is, one without an article) predicate nominative *must certainly* then be definite, thus solving the problem of reading "a god" instead of "God." Unfortunately, Colwell's rule does not claim that a noun in this grammatical construction *must* be definite. A closer examination of the grammar involved provides not only a satisfactory answer to the problem, but one that is theologically sound as well.

First, Colwell's rule offers three options for the noun in question: indefinite, definite, or qualitative. If *theos* were indefinite in John 1:1, it would be the only such indefinite noun in the Gospel of John, meaning that the indefinite translation does not conform to the literary evidence and thus runs contrary to a basic principle of the historical-grammatical method.[77] Second, Colwell's rule applies best to nouns already determined to be definite; it does not specify that a noun in this grammatical construction (anarthrous preverbal predicate nominative) *will be* definite.[78] Instead, the definiteness of the noun must be determined from context. Because the previous use of *theos* is definite, extending this definiteness to the second use of *theos* is grammatically possible.

However, Daniel Wallace argues that the best candidate for this particular text is actually qualitative, not definite. He points out that if the second *theos* were definite, it would be equating Jesus ontologically with the Father, saying essentially that "the Word was the *Father*."[79] Such a translation opens the way for modalism, which the entire Gospel of John argues against. On the other hand, understanding *theos* as qualitative affirms the deity of the Word yet draws the comparison to the Father in nature but not in person, thus proclaiming the essential unity of the two while also declaring the difference in persons between the Word and the Father.[80]

---

77. Wallace, *Greek Grammar beyond the Basics*, 267.

78. Contra Bruce M. Metzger, "On the Translation of John i. 1," *ExpTim* 63 (1951–1952): 125–26.

79. Wallace, *Greek Grammar beyond the Basics*, 268.

80. Wallace, *Greek Grammar beyond the Basics*, 269.

From a historical perspective, John's choice of the term "Word" (*logos*) is particularly telling as well. He commandeers and then subverts a key concept in Stoicism, the most popular philosophy in the Hellenistic world at that time, to both compare and redefine how Hellenistic readers conceptualize the driving force of the world.[81] Instead of using *logos* as a Stoic would, John redefines the term in light of Christ to show that the true *logos* is no impersonal guiding force but a supremely personal, divine answer to the problems of human sin and death. John's concept of *logos* appears, then, to intentionally serve as an alternative or corrective to the Stoic concept of *logos*.

Thus understanding both the grammar and the world of the text not only reveals layers of meaning in John 1:1 but also leads to a more robust theology of the Trinity.

2.4 LIMITATIONS OF THE HISTORICAL-GRAMMATICAL APPROACH

Because the historical-grammatical approach has been defined in multiple ways, it is difficult to pinpoint its limitations. However, some trends in methodology do place definite limits on the approach as an overall hermeneutical strategy. In general, the insistence of some scholars on one correct meaning per text represents a failure to appreciate the polysemous potentiality of language itself.

A text may deliberately carry more than one meaning or may consciously evoke stories or cue concepts that add meaning to the literal text. Overlooking these possibilities reflects an incomplete understanding of the potential of language and risks missing a greater point that an author might seek to communicate. For example, the symbolic language of John's Gospel and the stories of Paul evoke many concepts and ideas with key phrases and allusive language. Reading the text in light of these stories and symbols may change the sense of the interpretation—and should change it if the interpretation is to realize the fullness of meaning intended by the author. In short, the complexity of language in general and the sophistication of many of the biblical authors require the biblical scholar to either

---

81. Raymond E. Brown, *The Gospel according to John (I–XII)* (Garden City, NY: Doubleday, 1966), 519–20.

intentionally limit their interpretation or expand the concept of the historical-grammatical approach in order to appreciate the text more fully.

In addition, limiting one's hermeneutical strategy to simply the core historical-grammatical methods may lead to confusion as students seek to understand the hermeneutics and intertextuality they see at work within the Bible.[82] A variety of approaches, especially those well-grounded in history, may enable students to make better sense of the internal hermeneutics of the Bible, especially the intertextuality of the NT (e.g., Paul's use and interpretation of the OT).

Finally, external limitations placed on the historical-grammatical approach may not actually be helpful. Some scholars argue against integrating secular principles into the hermeneutical process.[83] This limitation may simply miss out on new hermeneutical insights due to a conviction that "secular" truths should not be incorporated into an interpretation of sacred text.

However, it must be noted that most of the limitations are reflections of external limitations on how far one may extend the concepts of grammatical and historical analysis. Those who have been willing to expand their horizons within these principles have found ample reward in both interpretation and in their impact on biblical studies and methodology in general.

2.5 CONTEMPORARY INFLUENCE OF THE HISTORICAL-GRAMMATICAL APPROACH

As what is included in "history" continues to expand, the implications of a historical text become more inclusive, and new methodologies are developed in their turn. For example, social history, cultural history, gender studies, and the role of social sciences in history have all become legitimate facets of history, and thus, as they are applied to the biblical text, become new ways of reading the text historically.

---

82. On the influence of intertextuality on biblical interpretation, see Jeffery M. Leonard, "Inner-Biblical Interpretation and Intertextuality," in *Literary Approaches to the Bible*, ed. Douglas Mangum and Douglas Estes, Lexham Methods Series 4 (Bellingham, WA: Lexham Press, 2017).

83. Thomas, *Evangelical Hermeneutics*, 129.

Linguistic developments over the past century have focused on the actual use of language and on the relationship of language to reality.[84] These studies, applied to the biblical text, have engaged and contributed to the issues of signification, real referents, symbolic language, insider/outsider language, and the play of language in a variety of literary genres.

The emphasis within the historical-grammatical approach on reading the text historically has influenced other reading strategies, including genre studies and rhetorical criticism.[85] Scholars have sought historical grounding for these, recognizing the danger of applying modern, generic labels and conventions of speech to ancient texts.

In short, any approach that recognizes the primacy of grammatical analysis and the essential role of historical contextualization in understanding and interpreting the text has been influenced by the historical-grammatical approach. As John Bright observes, the first stage of exegesis is historical-grammatical analysis.[86] Any next steps in the hermeneutical process occur within the boundaries established by and informed by the results of that analysis, whether those steps be rhetorical criticism, narrative criticism, literary criticism, social-scientific criticism, or any combination of these or other approaches.

Thus, analysis of the language of a text within the world of that text remains the primary step in interpretation, whether the interpreter be a scholar, minister, or a lay reader of the Bible. William Tolar captures the spirit and significance of the method in his commendation to students:

> Without an honest, careful, intelligent use of grammatical and historical knowledge, there is little or no hope for a correct interpretation of documents written in foreign languages within several different ancient historical contexts. To fail to use proper grammatical rules or to ignore those historical contexts is most certainly to guarantee failure in understanding the writer's intended meanings.[87]

---

84. For more on linguistics, see Douglas Mangum and Josh Westbury, eds., *Linguistics & Biblical Exegesis*, Lexham Methods Series 2 (Bellingham, WA: Lexham Press, 2017).

85. On the study of biblical genres, see chap. 4 on form criticism. On rhetorical criticism and other literary approaches, see Douglas Mangum and Douglas Estes, eds., *Literary Approaches to the Bible*, Lexham Methods Series 4 (Bellingham, WA: Lexham Press, 2017).

86. Bright, *Authority of the Old Testament*, 169.

87. Tolar, "Grammatical-Historical Method," 21.

2.6 RESOURCES FOR FURTHER STUDY

Aune, David E. "Historical Criticism." In *The Blackwell Companion to the New Testament*, edited by David E. Aune, 101–15. Malden, MA: Wiley-Blackwell, 2010.

> Aune provides a helpful overview of historical criticism and explains its relationship to the historical-grammatical method. He notes that the historical-grammatical method could be considered a "theologically sanitized form of the historical-critical method" adopted "as a conscious alternative to historical criticism" (102). In conservative approaches to biblical criticism, the interpretive process is guided by orthodox doctrines about the nature of the Bible.

Krentz, Edgar. *The Historical-Critical Method*. Philadelphia: Fortress Press, 1975.

> Krentz offers a concise and largely favorable discussion of the historical-critical method. His overview of the development of the method from the Reformation and Enlightenment up through the mid-twentieth century emphasizes the constructive and positive effect the historical-critical method had on improving biblical interpretation.

Terry, Milton S. *Biblical Hermeneutics: A Treatise on the Interpretation of the Old and New Testaments*. New York: Phillips & Hunt, 1883.

> Terry's work is one of the more influential books on hermeneutics for conservative biblical scholarship. According to Terry, the "grammatico-historical sense of a writer is such an interpretation of his language as is required by the laws of grammar and the facts of history" (203). He contrasts a grammatical-historical approach with mystical, mythical, or allegorical approaches that tend to ignore the ordinary, straightforward meaning that the words would have had in the author's historical context.

Tolar, William B. "The Grammatical-Historical Method." In *Biblical Hermeneutics: A Comprehensive Introduction to Interpreting Scripture,* edited by Bruce Corley, Steve W. Lemke, and Grant I. Lovejoy, 21–38. Nashville, TN: Broadman & Holman, 1996.

Tolar discusses the historical-grammatical approach as an essential part of properly interpreting the Bible because understanding the grammatical rules and historical circumstances of an ancient text is the only way to really understand the intended message of the text. Tolar describes the method in fairly neutral terms. His overview explains the methodology as commonly used by evangelical Bible scholars.

Torrey, R. A., A. C. Dixon, and Louis Meyer, eds. *The Fundamentals: A Testimony to the Truth.* 4 vols. Los Angeles, CA: Bible Institute of Los Angeles, 1917.

The Fundamentals is a collection of 90 articles by conservative Christian authors, first published between 1910 and 1915 in twelve volumes. The essays were reorganized and reprinted in a four-volume set in 1917. A number of the essays in volume one of the four-volume set present a conservative Protestant view of biblical criticism that is highly critical of the methodology for what is seen as the attempt from historical criticism to undermine the Bible as the inspired word of God. The essay on the history of higher criticism provides a view of the development of the method that is instructive for better understanding the ongoing debate in conservative circles over whether critical methods are acceptable for Christian interpreters.

3
SOURCE CRITICISM

Amy Balogh, Dan Cole, and Wendy Widder

The dean's office of any university will tell you that plagiarism is a problem on campus. Plagiarism has always been a temptation for students, but the internet has made finding and copying sources possible with the click of a mouse. When a professor grades a cut-and-pasted paper, she can often easily recognize the presence of different sources. The first clue that the material is not original to the student is usually that it outsmarts the student; that is, the professor knows that Student X does not have the mastery of language and material evident in the paper. Other clues are the "seams" between stolen sources; when certain paragraphs differ significantly from others in style and syntax, they most likely came from another source (probably the student). The same Internet at the disposal of the student is at the disposal of the professor, who—through a Google search of phrases and clauses—can often determine what sources the student used to put together the paper. The student may have failed, but the professor has successfully carried out a modern version of source criticism.

3.1 DEFINITION AND GOAL OF THE METHOD

Source criticism is the scholarly attempt to identify the literary sources behind biblical books (such as the book of Isaiah or the Gospel of Luke) or collections of books (such as the Pentateuch).[1] It is one of the most

---

1. Source criticism used to be called "literary criticism" in biblical studies because of its focus on literary sources. For example, Norman Habel's 1971 book introducing source criticism was called *Literary Criticism of the Old Testament* (Philadelphia: Fortress). As biblical

widely known methods arising from nineteenth-century critical scholarship. Source criticism works on the assumptions that many biblical books
are anonymous, written over a long period of time, and based on several
sources. In various places throughout the Old Testament, the text names
the sources behind it; for example, Num 21:14 refers to the Book of the Wars
of Yahweh, and Josh 10:13 cites the Book of Jashar (see also 2 Sam 1:18). Some
of the material in 1-2 Kings and 1-2 Chronicles—namely, the genealogies of
the monarchs in Israel and Judah—are attributed to ancient court records
(see, e.g., 1 Kgs 11:41; 14:29; 16:5). Unfortunately, these sources are lost to us
and known only from the references in the Old Testament.

However, the majority of books in the Bible are silent on the sources
of their material. The task of source critics is to determine what written
documents might lie behind the final form of the biblical text and also to
propose a historical setting and purpose for each document.[2] Source critics
analyze complete texts in order to separate them into sources, and then
synthesize the sorted material into separate documents, that is, what they
propose to be the original documents behind the extant version. Since
ancient authors did not have the same concerns that we have today about
the ownership of our written material, the practice of blending various
sources into a composite document was not unheard of in the ancient world.

3.1.1 SOURCE CRITICISM, TEXTUAL CRITICISM, AND "LITERARY" CRITICISM

This scholarly inquiry into the written sources behind the Bible emerged
at the same time that scholars were investigating various manuscripts
of the Bible and trying to determine which reading of the text was most
likely to be the original (i.e., text criticism). As a way to distinguish these
two areas of focus—one on the history of the text and the other on the text
itself—textual criticism came to be called "lower criticism," while source
criticism was called "higher criticism" (as well as "literary criticism" or
"historical criticism"). The label "lower criticism" reflects textual criticism's
focus on the most basic level of interpretation, the individual words on

---

scholarship drew more from secular literary criticism in the last quarter of the twentieth century, the use of the label "literary criticism" was no longer a clear reference to source criticism.

2. J. Coert Rylaarsdam, "Foreword," in Norman C. Habel, *Literary Criticism of the Old
Testament*, OTS (Philadelphia: Fortress, 1971), iii-vi.

the page. By contrast, "higher criticism" engages more abstract notions of authorship, date, setting, motivation for writing, and composition. While these terms appear in many written materials of the past two hundred years, the majority of scholars no longer use the labels "lower" and "higher" criticism; now the two approaches are known mainly as textual criticism and source criticism. Furthermore, the term "literary criticism" is now reserved for the analysis of literary features in the final form of the text, such as metaphor and imagery.

3.1.2 UNDERLYING ASSUMPTIONS

Several assumptions underlie the attempt to identify written sources that may have been brought together in the composition of the Bible. The first is that some biblical books are composite documents that reflect the hand of more than one author or editor, but do not indicate explicitly which authors or editors were responsible for the sections. The second assumption is that differences in such elements as vocabulary, style, and theme provide enough information for scholars to be able to suggest where the text may switch from one source to another, thus providing an overall picture of how the biblical book(s) at hand may have been put together. Source critics make these suggestions based on the stylistic features that characterize the hypothetical sources and often use statistical studies of the language and grammar of the passages at hand.

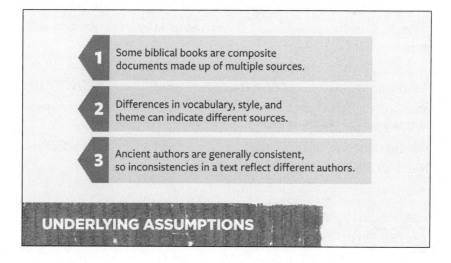

1 Some biblical books are composite documents made up of multiple sources.

2 Differences in vocabulary, style, and theme can indicate different sources.

3 Ancient authors are generally consistent, so inconsistencies in a text reflect different authors.

UNDERLYING ASSUMPTIONS

Another underlying assumption is that the ancient authors are generally consistent in their vocabulary, ideology, ability to narrate clearly, and ability to remember and read what they themselves have already written. Inconsistencies reflect different authors because authors generally do not contradict themselves. Furthermore, every author has his or her own voice and markedly different way of writing, because each comes to the task with a different background and authorial purpose.

3.1.3 KEY CONCEPTS

Source criticism is based on the idea that biblical books were edited together from various written sources. For the study of the Pentateuch, the Documentary Hypothesis is a fundamental concept for source criticism.

> Stated briefly and in purely literary terms, the Documentary Hypothesis states that the Pentateuch took shape in a series of stages in which, during the space of several centuries, four originally distinct books ("documents"), each written at a different time, were dovetailed together by a series of "redactors" to form a single work.[3]

Source critics commonly use specialized terms to describe aspects of their work. For example, the editing process is called "redaction," and the person responsible for the editing or compiling of source material is called a "redactor." Source criticism of the Pentateuch also commonly uses the initials J, E, D, and P to refer to different sources, following Julius Wellhausen's labeling of Pentateuchal sources. Over time, this shorthand for referring to parts of the Pentateuch as J, E, D, or P was adopted by other methods, such as form criticism, tradition history, and redaction criticism.

J for "Jahwist" is the German equivalent of "Yahwist." The name of the document comes from its use of the divine name "Yahweh" (YHWH), also known as the Tetragrammaton. The first occurrence of the divine name is in Gen 2:4b and signals the beginning of the J source. The J source, a continuous narrative, includes much of Genesis and sections of Exodus and Numbers. Wellhausen dated it loosely to the "Assyrian period" and said it

---

3. R. N. Whybray, *The Making of the Pentateuch: A Methodological Study* (Sheffield: Sheffield Academic, 1994), 20.

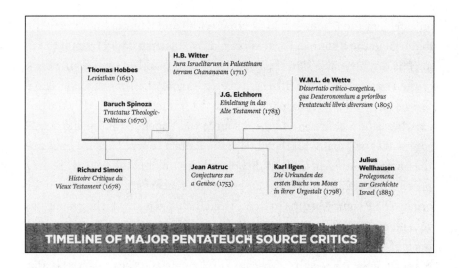

TIMELINE OF MAJOR PENTATEUCH SOURCE CRITICS

describes the religious situation of the early divided monarchy, especially in the southern kingdom.[4]

E for "Elohist" is the name for the document characterized by use of the name "Elohim" (God) to refer to the deity. It begins in Gen 15 and covers much of the same content as the J source. Prior to the revelation of the divine name "Yahweh" to Moses in Exodus, the E source uses only the name "Elohim" for God. Beyond the difference in divine names, it is difficult to distinguish between the J and E sources, leading some to refer to J/E rather than dividing between the two. E dates to the mid-eighth century and originated in the northern kingdom, Israel. The Hypothesis suggests that an author combined the J and E sources in the southern kingdom, some time after the fall of the northern kingdom in 722 BC.

D is for "Deuteronomist." This third document refers to the book of Deuteronomy (cf. Deuteronomistic History), which possibly developed from the "book of the law" that priest Hilkiah discovered in the temple in 622/621 BC, thus inspiring King Josiah's reforms (2 Kgs 22:3—23:25; cf. 2 Chr 34:3—35:19). The Hypothesis proposes that the core of Deuteronomy was created to propagate these reforms. Wellhausen argues that the

---

4. Julius Wellhausen, *Prolegomena to the History of Israel*, trans. J. Sutherland Black and Allan Menzies (Edinburgh: Adam & Charles Black, 1885), 13, 32. He also referred to the time frame as "the pre-prophetic period" (33). Wellhausen first published his work on the sources of the Pentateuch in 1876. The widely used English translation is based on the second German edition of 1883: *Prolegomena zur Geschichte Israels* (Berlin: G. Reimer, 1883).

author(s) of the D source was familiar with J and E but did not know the material in the P source. For this reason, Wellhausen dated P last.

P is for "Priestly." This last source determined the final framework of the Pentateuch in the fifth century BC, during the time of Ezra. The P source integrated its own materials into the framework offered by the pre-existing J and E sources, and the D source was appended at the end. The P source was originally conflated with the Elohist source because both use the name "Elohim" in Genesis. Scholars later isolated the Priestly source based on its affinity with priestly language, concerns, and a penchant for order. The P source begins in Gen 1:1 and includes many of the narratives, genealogies, and laws in Genesis, Exodus, and Numbers, plus the entire book of Leviticus.[5] Wellhausen argued that the P source was the "easiest to recognize with certainty" because of its style and vocabulary.[6] He also contended that it showed "an evolutionary development of religious practice leaving sole authority in priestly hands."[7]

Apart from labeling their hypothesized sources, source critics devote most of their attention to close study of the literary features of the text. A key concept for source criticism is that literary inconsistencies like repeated stories or shifts in vocabulary reveal where two sources may have been edited together. For example, an overall shift of literary style from Isa 1–39 to Isa 40–66 is generally assumed to mark a shift in authorship. The shift in usage of names for God between Gen 1 and Gen 2 is thought to indicate two different sources.

Since the development of source criticism progressed largely with research on the Pentateuch, so the labels and concepts associated with source criticism first emerged in that context. However, the core idea about finding the origins of biblical books in written sources that can be isolated through literary analysis was influential for studies far beyond the Pentateuch.

---

5. In later scholarship on the Documentary Hypothesis, Lev 17–26 comes to be called the "Holiness Code" and is attributed to a later fifth source, H ("Holiness").

6. Wellhausen, *Prolegomena*, 6.

7. David W. Baker, "Source Criticism," in *Dictionary of the Old Testament Pentateuch*, ed. T. Desmond Alexander and David W. Baker (Downers Grove, IL: InterVarsity, 2012), 802.

3.2 DEVELOPMENT OF SOURCE CRITICISM

Source criticism developed in post-Enlightenment biblical scholarship, but its roots lie in the Middle Ages. Until the advent of modern biblical scholarship in the seventeenth to twentieth centuries, most people simply accepted traditional views on the authorship of biblical books. For example, most people assumed that Moses was the author of the Pentateuch (Genesis–Deuteronomy), though some acknowledged that he may not have written about his own death (Deut 34). A handful of church fathers thought the sacred books of the OT had been destroyed during the exile in Babylon and then rewritten by Ezra (c. 450 BC), who was given divine revelation of their contents (see 2 Esdras 14). In the twelfth century,[8] Spanish scholar Abraham Ibn Ezra hinted in a commentary on Deuteronomy that there were other things in the book that Moses could not have written. However, no one developed Ibn Ezra's ideas until centuries later.

Scholars have applied source criticism to many different parts of the Bible, but three sections have received more attention than others: the Pentateuch, the book of Isaiah, and the Synoptic Gospels (Matthew, Mark, and Luke). Source criticism was foundational to the development of present-day approaches to biblical scholarship, and while not all agree on the value of this method or its findings, many scholars continue to employ the method as a critical, early step in the interpretive process.

3.2.1 EARLY DAYS OF SOURCE CRITICISM
(SEVENTEENTH AND EIGHTEENTH CENTURIES)[9]

In 1651 English philosopher Thomas Hobbes published what would later become a classic on the structure of society and government. His book *Leviathan* included a significant section on the "Christian Commonwealth," in which Hobbes discussed revelation and the authorship of the Bible. He asserted that determination of authorship must be based on internal evidence, not external tradition. Therefore, any Pentateuchal passages that explicitly identified Moses as their author, Hobbes attributed to Moses.

---

8. All dates are AD unless otherwise noted.—Eds.

9. For brief surveys of the early works in source criticism, see Edward J. Young, *An Introduction to the Old Testament* (Grand Rapids: Eerdmans, 1977), 117-22; Joseph Blenkinsopp, *The Pentateuch: An Introduction to the First Five Books of the Bible* (New York: Doubleday, 1992), 1-4.

However, the anonymity of the completed work, combined with a number of passages that reflect a time period after Moses (e.g., Deut 34; Gen 12:6), led him to conclude that Moses did not write the final document: "It is therefore sufficiently evident that the five Books of Moses were written after his time, though how long after it be not so manifest. But though Moses did not compile those Books entirely, and in the form we have them, yet he wrote all that which he is there said to have written."[10] Hobbes' ideas and conclusions thus helped lay the foundation for the "secular" study of the Bible.

In a similar vein, Baruch Spinoza, a seventeenth-century Jewish philosopher from Amsterdam, laid out a program for modern biblical scholarship in *Tractatus Theologico-Politicus* (1670). Spinoza explicitly identified verses in Deuteronomy and Genesis that Moses could not have written. For example, the first verse of Deuteronomy refers to Moses' words to Israel "beyond the Jordan," a geographical reference most likely to be made by someone in the land of Israel (Deut 1:1). Similarly, in Genesis 12:6 the narrator describes Abraham's journey through the land of promise at a time when "the Canaanites were in the land," a temporal statement that suggests the account comes from a later time when the Canaanites are *not* in the land, that is, after the events of the book of Joshua. Since Moses neither entered the promised land nor saw the time when Canaanites were not there, he could not be the author of statements like this, which are attested throughout the Pentateuch. Spinoza concluded, "From what has been said, it is thus clearer than sun at noonday that the Pentateuch was not written by Moses, but by someone who lived long after Moses."[11]

A contemporary of Spinoza, the French priest Richard Simon suggested that the nonlegal materials of the Pentateuch owe their authorship to someone other than Moses. He also noted the diversity of style and structure in the narrative portions of the Pentateuch, as well as the occurrence of "doublets," or accounts that appear more than once (e.g., the matriarchs in danger in Gen 8:10–20; 20:1–18; 26:1–11).[12] The Roman Catholic Church penal-

---

10. Thomas Hobbes, *Leviathan* (London, 1651), 3.33.

11. Benedict Spinoza, *Tractatus Theologico-Politicus* (Amsterdam, 1670), caput VIII.

12. Richard Simon, *Histoire critique du Vieux Testament* (Paris, 1678), livre premier, chapitre V.

ized Simon for his book, *Histoire Critique du Vieux Testament*, destroying most of the thirteen hundred copies in print and effectively banishing him.

Suggestions that someone other than Moses wrote the Pentateuch—or at least the sources behind the Pentateuch—took more definitive shape in the work of several eighteenth-century scholars, including Henning Bernhard Witter, Jean Astruc, and Johann Gottfried Eichhorn. In his 1711 monograph, Witter observed that Gen 1:1–2:4 is parallel to Gen 2:5–3:24, but each account uses different names for God: in Gen 1, the name Elohim is used, and in Gen 2–3 the divine name YHWH is used.[13] Witter proposed that Gen 1–17 contained two narrative strands, which were distinguishable by their use of the divine name and by the occurrence of doublets. According to Witter, Moses did write the Pentateuch, but used earlier materials as sources in order to do so. In 1753, Jean Astruc, a French royal physician and "amateur Old Testament scholar,"[14] seconded the findings of Spinoza, Simon, and Witter, then accounted for some of the Pentateuch's diversity by proposing further "that Moses had arranged these early sources synoptically, rather like a synopsis of the gospels, but that the pages got mixed up in the course of transmission."[15]

Like Astruc and his predecessors, Eichhorn originally believed that Moses had compiled Genesis using several smaller documents from two distinct sources, distinguishable by their use of the divine name. He further believed that Exodus-Deuteronomy had been written by Moses. Eichhorn later abandoned this view of Mosaic authorship and held that an unknown redactor had combined the Pentateuchal sources into the document known today.[16] A major difficulty scholars had with Eichhorn's theory is that one of his sources, known as the "Elohist" source, was too diverse to represent a single tradition. In 1798 Karl Ilgen resolved this problem by dividing the "Elohist" source into two documents, which both used the name "Elohim" (gods, God) for the deity.[17] The combined efforts of these scholars produced the theory that later scholarship would call the Older Documentary Hypothesis. Once scholars had adopted the idea of multiple

---

13. Young, *Introduction*, 118.
14. Blenkinsopp, *Pentateuch*, 3.
15. Blenkinsopp, *Pentateuch*, 3.
16. Blenkinsopp, *Pentateuch*, 5; Young, *Introduction*, 126.
17. Blenkinsopp, *Pentateuch*, 5.

sources composing biblical books, they began to ask questions about the origins of these sources. As a result, scholars became increasingly interested in matters such as the date, audience, and original purpose of the biblical writings.

While the Documentary Hypothesis regarding the Pentateuch was taking shape, source-critical theories on the three Synoptic Gospels were also developing. As early as Augustine (fourth century AD), scholars assumed literary interdependence among the three books. Two of the Gospel writers seem to have used one or more of the other Gospels and perhaps other lost sources to write their own books. Determining the nature of these literary relationships was the goal of NT source critics.

In 1771 G. E. Lessing proposed the idea of an "Ur-Gospel," a single hypothetical Gospel that each of the Synoptic Gospel writers used to create their compositions, and argued that the similarities among the Synoptics are because all of the authors used this Ur-Gospel.[18] Eichhorn later modified this view, suggesting several lost Gospels in addition to the Ur-Gospel. Both Lessing and Eichhorn proposed that the original Ur-Gospel was an Aramaic document that had been translated into Greek and then revised several times. These different Greek recensions accounted for the differences among the Synoptics: the authors had used different Greek versions of the Aramaic Ur-Gospel.

Twenty years later, a more popular theory was developed by J. J. Griesbach, who expanded on an idea originally presented in 1764. Eventually known as the Griesbach Hypothesis or the Two-Gospel Hypothesis, Griesbach contended that the Gospel of Matthew was written before both Mark and Luke. Luke then used Matthew, and Mark used both of the earlier Gospels. This hypothesis fell out of favor, only to be revived in the twentieth century by W. R. Farmer (1964).[19]

---

18. D. A. Carson and Douglas J. Moo, *An Introduction to the New Testament*, 2nd ed. (Grand Rapids: Zondervan, 2005), 89–90.

19. William R. Farmer, *The Synoptic Problem: A Critical Analysis* (New York: Macmillan, 1964).

3.2.2 THE HEYDAY OF SOURCE CRITICISM
(NINETEENTH AND TWENTIETH CENTURIES)

At the same time that source critics were deconstructing the composition of biblical books, other (i.e., textual-critical) scholars were studying a variety of biblical manuscripts in several languages. The findings of textual critics made biblical scholars aware of the great complexity behind the *transmission* of the text, while the hypotheses of source critics suggested a similar complexity behind the *formation* of the texts.

By the beginning of the nineteenth century, source critics of the Pentateuch had reached the consensus that Moses did not write these books, though he may have written bits and pieces, and maybe even most of Deuteronomy. The Documentary Hypothesis and source criticism in general took an important turn in 1805 with the publication of Wilhelm Martin Leberecht de Wette's dissertation on Deuteronomy.[20] De Wette concluded that the law book found by Josiah's men in 622/621 BC (2 Kgs 22:8–20) was written during Josiah's reign to propagate his reforms and formed the core of what would later become the book of Deuteronomy. According to de Wette, Deuteronomy was the latest source in the Pentateuch, preceded by a collection of annals and materials from the time before the monarchy (e.g., pre-David), which the author of Deuteronomy—most likely a prophet—combined and expanded. Thus, de Wette postulated four sources that roughly corresponded to what would eventually be called J, P, E, and D.[21] The contributions of de Wette came to represent a shift in critical scholarship, because he was the first to propose the four-source framework and also looked beyond the figure of Moses for possible movers behind the project of the Pentateuch.

While source-critical scholars were still interested in the literary sources behind the biblical compositions, they had shifted their attention toward understanding the development of Israelite religion from its earliest days to the post-exilic period. For some scholars, this interest in Israel's developing religion reflected romantic trends in broader scholarship that viewed human religious institutions as degenerative developments from the "pure," nature-based spiritual practices of earlier times.

---

20. Young, *Introduction*, 124–25.
21. Blenkinsopp, *Pentateuch*, 6.

This "romanticism," as it was called, led to a deep anti-institutional bias evidenced in much nineteenth-century scholarship and shaped scholarly attitudes against the church and especially against the synagogue. Thus, Israel's religion before the exile and even before the monarchy was thought to be a more spiritual version of religious practice, connected to nature, than the Judaism that emerged in the post-exilic period. For others, however, post-exilic Judaism represented an evolutionary process in which the legal material was a positive development. Regardless of the perceived quality of the legal material, the idea that Judaism was a relatively late development—not revealed to Moses on Mount Sinai—became a cornerstone of mid-nineteenth-century versions of the Documentary Hypothesis.

In the years leading up to Julius Wellhausen, the scholar most famously associated with the Documentary Hypothesis, several other European scholars contributed important ideas to the development of the theory.[22] Wilhem Vatke concluded that the legal portions of the Pentateuch came later and represent a positive development of Israelite religion. Hermann Hupfeld identified three complete and independent documents in Genesis: the J source, an earlier E source, and a later E source. Hupfeld dated the law to the Persian period (538–332 BC), after the time of the Prophetic Books. Similarly, Edouard Reuss dated the law after the prophets. Reuss' student Karl Heinrich Graf further developed the ideas of Vatke, Reuss, and Hupfeld, proposing that Hupfeld's second E source was a late priestly document—the P source. At about the same time, Abraham Kuenen independently reached conclusions similar to Graf's. Their ideas put all the pieces in place for Wellhausen to synthesize the information and to write his seminal work *Prolegomena to the History of Israel* (in German) in the 1880s. In brief, Wellhausen claimed that the Pentateuch was composed of four distinct written sources, J, E, D, and P, and that this was the order of their composition.[23] This "New Documentary Hypothesis" is also known as the Graf-Wellhausen Hypothesis, though it represents the synthesis of the work of many more scholars.

---

22. See Blenkinsopp, *Pentateuch*, 4–9, for a survey of Pentateuch scholarship in the mid-nineteenth century prior to Wellhausen.

23. For more details on the four sources, see §3.1.3 Key Concepts, above.

At around the same time, other scholars were focused on the book of Isaiah, echoing an idea expressed centuries earlier by the Jewish commentator Abraham Ibn Ezra. In the mid-twelfth century Ibn Ezra argued that the second half of Isaiah had been written by "an anonymous prophet who began to prophesy in Babylon on the eve of the Persian conquest."[24] Ibn Ezra's reason for dividing the book of Isaiah was his belief that prophets spoke intelligibly to their audiences with messages that were meaningful to their situations. In this framework, the news in the second half of Isaiah that King Cyrus of Persia would restore the exilic community in Babylon to its land would have been meaningless to the historical audience of the eighth-century prophet because at that point the Judaeans were still living in their land and tangling with the Assyrian King Sennacherib. Ibn Ezra's ideas did not take hold in biblical scholarship until the late eighteenth century, when J. G. Eichhorn and others reached a similar conclusion, namely that the book of Isaiah had two authors: the eighth-century prophet Isaiah (Isa 1-39) and an anonymous sixth-century prophet of the exile (Isa 40-66).

Wellhausen's student Bernhard Duhm developed the Three-Source Hypothesis on the book of Isaiah. First, he argued that the second half of Isaiah (Isa 40-66) was better divided into two sections written by two different authors in two different time periods: "Second Isaiah" (or Deutero-Isaiah) consists of chapters 40-55 and was written during the Babylonian exile; "Third Isaiah" (or Trito-Isaiah) consists of chapters 55-66 and was written in the early years of post-exilic restoration. Duhm proposed that the writings of the different prophets had originally circulated "as independent collections of [their] sayings," and, with a handful of other collections (e.g., Isa 24-27; 34; 36-39), were eventually compiled into the book of Isaiah.[25] This happened during the Maccabean era in "a relatively mechanical process" (c. 70 BC).[26] Later scholars would refine Duhm's hypothesis, placing Second Isaiah in exile and Third Isaiah in Jerusalem during the

---

24. Uriel Simon, "Ibn Ezra between Medievalism and Modernism: The Case of Isaiah xl-lxvi," in *Congress Volume: Salamanca 1983*, ed. J. A. Emerton (Leiden: Brill, 1995), 257.

25. Marvin A. Sweeney, "The Latter Prophets: Isaiah, Jeremiah, Ezekiel," in *The Hebrew Bible Today: An Introduction to Critical Issues*, ed. Steven L. McKenzie and M. Patrick Graham (Louisville: Westminster John Knox, 1998), 76.

26. Sweeney, "Latter Prophets: Isaiah, Jeremiah, Ezekiel," 76.

Persian period.[27] Duhm's second hypothesis was that the four "Servant Songs" of Second Isaiah were not part of the original composition but had been worked into the text over time from marginal writings. Finally, Duhm hypothesized that Isaiah of Jerusalem, the eighth-century prophet, was not the author of everything in chapters 1–39. For example, the diversity of the material in Isa 24–27 suggested to Duhm that the section had been written by someone else and added to Isaiah later.[28] In the decades that followed Duhm, scholars further divided the book into fragments studied in isolation from their surrounding contexts.

At the same time that source-critical theories of the Pentateuch and Isaiah were under construction, in NT studies the idea of an "Ur-Gospel" that lay behind the three Synoptics was encountering difficulty. The more scholars evaluated the possibility of a single source, the more that source looked like an earlier form of the Gospel of Mark. This introduced a scholarly framework that still dominates the field of Gospel studies today, namely the textual priority of the Gospel of Mark, also known as Markan Priority. However, there remains a fair amount of material shared by Matthew and Luke that does not match anything in Mark. In 1861 the NT scholar H. J. Holtzmann addressed this problem by proposing a second main source behind Matthew and Luke, a collection of 230 or so sayings of Jesus. This hypothetical source was called "Quelle," meaning "source" in German, and eventually came to be known simply as "Q."[29] The introduction of Q put into place the Two-Document Hypothesis of the literary relationship among the three Synoptic Gospels. The theory of Markan priority also lay behind another hypothesis of the twentieth century, the Farrer-Goulder Hypothesis, which asserted that Matthew used Mark and then Luke used both Matthew and Mark. Also during the twentieth century, the Griesbach Hypothesis or Two-Gospel Hypothesis regained standing through the scholarship of W. R. Farmer and others.

---

27. Sweeney, "Latter Prophets: Isaiah, Jeremiah, Ezekiel," 76.

28. H. G. M. Williamson, "Isaiah: Book of," in *Dictionary of the Old Testament Prophets*, ed. Mark J. Boda and J. Gordon McConville (Downers Grove, IL: InterVarsity, 2012), 366–67.

29. G. N. Stanton, "Q," in *Dictionary of Jesus and the Gospels*, ed. Joel B. Green, Scot McKnight, and I. Howard Marshall (Downers Grove, IL: InterVarsity, 1992), 644.

3.2.3 SOURCE CRITICISM IN CONTEMPORARY RESEARCH

As the limitations of source criticism became apparent in the twentieth century, many scholars developed other ways to resolve the questions that lie behind the creation and compilation of the biblical material. Source criticism led to form criticism and tradition-history criticism, which, in turn, led to redaction criticism. While many scholars have turned their attention to the final form of the text, many source-critical issues still persist.

The Documentary (Graf-Wellhausen) Hypothesis stood as the primary model by which scholars understood the Pentateuch for over one hundred years. Its support began to wane in Europe in the 1970s, primarily under the influence of Rendtorff's *The Problem of the Process of Transmission in the Pentateuch* (German; 1975), which amplified the Traditio-Critical Hypothesis—the only viable competition for the Documentary Hypothesis on the issue of the composition of the Pentateuch (see below, under "Application"). Yet despite the amount of anti–Documentary Hypothesis literature, many scholars, particularly in the United States, still hold to modified versions of the theory, though specifics regarding the nature and date of the various sources remain major points of contention.[30]

Since the mid-1990s, and even more since the turn of the twenty-first century, scholars in the United States and around the globe have come to the defense of the Documentary Hypothesis, leading to what is now referred to as the Neo-Documentary Hypothesis. These scholars argue for the validity of the core of the original theory—that the Pentateuch is a combination of four literary sources that reached its final form sometime after Judah's exile (586 BC). These arguments stem from the conviction that the presence of distinct vocabulary, style, and ideology in certain portions of the Pentateuch, plus the existence of inconsistencies, doublets, and repetitions, must be theoretically explained. Furthermore, this cannot be done without positing the existence of different sources. Few scholars today hold to a strict view of Wellhausen's version of the Documentary Hypothesis, in all of its detail, but many hold to its core tenets, or at least modified versions of them. The nature and extent of the sources behind

---

30. Jean-Louis Ska, *Introduction to Reading the Pentateuch*, trans. Sr. Pascale Dominique (Winona Lake, IN: Eisenbrauns, 2006), 131–61.

the Pentateuch continue to be a source of scholarly discussion and will likely never be resolved.

The most extensive and influential volumes in support of the Neo-Documentary Hypothesis are *J, E, and the Redaction of the Pentateuch* (2009) and *The Composition of the Pentateuch: Renewing the Documentary Hypothesis* (2012), both by Joel S. Baden. Baden concludes that "what is most necessary in contemporary source-critical scholarship is a return to the simplest possible explanations for the various problems presented by the canonical text of the Pentateuch, based first and foremost on the literary evidence, before any historical or theological conclusions can be made."[31] This sentiment resonates with supporters of the (Neo-)Documentary Hypothesis because alternative theories that have been proposed thus far fail when applied to the problems inherent in the text of the Pentateuch.

As for the book of Isaiah, most critical scholarship assumes two or three sources, though some evangelical critical scholars continue to advocate for a single author. For the most part, Isaiah studies have moved past the source-critical debate and focus on other areas of interest. Many scholars have shifted attention to reading the book as a whole and trying to understand how the different authors and the final redactors established thematic relationships among the different sources.

The source-critical questions associated with the Synoptic Gospels remain an active point of debate. The two main approaches assert Markan priority: the Two-Document Hypothesis, which advocates the existence of Q, and the Farrer-Goulder Hypothesis, which argues that Luke used Matthew and Mark instead of sharing a second common source (Q) with Matthew. A third approach, the Griesbach Theory, held by a "weighty and vocal minority," holds to the priority of Matthew.[32] More detail on this issue appears below.

3.3 APPLICATIONS OF SOURCE CRITICISM

How does one put source criticism into practice in order to arrive at a hypothesis? Throughout the course of its development, source criticism

---

31. Joel S. Baden, *J, E, and the Redaction of the Pentateuch* (Tübingen: Mohr Siebeck, 2009), 313.

32. Mark Goodacre, *The Synoptic Problem: A Way through the Maze* (London: T&T Clark, 2001), 23.

developed general criteria that take center stage in critical analysis. However, the addition of other criteria and concerns by subsequent scholars often leads to strong criticism of the main theories and the development of alternative hypotheses. This is why no single theory for the authorship of the Pentateuch, the book of Isaiah, or the Synoptic Gospels has been universally adopted, though some proposed solutions do find more support than others.

3.3.1 PENTATEUCH

The basic claim of the classic Documentary Hypothesis is that the Pentateuch is composed of four separate, essentially complete, documents that an author or redactor combined into one work, most likely during the time of Ezra (fifth century BC). The order of the initials J-E-D-P reflects the order in which the documents behind the Pentateuch were written, beginning during the time of the first temple and ending with a completed document under Ezra during the postexilic period. Drawing heavily from the work of his predecessors, Wellhausen's primary thesis is that the Mosaic law (i.e., the formation of the covenant community at Mount Sinai) was not the starting point of Israel's history, but rather a later fabrication that served as the starting point of Judaism, the religious community that emerged out of the exile.[33] The Hypothesis has developed and changed many times since its beginnings, but after well over one hundred years in the academy, it remains the main theory regarding the composition of the Pentatuech.

3.3.1.a *Criteria for Identifying Sources*

The Pentateuch is a lengthy body of literature containing diverse subject matter and literary genre. In order to manage the task of applying source criticism to the Pentateuch as a whole, one must narrow the scope of investigation by deciding beforehand which criteria and historical concerns are to be prioritized. These data points and their underlying assumptions may vary from scholar to scholar, but there are a few major criteria that have garnered the attention of the majority of source-critical scholars. For the Pentateuch, these include distinct vocabulary and style, problems

---

33. Wellhausen, *Prolegomena*, 1.

with consistency or coherence, and doublets and repetition. Perhaps the most illustrative case study of the distinctiveness of each source's language is in how they talk about the deity, including which divine name each uses. The J (Yahwist) source always refers to the deity with the name "Yahweh" ("the LORD") and speaks about him in anthropomorphic terms. For example, Yahweh literally gets his hands dirty in the work of creation (Gen 2:7–9, 19–22) and goes for regularly scheduled walks in the garden of Eden, where he seeks the company of the first humans (Gen 3:8–10). The D (Deuteronomistic) source also uses the name Yahweh, but shies away from anthropomorphism by focusing on the work of Yahweh in history, specifically the exodus from Egypt and miracles in the wilderness, as grounds for morality and loving the deity "with all of your heart and with all of your soul and with all of your might" (Deut 6:5 LEB).

The E (Elohist) source uses only the generic terms "El" ("god," "God") or "Elohim" ("gods," "God") for the deity, until the name Yahweh is formally introduced into the narrative by the J source in Exod 3. After that point, it is difficult to distinguish between J and E, since E also speaks of God using anthropomorphism. At that point, another criterion is introduced. Scholars often divide J and E according to the notion that the J source is primarily concerned with locations in Judah, the southern kingdom of Israel after the united kingdom divides in two under King Rehoboam (1 Kgs 12), while the E source concerns itself with only locations in the northern kingdom, Israel. As for the D source, it is concerned about a different place altogether—an unnamed place—"the place that Yahweh your God will choose." This place is mentioned twenty-one times in the book of Deuteronomy as the site where Yahweh will cause his name to dwell once the people enter the promised land and likely refers to either Shiloh or Jerusalem.

Like the E source, the P (Priestly) source also uses only the terms "El" and "Elohim" to refer to the deity until the name Yahweh is formally introduced in Exod 6 (for E, this is Exod 3). However, P remains distinct because it portrays the divine as wholly other and therefore dangerous (e.g., Exod 40:33–38; Lev 10:1–7). P is also marked by repeated phrases, such as "in that day," "this word which Yahweh commanded," and "thus he did according to." Since the P source is primarily concerned with matters pertaining to daily life in the tabernacle or temple, including priestly and ritual traditions that are not discussed outside this source, it often uses subject-specific vocabulary and a distinctive mechanical style not found elsewhere in the Hebrew Bible (e.g., Gen 1; Lev 1–16). P's additional task of preserving genealogies, ages, and locations also adds to its narrative style (e.g., Gen 5).

All of these differences in language, style, and focus are by-products of what is truly different about each source, and that is their ideology. Different ways of talking about the divine draw the audience's attention to not only the coexistence of different literary sources, but also the different kinds of people and ways of thinking behind those literary sources, all of which are preserved and represented in a single work. For example, although the P source does not share J and E's anthropomorphic view of God, the redactor(s) do not edit out either P's or J/E's conception of the divine, but allow for a plurality of views to coexist within the text.

Another criterion that is central for source critics is attention to inconsistency and problems with coherence. Sometimes these appear as contradictions. For example, the number of prescribed animals in Noah's ark: according to the P source, God prescribes two of each species, male and female (Gen 6:19–20), whereas the J source specifies seven pair of each species, plus one pair of each unclean species (Gen 7:2–3). At other times, occurrences of inconsistency affect the clarity of a plot. For example, when Abraham banishes Hagar and Ishmael, Ishmael appears to be an infant (Gen 21:15–16), yet the surrounding narrative conveys that he was well over fourteen (Gen 16:16, 21:5)—an age at which he found mockery amusing (Gen 21:9). Although the ancient redactor did not mind such inconsistency, this is the sort of occurrence that draws the attention of source critics to the possibility that the section of text under consideration is a composite text. These critics then further their investigation regarding the textual boundaries of each source by using additional tools and criteria.

One of the features of the Pentateuch that first alerted scholars to the possibility of multiple literary traditions within a single text is the appearance of doublets or repetition. The mere existence of doublets does not necessarily prove that there are different sources, as there are a variety of explanations for this phenomenon (e.g., variant traditions regarding the same event, an author's reworking, literary type-scene). This must be assessed on a case-by-case basis. However, if there are other telling factors, such as notable differences in diction and issues of coherence, then this gives the critic an environment in which to isolate sources. Doublets may appear as either two or more separate tellings of the same event, such as the wife/sister scene (Gen 12:10–20; 20:1–18; 26:1–11), or two sources may be blended into a single narrative, such as the story of Noah (Gen 6–9), which often results in repetition and narrative inconsistencies.

It is often a combination of inconsistency and distinct vocabulary that leads source critics to conclude they are looking at a doublet. For example, one of the inconsistencies that first alerted scholars to the possibility of multiple sources in the Pentateuch occurs as early as Gen 1 and 2, in the order of creation. In Genesis 1:9–28, plants precede all living creatures, and humankind, male and female together, is the capstone. However, in Genesis 2:4–7, there are no plants at the time that the first male is formed because there is neither rain nor a human to till the ground. In response to the aloneness of the man, Yahweh forms both wild and domesticated beasts, plus birds, finally leading to the creation of the first female (Gen 2:19).

One also notices distinct vocabulary consistent with the P and J sources, respectively. Genesis 1 uses the terms "create" and "cause to divide" to describe the act of creation, which God—Elohim—directs through speech without directly engaging in the material world. This emphasizes the power and otherness of God that is characteristic of the P source's conception of the deity. In comparison, Genesis 2 uses "formed" and "planted" and portrays the LORD—Yahweh—in anthropomorphic terms. In Genesis 2–3 Yahweh gets his hands dirty (2:7–9, 19–22) and walks in the garden, conversing with humans (3:19). All of these observations suggest to many readers

SOURCE	IDENTIFYING MARKERS	CONTENT	DATE
J (Jahwist)	Uses the divine name YHWH, presents a God who walks and talks with us	Much of Genesis and sections of Exodus and Numbers	Assyrian period, particularly the early divided monarchy in the southern kingdom
E (Elohist)	Uses the name Elohim, presents a God who speaks in dreams	Begins in Genesis 15 and covers much of the same material as J.	The northern kingdom in the mid-eighth century BC
D (Deuteronomist)	Stresses a central place of worship, uses a moralistic approach	The book of Deuteronomy	622/621 BC, sparking King Josiah's reforms
P (Priestly)	Uses priestly language and has a penchant for order, uses a cultic approach	The entire Pentateuch in its final form	Sixth–fifth century BC.

THE SOURCES OF THE DOCUMENTARY HYPOTHESIS

of Gen 1–3 that Gen 1 is associated with the P source and Gen 2–3 with the J source. The outcome is that scholars now understand Gen 1 and 2 as a doublet—two different accounts placed side by side by an ancient author or redactor. This is a classic example of how source criticism works and is used as an illustration in classrooms throughout the world today.

3.3.1.b Arguments for Overall Composition

The Documentary Hypothesis has never been without its critics. So numerous are the alternative theories that have been proposed in the years since Wellhausen first popularized the hypothesis that one simply cannot catalog all of them, let alone describe them in full. Many theories have fallen in and out of fashion over the decades, but as the issue stands there are two main theories vying for support—the Documentary, or neo-Documentary Hypothesis, and the Traditio-Historical Hypothesis, also known as the Supplementary Hypothesis. As this latter proposition represents a method different from source criticism, it is not dealt with in full here, but introduced in the spirit of offering a complete picture of the major, available theories regarding the composition of the Pentateuch.

3.3.1.c Documentary Hypothesis

Until this point, we have discussed only the Documentary Hypothesis as a viable solution to the problems presented by the text of the Pentateuch. This remains the dominant theory about the composition of the Pentateuch, especially in the United States, where it has been reinvigorated as the Neo-Documentary Hypothesis.

3.3.1.d Traditio-Historical (Supplementary) Hypothesis

In the mid-1900s in Germany, Gerhard von Rad (1938) and Martin Noth (1948) approached the problem of the composition of the Pentateuch anew, with the premise that the books of Genesis through Deuteronomy began with a core of tradition that was supplemented throughout various stages of history.[34] This is not source criticism per se, but a combination of tradition

---

34. Gerhard von Rad, "The Form-Critical Problem of the Hexateuch (German, 1938)," in *The Problem of the Hexateuch and Other Essays* (Edinburgh: Oliver & Boyd, 1966), 1–78; Martin Noth, *A History of Pentateuchal Traditions*, trans. Bernhard W. Anderson (Englewood Cliffs, NJ: Prentice Hall, 1972).

criticism and historical criticism, hence the name Traditio-Historical Hypothesis. It is also referred to as the Supplementary Hypothesis. Scholars who use this approach look at reoccurring themes in order to arrive at a timeline of literary strata. For example, von Rad looks exclusively at the single theme of credo, whereas Noth looks at five themes, each of which he assigns to an originally separate block of tradition: (1) exodus from Egypt, (2) entrance into Canaan, (3) promise to the patriarchs, (4) divine guidance in the wilderness, and (5) Sinai.[35] Traditio-historical critics generally avoid the labels J, E, D, and P, so as not to be confused with supporters of the Documentary Hypothesis.

Rolf Rendtorff, a student of Gerhard von Rad, continued to develop the Traditio-Critical Hypothesis in *The Problem of the Process of Transmission in the Pentateuch* (German, 1975), in which he deemed the Documentary Hypothesis unnecessary and strongly critiqued other scholars' search for the so-called Yahwistic source.[36] He also presented the argument that the Documentary Hypothesis does not bridge the gap between small textual units and the whole of the Pentateuch, which is another way of saying that the hypothesis works in theory but not in practice. Rendtorff's work, often referred to as his theory of "complexes of tradition," broadened the influence and support of the Traditio-Historical Hypothesis, particularly within European scholarship, where it is still alive and well today.[37] Yet, like the Documentary Hypothesis, many competing variations of the Traditio-Historical Hypothesis have arisen in the decades following Rendtorff.

3.3.1.e Strengths and Weaknesses of the Solutions

The strength of the Documentary Hypothesis is in the simplicity and practicality of its most basic iteration—that the Pentateuch is a compilation of sources that was put together at a certain point in history. This approach begins with the text as it is, with all of its different vocabularies, inconsistencies, and repetitions, and then, after much analysis, posits a timeline

---

35. John Van Seters, "The Pentateuch," in *The Hebrew Bible Today*, ed. Steven J. McKenzie and M. Patrick Graham (Louisville: Westminster, John Knox, 1998), 11.

36. John Van Seters, *The Edited Bible: The Curious History of the "Editor" in Biblical Criticism* (Winona Lake, IN: Eisenbrauns, 2006), 270–78.

37. For an example of a volume that engages and expounds on Rendtorff's ideas, see Thomas B. Dozeman and Konrad Schmid, ed., *A Farewell to the Yahwist? The Composition of the Pentateuch in Recent European Interpretation* (Atlanta: Society of Biblical Literature, 2006).

of when various sources were written and assembled. No theory has been able to explain these literary phenomena without appealing to the idea of different sources, therefore reiterating the main tenets of the Documentary Hypothesis.

The weakness of the Documentary Hypothesis is in the details, specifically regarding the exact nature and dating of J, E, D, and P. Even 130 years after Wellhausen (1883; English translation 1885) popularized the theory, the difficulties of clearly distinguishing between the J and E sources and the dating of the P source are still the two main issues that prevent scholars from accepting the theory in full.[38] As previously mentioned, J and E are so similar that the line between them blurs once the name Yahweh is introduced in Exod 3, which leaves many to question whether source critics can divide the two with any degree of certainty. The dating of the P source was the first element of Graf and Wellhausen's iteration of the Documentary Hypothesis to come under fire, and it remains a divisive issue to this day.[39]

Much discussion of the validity of the Documentary Hypothesis revolves around Wellhausen's particular iteration of it. However, none of the major arguments are original to Wellhausen; what he presents is a synthesis of the work of his source-critical predecessors. One of Wellhausen's colleagues, August Dillmann (1886; followed by S. R. Driver, 1891), almost immediately pointed out that Wellhausen's arguments often suffer from gaps in logic, incomplete assessment of key assertions regarding history, lack of attention to detail, and the use of arguments from silence.[40] Furthermore, Wellhausen's unabashedly anti-Semitic and anti-institutional rhetoric causes many to seriously consider whether *Prolegomena*, at its very core, is legitimate scholarship.[41] Either way, one has to rethink what happens to Wellhausen's presentation of the data if the motives of

---

38. Ska, *Introduction to Reading the Pentateuch*, 131–61.

39. August Dillmann, *Die Bücher Numeri, Deuteronomium und Josua* (Leipzig: S. Hirzel, 1886).

40. Dillmann, *Die Bücher Numeri, Deuteronomium und Josua*; S. R. Driver, *An Introduction to the Literature of the Old Testament* (New York: Scribner's, 1914).

41. Moshe Weinfeld, *The Place of the Law in the Religion of Ancient Israel* (Leiden: Brill, 2004), 65–68.

the P source in particular are not as egomaniacal, heartless, and heathen as he describes.[42]

As for the Traditio-Historical Hypothesis, or Supplementary Hypothesis, its strength lies in the value of its contributions to the discussion of how the various traditions preserved in the Pentateuch, whether written or oral, came to be. Thinking through this issue provides much insight into how a largely illiterate society may have developed and maintained its traditions throughout the course of an often dangerous and unsettled history. The simple idea of a core of tradition that is supplemented throughout the ages, and eventually and organically arrives at a final form, appeals to many who find the division of sources, timeline, and easily complicated discussions of the Documentary Hypothesis too rigid to be certain.

The weaknesses of the Traditio-Historical Hypothesis lie in three main areas. The first is the speculative nature of tradition criticism, which theorizes about the original content of traditions and the mechanisms by which they are passed down. The problem is that there are no extant records about how the ancient, largely illiterate, Israelite population passed down tradition, and neither can the oral stage of tradition be retrieved. It can only be guessed at, imagined, and surmised. The second is tradition criticism's dependency on the criteria of theme. This is one area of biblical scholarship that has been heavily critiqued in recent years because (1) it is also speculative in practice and (2) does not acknowledge the subjectivity of the scholar. Whatever theme the scholar is using as a lens through which to analyze the text, the theme is one the scholar has chosen for his or her own purpose, whether this is acknowledged or not. For example, von Rad's use of credo as the theme by which he constructs the textual history of the entire Pentateuch might say more about his vocation as a German Lutheran minister in the mid-1900s than it does about the ancient Israelites, from whom we have no word that expresses any concept similar to that of credo. Furthermore, the theme one chooses as criterion for analysis will result in different analysis.

The third major weakness of this hypothesis is that it is incomplete. No scholar has yet produced a version of the theory that deals with all of the textual and historical issues that arise, even in the first two chapters of the

---

42. For example, see Wellhausen, *Prolegomena*, 425.

Pentateuch, including passages with distinct language, inconsistency, and doublets. Joel Baden critiques the generations of Rendtorff's students who continue to develop his ideas, saying that their works are unified only in their refusal to accept the methods and conclusions of the Documentary Hypothesis. Taken together, their works do not put forth a unified theory of Pentateuchal composition that may serve as an alternative.[43]

Lack of attention to matters that are expressly in the text of the Pentateuch suggests that, although the Traditio-Historical Hypothesis may work on the theoretical plane, when put into practice it does not sufficiently explain the main problems of the composition of the Pentateuch.

3.3.2 ISAIAH

A second focus of source-critical scholarship in the Old Testament was the book of Isaiah. As with the Documentary Hypothesis of the Pentateuch, source critics of the book of Isaiah focus on identifying the setting, purpose, and relevance of each section for their respective intended audiences. In so doing, scholars also set out to uncover the voices of the individual authors behind each section. By determining where a text is edited and in what way, one can begin to see glimpses of what is original to the authors who penned the hypothetical first draft and what is original to those who continued to develop the text throughout the centuries. In the last quarter of the twentieth century, scholars of Isaiah began to develop a second approach, which focuses on how the different parts of the book relate to one another.

3.3.2.a Criteria for the Major Divisions

Source critics focus on two main criteria for arriving at the threefold division of the book of Isaiah. The first is historical reference and, by extension, relevancy for the intended audience. The book contains several personal names, the earliest being King Uzziah (Azariah), who reigned in Judah from 783-742 BC (Isa 1:1; 2 Kgs 15), and the latest being Cyrus the Great, emperor of Persia, who conquered Babylon in 539 BC (Isa 44:24, 28; 52:11; 54:11–12; Ezra 1:2–3). The book also refers to the Syro-Ephramite crisis (735–732 BC), the aggression of the Assyrian Empire toward Judah and Jerusalem

---

43. Baden, *J, E, and the Redaction of the Pentateuch*, 1.

(705–701 BC), and the threat of the Babylonian Empire (610–587 BC). There are also allusions to the life of the Judahite community after the temple was rebuilt. Since its rededication was in 515 BC (Ezra 6), it appears as though the book of Isaiah reflects roughly 250 years of Judahite history.[44]

The variety of historical situations reflected in the book alerts source critics to the possibility of multiple sources, leading to the division of First ("Proto") Isaiah and Second ("Deutero") Isaiah. In the first thirty-nine chapters of Isaiah, Assyria is the main threat, and it is not named again after Isa 38:6. Isaiah 40 begins with "Comfort, comfort my people, says your God. Speak tenderly to Jerusalem, and cry to her that her warfare is ended" (Isa 40:1–2a ESV). The declaration that war has ended in Jerusalem is irrelevant until Cyrus' conquest of Babylon and empire-wide decree to send exiles back to their lands (539 BC). Cyrus is glorified by name for his deeds several times in the book of Isaiah and is portrayed as a type of messiah (Isa 44:24, 28; 52:11; 54:11–12). These references to Assyria, then Cyrus, suggest that chapters 1–39 and 40–66 originate in two separate periods, the eighth century and the sixth century, respectively.

Furthermore, the name of Isaiah—the prophet in the days of eighth-century Judaean kings Uzziah (Azariah), Jotham, Ahaz, and Hezekiah—does not appear after Isa 39:8. The oracles of Isa 40–66 are anonymous and have been associated with the eighth-century prophet by virtue of their location in the scroll that bears his name. However, the criteria that source criticism uses to examine the book of Isaiah suggest that these chapters were written much later than the historical prophet.

The second criterion for dividing Isaiah is a shift in message. As already remarked, Isa 40 opens with a call to comfort, which is something that is foreign to Isa 1–39. The optimistic themes of comfort after exile and restoration that characterize Isa 40–55 are most relevant for those in exile in the sixth century, whereas the themes of warning and judgment that characterize Isa 1–39 are most relevant to the eighth-century political crises. This lends further support to the idea that Isa 1–39 stems from the eighth century and Isa 40 onward stems from the sixth.

---

44. David L. Petersen, *The Prophetic Literature: An Introduction* (Louisville: Westminster John Knox, 2002), 50–60.

While looking at the issue of theme in the book of Isaiah, one cannot help but notice another marked shift beginning at Isa 56. The theme suddenly shifts from comfort and reconciliation to a blend of judgment and redemption. Isaiah 56–66 lacks the overall optimism of Isa 40–55 "and instead anticipate[s] YHWH's judgment against the wicked within the people and among the nations."[45] Although some scholars continue to treat Isa 40–55 and Isa 56–66 as a single unit, others hold that they are indeed separate compositions—Second Isaiah and Third ("Trito") Isaiah.

3.3.2.b Arguments for Overall Composition

Today, there are two main theories of the composition of Isaiah. The first is that of Duhm and decades of scholars after him, who divided the text into First, Second, and Third Isaiah. The theory of three Isaiahs focuses on the prophetic figure behind each literary unit and the relevance of various oracles for their intended audience. The second theory is a furthering of Duhm's original proposal, but with a focus on the literary unity and interdependence of the book's parts.

3.3.2.c The Three-Source Hypothesis

The opening verse of Isaiah identifies the source of the material as Isaiah's vision during the reigns of four kings of Judah: Uzziah, Jotham, Ahaz, and Hezekiah (Isa 1:1; compare Isa 2:1). This locates the historical prophet Isaiah in the eighth century, when Assyria invaded Syria-Palestine, destroying both Syria and the northern kingdom of Israel. This tumultuous century ended with Assyrian subjugation of Judah under Hezekiah in 701 BC. Much of this history is recounted in the first thirty-nine chapters of the book, and scholars readily associate the eighth-century prophet with the content of this section of the book.

By the late eighteenth century AD, scholars posited at least three authors of the book: Isaiah of Jerusalem, or "First Isaiah," who wrote 1–39 in the eighth century; "Second Isaiah," who was an anonymous prophet of the Babylonian exile and wrote chapters 40–55; and "Third Isaiah," who

---

45. Sweeney, "Latter Prophets: Isaiah, Jeremiah, Ezekiel," 76.

wrote chapters 56–66 in Jerusalem, just before the time of Nehemiah in the fifth century.[46]

As previously mentioned, Bernhard Duhm inherited the hypothesis associated with his name from his predecessors, but his detailed arguments firmly set the theory into the mainstream of biblical studies in the early twentieth century. Duhm adopted the division of Isaiah into First Isaiah (Isa 1–39) and Second Isaiah (Isa 40–66) from Abraham Ibn Ezra and J. G. Eichhorn, but furthered the theory by continuing to divide the sources.[47] He is credited with being the first to argue that Third Isaiah (Isa 56–66) is a distinct unit, and it is for this reason that the Three-Source Hypothesis is associated with Duhm. He also argued that there were a handful of other collections (e.g., 24–27; 34; 36–39; Servant Songs) that had been incorporated into the book at a later stage and, therefore, the authors of First, Second, and Third Isaiah were not the authors of everything in their respective sections.[48]

SECTION	AUTHOR	DATE
Chapters 1–39	The prophet Isaiah ("First Isaiah")	Eighth century BC Jerusalem
Chapters 40–55	"Second Isaiah"	Sixth century BC Babylonian exile
Chapters 56–66	"Third Isaiah"	Fifth century BC Jerusalem

THE THREE-SOURCE HYPOTHESIS OF ISAIAH

3.3.2.d The Unity of the Book of Isaiah

In the last quarter of the twentieth century, scholars began to revisit the issue of the composition of Isaiah, but with an eye for how its diverse

---

46. Williamson, "Isaiah: Book of," 366–67.

47. In Duhm's original version of the theory, Second Isaiah lived in Phoenicia (Sweeney, "Latter Prophets: Isaiah, Jeremiah, Ezekiel," 76).

48. Williamson, "Isaiah, Book of," 366–67.

sources relate to one another. The starting assumption is that the Three-Source Hypothesis, as Duhm described it, is a useful starting point, but ought to be furthered. The main question is: How do First, Second, and Third Isaiah and all of the later additions relate to one another? In other words, how does one make sense of how all these sources are put together? As with many theories of biblical authorship, there are many subtheories of how this all works, and innumerable discussions regarding the exact details of dividing sources and assigning historical periods. However, there are a few agreed-upon pieces regarding the unity of Isaiah.

The basic conclusion of this movement toward an understanding of the book's unity is that Isa 33–35 are transitional chapters that serve as a hinge connecting Isa 1–32 and 36–66. The first part, Isa 1–32, focuses on the problems of Judah and Jerusalem, including sin, punishment, politics, and international relations, and is concerned with the time period of the Assyrian Empire. The second part, Isa 33–66, focuses on the process of exile and return and personifies Jerusalem as one who deserves comfort (Isa 40:2). These chapters are also concerned with what comes after the Assyrian Period—the Babylonian exile (586 BC), Cyrus the Great of Persia (who conquered Babylon in 539 BC), and the restoration of the Judaeans to the land of Judah (539–480 BC).[49] Many scholars have also noticed that the first and last chapters (Isa 1; [65-]66) of the book function as a literary envelope, uniting the bundle of oracles and narratives into a single package. The function of Isa 33–35 as a hinge and chapters 1 and 66 as an envelope suggest a deliberate arrangement around certain chronological and thematic concerns.

In terms of how Isa 2–32 and 36–65 are assembled, those who argue for the unity of Isaiah agree that the process by which the text arrived at its form is a complicated matter. Although there is little consensus on the minutiae of who wrote exactly what and when, most agree that the author of Second Isaiah both assumes the existence of First Isaiah and edits the previous edition of the work while adding his own related material, both

---

49. Petersen, *Prophetic Literature*, 61–63.

within the first edition and at the end.[50] Third Isaiah is an even later combination of sources that was added to round out the distinct differences between First and Second Isaiah. The author of Third Isaiah may have also acted as an editor, though this is not clear.

3.3.2.e Strengths and Weaknesses of the Solutions

The strength of the Three-Source Hypothesis is its ability to explain the variety of historical situations that are reflected in the book of Isaiah. The idea of multiple sources addresses the problem of the relevance of specific proper names to the audiences of the historical prophets, as well as the problem of shifting theme and language.

The main problem with the Three-Source Hypothesis is the inclusion of more than three sources. In the decades since Duhm, source critical scholars have isolated more added units and have looked to additional themes to get a more informed view of the composition of the book. For example, when one looks at references to Assyria and Persia, especially King Cyrus, the division between Isa 1–39 and Isa 40–66 is very clear. When one looks at references to Babylon, the picture is quickly muddied. References to Babylon as a violent threat begin in a vision of the prophet as early as Isa 13:1, yet Babylon was barely on the world scene during the eighth century. In fact, the narrative of Isa 1–39 ends with envoys from Babylon bringing get-well letters to King Hezekiah of Judah, who welcomes them into closed quarters (Isa 39; 2 Kgs 20). Isaiah then prophesies that the day is coming when the Babylonians will attack and plunder Jerusalem, yet even the king does not see Babylon as a threat at the close of First Isaiah. This sort of inconsistency has led source critics to dig deeper into Isaiah and to further divide the three main sections into separate sources or collections of sources.

The strength of the current hypothesis regarding the unity of Isaiah is in its consideration of weaknesses of the Three-Source Hypothesis and the increased complexity of the final form. Although the focus of this project is to put the text back together after the source critics have done their part, it is heavily dependent on the findings of source-critical scholars. The

---

50. H. G. M. Williamson, *The Book Called Isaiah: Deutero-Isaiah's Role in Composition and Redaction* (Oxford: Clarendon, 1994).

general theory, as it now stands, explains the problems caused by historical references and, by extension, their relevance, plus differences in language and theme. It also refuses to oversimplify the process of composition and attempts to honor all who were involved in the process over the centuries.

The weakness of the theory regarding the unity of Isaiah is that there is, as yet, no single unified theory as to how the entire work reached its final form. This is partially because the level of attention to detail and time period that theorizing about the authorship of Isaiah requires often leads to disagreement regarding individual verses and their relationship to other individual verses. In a book as lengthy as Isaiah, these kinds of issues take a great deal of time, often decades, to sort out, and even then the conclusions remain hypothetical.

3.3.3 GOSPELS

While source criticism has been applied to many parts of the New Testament—such as studying whether parts of 1 and 2 Corinthians began as a number of smaller, separate letters—its primary application has been to the sources behind the Gospels. Throughout the history of the church, Christians have worked to explain and integrate the fourfold witness of the Gospels, doing so most often through the harmonization of the accounts into one continuous narrative.[51] With the Enlightenment, NT scholars started to apply source criticism to the Gospels, leading Jakob Griesbach to develop the synopsis—a tool for examining the connections between the four accounts, by laying out the text of the four Gospels in four columns with similar events appearing in corresponding rows.[52]

3.3.3.a *Criteria Leading to the Synoptic Problem*

Viewed through the synopsis, it is clear that Matthew, Mark, and Luke bear a strong resemblance to one another, earning them the label "Synoptic Gospels." In light of these resemblances, source critics divide texts within the Synoptic Gospels into three major categories. First, the triple tradition denotes material and wording that is common to all three Gospels. Second,

---

51. Goodacre, *The Synoptic Problem*, 14.

52. Scholars still use such synopses, the most common being the English and Greek ones edited by Kurt Aland (e.g., Kurt Aland, *Synopsis of the Four Gospels: Greek-English Edition of the Synopsis Quattuor Evangeliorum* [Stuttgart: German Bible Society, 1993]).

although the term can refer to any material where two of the Synoptic Gospels agree against the third, the double tradition normally denotes the 230 verses present in Matthew and Luke but absent from Mark. Third, special material refers to text unique to a particular Gospel, and is normally applied only to Matthew and Luke, given that over 90 percent of Mark appears in either or both of the other Synoptics.

Not only do the Synoptic Gospels recount similar events in contrast to John, but they also do so in four notably similar ways. First, the Synoptics generally present the triple tradition pericopae[53] in the same order, and where one evangelist diverges from the order by inserting or leaving something out, he resumes the order again afterward (e.g., Jesus' teaching on the way to Jerusalem, Matt 16:30—18:9; Mark 8:27—9:50; Luke 9:18-50). Second, in parallel pericopae, each evangelist uses very similar and often identical wording (e.g., the call of Levi, Matt 9:9-10; Mark 2:13-15; Luke 5:27-32). Third, these similarities in wording occur not only in the words of Jesus, but also in narrative descriptions and editorial comments ("let the reader understand," Matt 24:15-16; Mark 13:14). Fourth, each of the Synoptics quotes the OT in similar ways, unique from the Hebrew OT and its Greek translation, the Septuagint ("make his paths straight," Matt 3:3; Mark 1:3; Luke 3:4; compared to "make a straight path for our God," Isa 40:3).

In light of these similarities, the vast majority of scholars argue for a fundamentally literary relationship among the Synoptic Gospels. Along with these similarities, however, important differences exist among the Synoptic Gospels. Along with the most obvious differences, such as the lack of birth narratives and the Lord's Prayer in Mark, as well as the unique structure of Matthew around Jesus' five discourses, source critics must also account for smaller differences in wording, details, and the movement of individual pericopae. How to account for these similarities and differences together constitutes the synoptic problem.

3.3.3.b Main Theories to Solve the Synoptic Problem

Since the publication of the first synopsis, scholars have put forward a broad array of solutions to the synoptic problem, some with a staggering

---

53. "Pericopae" is the plural of "pericope," the term used for a small group of verses that function as a contained unit.

degree of complexity. Here we cannot trace the history of the synoptic problem or every answer given, but we will present in broad outline the three most prevalent hypotheses in current scholarship.[54]

3.3.3.b.1 Early Theories

In response to the synoptic problem, source-critical scholars of the eighteenth–nineteenth centuries devoted much research and imagination to the issue. By the mid-nineteenth century, four major approaches to the agreements among the synoptic texts had emerged. The first, mentioned previously, is G. E. Lessing's idea of an "Ur-gospel" (1771, 1776), or proto-Gospel, an original Gospel written in Aramaic that was translated into Greek several times. The Synoptics are similar because they all use this Ur-Gospel, and any differences arise from the authors using different versions of the Greek.

This approach eventually fell out of fashion because the more scholars tried to reconstruct the hypothetical Ur-Gospel, the more it looked like the canonical Gospel of Mark. This observation would later come up in discussions of "Markan priority," the idea that Mark was the first Synoptic Gospel to be written and was prioritized by Matthew and Luke as their main source. The idea that the Gospel writers may have had to deal with Aramaic and possibly even Hebrew sources, either oral or written, remains alive and well in the details of some of the later debates. Eichhorn's idea about there being lost Gospels remains valid due to the discoveries of the Gospels of Thomas, Mary, and others.[55]

Another early approach to the issue of synoptic agreement was to propose common dependence on oral sources. In 1797, J. G. Herder argued that the synoptic writers all relied on a fixed oral tradition that was solidified shortly after Jesus' life. J. K. L. Gieseler developed and defended this view (1818), which was popular in the nineteenth century and is still held by a

---

54. Dungan provides the most thorough history of the synoptic problem, although his work is in part motivated by demonstrating the influence of other factors, such as political ones, on the solutions given. David Laird Dungan, *A History of the Synoptic Problem: The Canon, the Text, the Composition, and the Interpretation of the Gospels* (New York: Doubleday, 1999). For a shorter history, see, A. D. Baum, "Synoptic Problem," in *Dictionary of Jesus and the Gospels*, 2nd ed., ed. Joel B. Green, Jeannine K. Brown, and Nicholas Perrin (Downers Grove, IL: InterVarsity, 2013), 911–19.

55. Francis Watson, *Gospel Writing: A Canonical Perspective* (Grand Rapids: Eerdmans, 2013).

handful of scholars today.[56] However, the tenuous nature of arguments for a specific oral tradition with any degree of certainty causes most scholars to focus their attention on other possibilities.

A third early approach was to think of synoptic agreement as the product of common dependence on gradually developing written fragments. F. Schleiermacher (1832) argued for a developing collection of fragmentary sayings of Jesus that existed in the early church and were available to all three synoptic writers. Since this was an evolving body of literature, it would have existed in various stages of development, depending on when and where each Gospel writer encountered it. Although Schleiermacher's theory did not catch on due to its purely hypothetical nature, his work remains significant as the first to argue that Papias (AD 70–163) refers to one of these fragments as "a collection of the sayings of Jesus."[57]

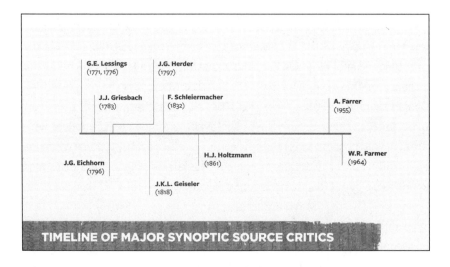

TIMELINE OF MAJOR SYNOPTIC SOURCE CRITICS

Finally, without negating the possible influence of an Ur-Gospel, oral tradition, or an early literary collection, we come to the idea of interdependence. The idea that Matthew, Mark, and Luke owe their literary agreements to one another was the standard view beginning with the fourth century AD, when Augustine first advocated that Matthew was written first, Mark borrowed from Matthew, then Luke borrowed from both Matthew

---

56. Carson and Moo, *Introduction to the New Testament*, 90.

57. Carson and Moo, *Introduction to the New Testament*, 90–91.

and Mark.[58] This theory remained standard until the nineteenth century, when scholars began to examine the texts even closer and to propose alternative theories. Although only a handful of modern scholars hold to Augustine's proposed chronology, the idea that the Synoptics owe their similarities only to borrowing from one another at the final literary level is at the core of all current theories regarding their composition and a position held by almost complete consensus.[59]

3.3.3.b.2 The Two-Source Hypothesis

H. J. Holtzmann first proposed the Two-Source Hypothesis (also called either the Two-Document Hypothesis or the Four-Source Hypothesis) in 1861, although its current ascendency in English-speaking countries owes more to the Oxford seminar on the synoptic problem,[60] and especially the work of one of its participants, B. H. Streeter.[61] So great was their influence that by the end of the Second World War the Two-Source Hypothesis had become "the one absolutely assured result" of New Testament study.[62] Although some challenge it today, it remains the most widely held answer to the synoptic problem.

The Two-Source Hypothesis rests on two fundamental concepts: Markan priority and the use of a sayings source. Scholars bring a range of evidence in favor of Markan priority. At the most basic level, while Mark is shorter than either Matthew or Luke, his individual pericopae tend to be longer, which could suggest that Matthew and Luke summarize Mark as a source and then add more material of their own. At a linguistic level, many scholars point to Mark's "inferior" Greek compared to that of Matthew and Luke, with the conclusion that it is more likely that Matthew and Luke cleaned up Mark.[63] On a theological level, scholars argue that Mark gives a less

---

58. Augustine, *The Harmony of the Gospels* 1.2.

59. Carson and Moo, *Introduction to the New Testament*, 91.

60. William Sanday, ed., *Studies in the Synoptic Problem, by Members of the University of Oxford* (Oxford: Clarendon, 1911).

61. Burnett Hillman Streeter, *The Four Gospels: A Study of Origins* (New York: Macmillan, 1925).

62. G. M. Styler, "The Priority of Mark," in *The Birth of the New Testament*, by C. F. D. Moule (New York: Harper & Row, 1962), 223.

63. Craig A. Evans, "The Two Source Hypothesis," in *The Synoptic Problem: Four Views*, ed. Stanley E. Porter and Bryan R. Dyer (Grand Rapids: Baker Academic, 2016), 29–31.

dignified portrayal of Jesus, such as his inability to perform many healings in Nazareth because of the unbelief of the people there (Mark 6:5), as opposed to Matthew's statement that Jesus did not do many miracles there (Matt 13:58).[64] Again, it appears more probable that Matthew would soften Mark's image of Jesus rather than Mark presenting Jesus in a less dignified light. Finally, given that Mark remains silent on elements of Jesus' life, many agree with Streeter that "only a lunatic would leave out Matthew's account of the Infancy, the Sermon on the Mount, and practically all the parables, in order to get room for purely verbal expansion of what was retained."[65]

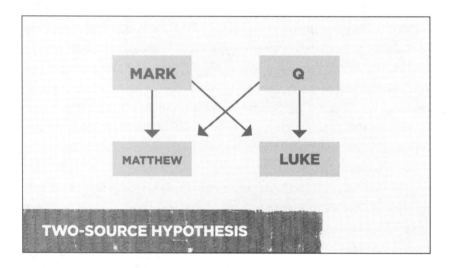

With respect to a sayings source, given the substantial amount of material in the double tradition with a very high level of agreement, advocates of the Two-Source Hypothesis postulate that Matthew and Luke made use of a second source that is no longer extant. As previously mentioned, scholars denote this source as Q and argue that it was composed of the sayings of Jesus with little narrative detail. A critical edition complete with its own versification exists.[66] Proponents of Q mount a number of arguments that Luke and Matthew did not know of each other, including

---

64. Evans, "Two Source Hypothesis," 31–34.

65. Streeter, *Four Gospels*, 158.

66. James M. Robinson, Paul Hoffmann, and John S. Kloppenborg, eds., *The Critical Edition of Q: Synopsis Including the Gospels of Matthew and Luke, Mark and Thomas with English, German, and French Translations of Q and Thomas* (Minneapolis: Fortress, 2000).

the radically different ordering of the double tradition in Matthew and Luke.[67] Yet many others voice skepticism about delineating Q—ranging from the impossibility of discerning the exact limits of such a document (particularly the degree to which it might have overlapped with Mark) to the number of "coincidences" necessary to posit an independent writing of Matthew and Luke.[68]

3.3.3.b.3 Farrer-Goulder Hypothesis

The final major alternative, the Farrer Hypothesis, receives its name from a 1955 article by Austin Farrer in which he argued that Q is an unnecessary postulate in the answer to the synoptic problem.[69] Thus, the Farrer Hypothesis sits between the Two-Source Hypothesis and the Two-Gospel Hypothesis, in that it accepts Markan priority yet also argues for a direct literary relationship between Matthew and Luke, thus rejecting the existence of Q. Therefore, the Farrer hypothesis argues that Mark wrote first, Matthew used Mark as a source, and then Luke wrote third, using both Mark and Matthew. Since Farrer's initial article, the arguments for the Farrer Hypothesis have been expanded by Michael Goulder (thus sometimes this argument is called the Farrer-Goulder Hypothesis),[70] and most importantly by Mark Goodacre,[71] as well as recently by Francis Watson.[72]

Because the Farrer Hypothesis consciously takes pieces of evidence from both the Two-Document and Two-Gospel Hypotheses, its proponents use much of the evidence already presented above concerning Markan priority—the dignity argument, the length arguments, the corrections

---

67. Delbert Burkett, *Rethinking the Gospel Sources, Volume 2: The Unity or Plurality of Q* (Atlanta: Society of Biblical Literature, 2009), 10–32.

68. Watson, *Gospel Writing*, 117–55. One scholar even quips, "I cannot help thinking that biblical scholarship would be greatly advanced if every morning all exegetes would repeat the mantra: 'Q is a hypothetical document whose exact extension, wording, originating community, strata, and stages of redaction cannot be known'" (John P. Meier, *A Marginal Jew: Rethinking the Historical Jesus, Volume 2: Mentor, Message and Miracles* [New York: Doubleday, 1994], 178).

69. A. M. Farrer, "On Dispensing with Q," in *Studies in the Gospels: Essays in Memory of R. H. Lightfoot*, ed. D. E. Nineham (Oxford: Blackwell, 1955), 55–88.

70. Michael D. Goulder, *Luke: A New Paradigm* (Sheffield: JSOT Press, 1989), 3–128.

71. Goodacre, *Synoptic Problem*; Mark Goodacre, *The Case against Q: Studies in Markan Priority and the Synoptic Problem* (Harrisburg, PA: Trinity Press International, 2002).

72. Watson, *Gospel Writing*.

argument—and that concerning a direct literary relationship between Matthew and Luke—particularly in light of the minor agreements.[73] Likewise, detractors of the Farrer Hypothesis marshal many of the same critiques leveled at the two other arguments above, especially that Luke's differences from Matthew are better explained through the independent use of the same source rather than selective emendation.[74] In addition to this evidence, Goodacre also introduces the concept of "editorial fatigue."[75] This idea denotes an evangelist correcting his source early in a pericope but relapsing to the incorrect grammar or terminology as the account progresses, such as Matthew's denotation of Herod as "tetrarch" (Matt 14:1) at first before later calling him a "king" (Matt 14:9), in line with Mark's usage throughout (Mark 6:14). Importantly, Goodacre uses editorial fatigue as evidence not only for Markan priority but also for Luke's knowledge and use of Matthew, thus ruling out Q.

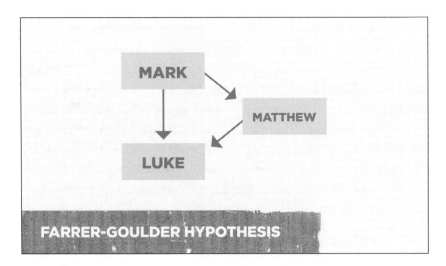

3.3.3.b.4 Two-Gospel (Griesbach) Hypothesis

The Two-Gospel Hypothesis claims the oldest pedigree of the three major theories, and its current form traces back to the work of Jakob Griesbach

---

73. Mark S. Goodacre, "The Farrer Hypothesis," in *The Synoptic Problem: Four Views*, ed. Stanley E. Porter and Bryan R. Dyer (Grand Rapids: Baker Academic, 2016), 49–58.

74. Michael F. Bird, *The Gospel of the Lord: How the Early Church Wrote the Story of Jesus* (Grand Rapids: Eerdmans, 2014), 168–70.

75. Mark S. Goodacre, "Fatigue in the Synoptics," *NTS* 44 (1998): 45–58.

(hence some also refer to this as the Griesbach Hypothesis). Proponents of the Two-Gospels Hypothesis also broke through the hegemony of the Two-Source Hypothesis, particularly in the work of B. C. Butler, who demonstrated that the circularity implicit in Streeter's arguments could be used just as easily against Markan priority as for it.[76] Since then, most credit William Farmer with the rise of the Two-Gospel Hypothesis, with others taking up the cause more recently.[77]

In contrast to the Two-Source Hypothesis, the Two-Gospel Hypothesis rejects both Markan priority and the existence of Q. Instead, the hypothesis states that Matthew wrote first, then Luke used Matthew as a source, and finally Mark conflated both Matthew and Luke into his Gospel. Evidence garnered in support of this arrangement includes Markan redundancies, whereby Mark's wording contains a redundant double phrase with half found in Matthew and half in Luke, and the possibility of isolating linguistic particularities.[78] Probably the weightiest argument for the Two-Gospel Hypothesis, however, comes from minor agreements—passages within the triple tradition where Matthew and Luke agree against Mark.[79] These could suggest a direct literary relationship between Matthew and Luke rather than identical independent additions. Those who favor the Two-Source Hypothesis generally acknowledge that these minor agreements pose the greatest challenge to their view, though many have also offered various solutions, from later scribal assimilation to the influence of oral traditions.[80] Further, in response to the challenge that Mark would never have left out core elements of Matthew and Luke, such as the birth narratives or the Lord's Prayer, Peabody argues that Mark would have found it easier to skip these sections than deal with their divergence in

---

76. B. C. Butler, *The Originality of St. Matthew: A Critique of the Two-Document Hypothesis* (Cambridge: Cambridge University Press, 1951), 62–71.

77. William R. Farmer, *The Synoptic Problem: A Critical Analysis* (New York: Macmillan, 1964).

78. However, the evidence from linguistic particularities is not conclusive. David Barrett Peabody, "The Two Gospel Hypothesis," in *Synoptic Problem: Four Views*, ed. Stanley E. Porter and Bryan R. Dyer (Grand Rapids: Baker Academic, 2016), 70–79.

79. Goodacre, *Case against Q*, 152–69.

80. Robert H. Stein, *Studying the Synoptic Gospels: Origin and Interpretation*, 2nd ed. (Grand Rapids: Baker Academic, 2001), 136–41.

testimony (e.g., Matthew's magi and Luke's shepherds, or Matthew's Sermon on the Mount and Luke's Sermon on the Plain).[81]

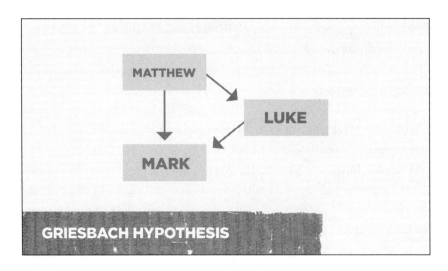

Beyond the evidence within the Synoptic Gospels themselves, those who hold to the Two-Gospel Hypothesis also draw on "external evidence"—the tradition of the early church. Although most of the church fathers showed little interest in the documentary relationship between the Synoptics, passing comments by Clement, Origen, and Augustine (as well as possible evidence from Irenaeus and Jerome) demonstrate their belief that Matthew wrote his Gospel first.[82] Most of this evidence, however, indicates their belief that Mark wrote second and Luke third, and some debate the evidence in Clement and Augustine for Mark writing third.[83] Given the general trend, therefore, for the early church to place Mark prior to Luke and also to posit the now generally dismissed argument that Matthew originally wrote in Hebrew, the question of evidence from tradition for all involved

---

81. David Barrett Peabody, "Reading Mark from the Perspectives of Different Synoptic Source Hypotheses: Historical, Redactional and Theological Implications," in *New Studies in the Synoptic Problem: Oxford Conference, April 2008, Essays in Honour of Christopher M. Tuckett,* ed. Paul Foster et al. (Leuven: Peeters, 2011), 173–74.

82. For a collection of the evidence, see Peabody, "Reading Mark," 182–85.

83. Stephen C. Carlson, "Clement of Alexandria on the 'Order' of the Gospels," *NTS* 47 (2001): 118–25; Rainier Riesner, "Orality and Memory Hypothesis Response," in *The Synoptic Problem: Four Views,* ed. Stanley E. Porter and Bryan R. Dyer (Grand Rapids: Baker Academic, 2016), 160–61.

in the synoptic question is not whether it should be accepted or ignored, but the degree to which it should be given a voice in the debates.

3.3.3.c Strengths and Weaknesses of the Solutions

It is clear that questions and challenges exist for each of the three major hypotheses concerning the source criticism of the Gospels, and the consensus of sixty years ago no longer exists.[84] Moreover, as much as previous generations of source critics strove to approach the synoptic problem with a scientific objectivism, numerous presuppositions shape the appraisal of the evidence outlined above. For example, Streeter bases his strongly worded argument about the Markan omission of the birth narratives and Sermon on the Mount, rightly or wrongly, on a value judgment regarding their importance for the Christian faith. Likewise, these theories rest on particular (and often quite unflattering) conceptions of ancient scribes and their use of sources, though recent research suggests that they used methods more complex than "cutting and pasting" or only using one source at a time.[85] Perhaps the most significant challenge to these presuppositions, however, comes from the field of orality and memory studies. While modern variants of the hypotheses above take a degree of orality into account, a strong emphasis on possible oral transmission of the accounts of the life and teaching of Jesus can give a very different shape to the answer of the synoptic problem.[86]

Far from being an intellectual riddle confined to the halls of academia, the answer given to the synoptic problem may have far-reaching consequences for theology. Thus, for instance, based on the existence of Q, Kloppenborg argues that the earliest Christians were not concerned with

---

84. Stanley E. Porter and Bryan R. Dyer, "What Have We Learned Regarding the Synoptic Problem, and What Do We Still Need to Learn?," in *The Synoptic Problem: Four Views*, ed. Stanley E. Porter and Bryan R. Dyer (Grand Rapids: Baker Academic, 2016), 176–78; Christopher M. Tuckett, "The Current State of the Synoptic Problem," in *New Studies in the Synoptic Problem: Oxford Conference, April 2008, Essays in Honour of Christopher M. Tuckett*, ed. Paul Foster et al. (Leuven: Peeters, 2011), 49–50.

85. James W. Barker, "Ancient Compositional Practices and the Gospels: A Reassessment," *JBL* 135 (2016): 109–21; John C. Poirier, "Why the Farrer Hypothesis? Why Now?," in *Marcan Priority without Q: Explorations in the Farrer Hypothesis*, ed. John C. Poirier and Jeffrey Peterson (London: Bloomsbury, 2015), 11–12.

86. See, for instance, Rainer Riesner, "The Orality and Memory Hypothesis," in *The Synoptic Problem: Four Views*, ed. Stanley E. Porter and Bryan R. Dyer (Grand Rapids: Baker Academic, 2016), 89–111.

the death and resurrection of Jesus but only with his teaching.[87] At the other end of the spectrum, Farnell argues that any documentary answer to the synoptic question undermines the doctrine of the inspiration of the Scriptures.[88] Most scholars, however, fall in between these two poles and view the source criticism of the Gospels as one necessary and useful tool for reading the Synoptic Gospels.[89] At the very least, regardless of the answer given with respect to the sources behind the Synoptic Gospels, an awareness of the synoptic problem should lead to a greater appreciation for the genius of each of the evangelists and a deeper engagement with the particularities of each perspective of Jesus.

3.4 LIMITATIONS OF SOURCE CRITICISM

Source criticism is one of the earliest methods of the academic study of the Bible and continues to be an indispensable approach in the field of biblical studies. By examining its history and some of its greatest applications, one sees the value of source-critical work and how it has shaped today's understanding of the biblical text. The limitations of this type of work lie in the specificity of its task, which we previously defined as to determine what written documents lie behind the final form of the biblical text and to propose a historical setting for each document (see §3.1 Definition and Goal of the Method, above). The job of the source critic is to scientifically and artfully dismantle ancient texts, then to categorize and describe the pieces. This is one stage in the assembly line of biblical studies. From there, a different criticism must be applied in order to put the pieces back together and describe the whole.

3.5 CONTEMPORARY INFLUENCE
OF SOURCE CRITICISM

Today's understanding of the early history of the biblical text is largely the result of source criticism. Within the academy, most graduate-level programs require that students obtain a certain level of familiarity with

---

87. John S. Kloppenborg, *Excavating Q: The History and Setting of the Sayings Gospel* (Minneapolis: Fortress, 2000), 412–16.

88. David F. Farnell, "How Views of Inspiration Have Impacted Synoptic Problem Discussions," *MSJ* 13 (2002): 33–64.

89. For a typical evangelical response, for instance, see Evans, "Two Source Hypothesis," 27.

Wellhausen, Duhm, and the synoptic problem. Any scholar who works on a text that has been debated using source criticism must be able to situate themselves and their work among the various theories. Although few modern scholars focus on source criticism as their primary mode of analysis, the theories provided by source critical work inform the vast majority of work done in biblical studies today, although this is not always explicitly stated.

Outside the academy, source criticism's influence continues to grow, albeit slowly. As more and more clergy, leaders, and laypeople learn about the Bible from an academic perspective, more perspectives on the Bible are shaped by the basic tenets of source criticism. Of course, one would be hard-pressed to find a church or synagogue that preaches Wellhausen, Duhm, or Griesbach, but the understanding of the biblical text that stems from their work has been part of the fabric of theological training in the West for decades.

3.6 RESOURCES FOR FURTHER STUDY

Blenkinsopp, Joseph. *The Pentateuch: An Introduction to the First Five Books of the Bible*. New Haven: Yale University Press, 1992.

> Blenkinsopp has written a thorough introduction to critical scholarship on the Pentateuch, especially centered on the source-critical conclusions of Wellhausen and their reception and modification by later scholars.

Garrett, Duane A. *Rethinking Genesis: The Sources and Authorship of the First Book of the Pentateuch*. Fearn, Great Britain: Christian Focus Publications, 2000.

> Garrett offers a theologically conservative perspective on the question of whether the Pentateuch was compiled from literary sources. Instead of rejecting the possibility outright, Garrett carefully evaluates the evidence and reveals the inadequacy of the Documentary Hypothesis for explaining the origin of the book of Genesis.

Goodacre, Mark. *The Synoptic Problem: A Way through the Maze*. London: T&T Clark, 2001.

> Goodacre's book is a good starting point for better understanding the source criticism of the NT. While Goodacre favors the Farrer-

Goulder hypothesis, he still represents the other options in a fair and balanced way.

McKnight, Scot. "Source Criticism." *Interpreting the New Testament: Essays on Methods and Issues,* eds. David Alan Black and David S. Dockery, 74–105. Nashville: Broadman & Holman Publishers, 2001.

McKnight provides a very readable introduction to source criticism of the Gospels. He clearly demonstrates its importance and relevance for continued research. The essay is especially valuable for his helpful illustration of the issues in the example of how Luke's account of Peter's confession relates to Mark's (Mark 8; Luke 9).

Wellhausen, Julius. *Prolegomena to the History of Israel.* Translated by J. Sutherland Black and Allan Menzies. Edinburgh: Adam & Charles Black, 1885.

In this book, Wellhausen presents the classic articulation of the Documentary Hypothesis, which continues to be influential in biblical scholarship despite significant revision and rejection of key components of Wellhausen's version of the concept.

Whybray, R. N. *The Making of the Pentateuch: A Methodological Study.* Sheffield: Sheffield Academic, 1994.

Whybray covers the major critical approaches used in research on the Pentateuch, including source, form, and tradition-historical criticism. His book provides a helpful introduction to biblical criticism in general, but it is especially useful for his clear summary and evaluation of Wellhausen's Documentary Hypothesis.

4

FORM CRITICISM

Gretchen Ellis

4.1 DEFINITION AND GOAL OF THE METHOD

Form criticism is a method of analyzing the biblical text that focuses on the relationship between a text's formal features and its communicative function in particular social or literary settings. Formal features include genre and discourse conventions that point to how and when a text was used. For example, the prophetic formula *wayhî dĕbar-yhwh ʾēlay* (וַיְהִי דְבַר־יְהוָה אֵלַי; "and the word of Yahweh came to me") is used throughout the book of Ezekiel to signal that what follows is a message from God (e.g., Ezek 6:1). Form criticism is concerned with both delineating short textual units and describing how those textual units fit into larger literary units. While initially focused on the potential origin of biblical texts in oral traditions, form criticism has come to address broader literary questions related to a text's overall composition and its effect on later audiences.

4.1.1 RELATION TO SOURCE CRITICISM

At the turn of the twentieth century,[1] the dominance of source criticism in the world of biblical studies began to diminish, due primarily to Hermann Gunkel's commentary on Genesis. In this work, which appeared in three editions from 1901 to 1910, Gunkel outlined a new methodology that he

---

1. All dates are AD unless otherwise noted.—Eds.

thought superior to the source criticism of his predecessors.[2] Source critics, according to Gunkel, saw the world of ancient Israel in too "academic" a light, imagining the compilers of the OT as fastidious scholars painstakingly reworking their sources into a cohesive text. In this framework, perceived inconsistencies in the text arose from the failure of the writers to smoothly stitch together the narratives from their sources. The systematic analysis of these "seams" in the text and their subsequent classification into various source documents was the goal of source criticism.

Gunkel was dissatisfied with the prevailing source-critical methodology and sought to approach the text in a different way; as a result, he introduced form criticism. Rather than stemming from individual writers copying and editing written documents, Gunkel argued that the Bible was the product of an *oral* tradition. Moreover, this tradition was situated within a culture with its own specific genres, which determined how stories could and should be told. Scholars of this new methodology—such as Gunkel and those he influenced, including Albrecht Alt and Sigmund Mowinckel—believed that searching out the oral traditions behind the sources allowed them to move beyond the stylistic, theological, and grammatical aspects analyzed by source critics, providing a more accurate picture of the original, oral sources of the text.

This new methodology did not stop at analyzing the text, however. Gunkel believed that the unique structures and genres used in storytelling reflected a specific social context that could be determined and described through close reading of the text. In other words, the Bible is the record of the very same communal activities that gave birth to the texts, and knowledge of biblical genres would inevitably lead to knowledge of Israelite society and culture. Discovering the various genres to which biblical texts belonged and relating them to their potential social setting within the community became the primary task of the biblical scholars who followed in Gunkel's footsteps—and thus form criticism was born.

---

2. Hermann Gunkel, *Genesis übersetzt und erklärt*, 3rd ed. (Göttingen: Vandenhoeck & Ruprecht, 1910). The first and second German editions appeared in 1901 and 1902, respectively. The third edition has been translated into English: *Genesis* (Macon, GA: Mercer University Press, 1997). Gunkel's views on Genesis became more widely known during this time primarily due to the publication of an English translation of the introduction from the 1901 edition of the commentary that appeared as *The Legends of Genesis*, trans. W. H. Carruth (Chicago: Open Court, 1901).

4.1.2 UNDERLYING ASSUMPTIONS

Like any methodology, form criticism relies on a set of assumptions that inform its approach to the text. The fundamental assumption for form criticism as outlined by Gunkel is its emphasis on oral culture and social and historical context.

Like their predecessors in source criticism, form critics like Gunkel[3] believe that the biblical text as it exists presently is a composite document— that is, it is made up of various sources that were compiled and recorded by many people. However, unlike source critics, form critics assumed the original sources to be oral rather than written. This may not seem like a revolutionary proposition, but its effects were far-reaching.

According to early form critics, the composite nature of the text and its heterogeneity[4] (i.e., diversity in character and content) were not the product of a few select scribes editing together their various source documents. Source critics had neglected to recall that throughout the history of Israel its culture was predominantly oral, and its various traditions would have been handed down through speech rather than writing. If, as form critics claimed, the heterogeneity of the text is due in large part to the *oral* nature of the original sources, one must approach this heterogeneity equipped to recognize the text's genre. The criticism was that the kind of "cut and paste" operation that form critics claimed source critics were doing did not account for the issues of genre or heterogeneity. Without a proper understanding of the oral forms in the text, any decision as to what in a text was original and what was secondary was arbitrary and most likely wrong.

If the texts were originally oral products of Israelite society, form critics assumed that they must have served a particular sociocultural purpose. Why else, they claimed, would *these texts* have been preserved instead of others? The Pentateuch, for example, could have been useful for teaching

---

3. For a description of the most influential form critics and their contributions to the discipline, see the section titled §4.2 Development of Form Criticism. For the sake of clarity, the phrase "form critics" will be used rather than listing every influential form-critical scholar. Although different scholars may not hold to these assumptions for the same reasons (for example, someone could hold to the assumption of oral traditions in the Pentateuch without necessarily agreeing with all the classical definitions of the Documentary Hypothesis), these are still common aspects of form-critical methodology.

4. The word "heterogeneity" is a useful neutral term for describing what higher critics such as source and form critics are trying to explain. Labels like "incoherence" and "inconsistency" are implicitly negative.

children the history of the nation and for defining the community's identity in contrast to the other sociocultural groups of the time. Psalms expressed the nation's attitude toward its deity and bound it together through ritual. The list could go on, but the basic premise is a utilitarian one: a society preserves those texts that are in some way useful to it.

Implied within the assumption of sociocultural utility is the existence of a specific sociocultural setting within which the genre under investigation functions. Psalms, for example, belong within the ritual sphere of Israelite life and can best be understood if their original setting in religious practice is defined: a festival, a pilgrimage, daily worship, the installment of a new king, etc. In fact, for form critics, the very existence of any genre implies a specific social setting that both gave birth to and shaped the texts of that genre into the form in which they exist today. To take an example from American culture, the well-known catchphrase, "Ladies and gentlemen, let's get ready to rumble!" belongs to the social setting of sports, specifically boxing and wrestling, and its creation is credited to announcer Michael Buffer.[5] This setting not only determines *what* is said but *how* it is said. However, unlike this example, form critics assign the development of a specific structure to the community rather than to a specific individual.

Moreover, early form critics such as Gunkel, Mowinckel, and von Rad believed that they could determine and describe these specific sociocultural settings solely by understanding the genres of oral tradition themselves. In other words, reading the biblical texts opened up windows into the past through which a form critic could perceive the life of the Israelite community, and it was the goal of form criticism to do just that. Later form critics would move away from this emphasis, but the assumed relationship between a genre and a social setting persists, albeit with far less prominence.

In sum, the four fundamental assumptions of form criticism are: (1) the biblical text is heterogeneous/composite; (2) the original texts of the Bible were oral rather than written; and (3) each oral text served a sociocultural purpose within (4) a specific sociocultural setting that can be determined and described.

---

5. Michael Buffer is the boxing announcer who invented and trademarked the phrase, "Ladies and gentlemen, let's get ready to rumble!" He created a unique style for announcers in this sport that has been utilized quite frequently ever since.

Taken as a whole, form criticism began as an attempt to reorient the nature of biblical criticism; form critics found serious flaws with source criticism's methodology and sought to correct them. Assuming with source critics that the biblical text is composite, form critics attempt to construct the best method for identifying the sources that lie behind the biblical text as it stands. Form critics shifted focus away from what they perceived as a haphazard approach to apportioning the text to arming the biblical critic with knowledge of the oral genres that gave birth to various texts of the Bible. With this knowledge in hand, they sought not only to clarify the divisions of the texts themselves, but also to gain insight into the social context within which these genres were utilized—that is, ancient Israel. In their own way, form critics sought to do what they held source criticism could not: namely, gain insight into the lived culture of Israel.

While form criticism is commonly associated with Gunkel and described as an OT enterprise, interest in the literary forms of the NT was also growing in the late nineteenth century.[6] These early studies were concerned with literary, not oral, forms, but eventually form criticism came to be applied to the NT with the same underlying assumptions described above. The main difference is that form critics of the NT were much more narrowly focused on the oral sources lying behind the Gospels rather than on the entire corpus of the NT. As with the OT, form critics of the NT followed closely on the heels of source criticism, with its interest in the four Gospels.

4.1.3 KEY CONCEPTS

Like source criticism, form criticism arose from German biblical scholarship, so some of the main concepts are known by their German names even in English publications. The next step in understanding form criticism, then, is exploring these German terms.

4.1.3.a Gattung

The German word *Gattung* does not approximate any English word. Although the word "genre" is a very common translation, the English usage of "genre" often implies categorizing literary works on a large scale rather

---

6. Martin J. Buss, *Biblical Form Criticism in Its Context* (Sheffield: Sheffield Academic, 1999), 263–67.

than as small segments of oral or written communication; *Gattung* includes both. "Form" is too narrow; *Gattung* refers more specifically to the nature of the text, which includes, but is not limited to, its structural features, as the term "form" implies. "Structure," again, is too narrow a definition for *Gattung*, and there are no other comparable words in English used to define literary categories. The best choice is, then, "genre," though anyone studying form criticism should be aware that "genre" refers to texts of all sizes and in both oral and written form. Yet what precisely does *Gattung* mean, specifically with respect to form criticism?

> A *Gattung* or genre is a *conventional pattern, recognizable by certain formal criteria* (style, shape, tone, particular syntactic or even gram-matical structures, recurring formulaic patterns), which is *used in a particular society in social contexts which are governed by certain formulaic conventions.*[7]

Thus *Gattung*/genre, in form criticism, encompasses not only textual structures and formulae but also the specific setting and purpose of that text; in other words, social setting is inherent within the definition of a genre itself.

4.1.3.b Sitz im Leben

The other important German phrase used in form criticism is *Sitz im Leben*. This phrase is most often translated as "setting in life," "situation in life," or sometimes "life setting" for short. It refers to the specific social setting within a society in which the genre took shape and was composed, recited, and utilized by the community. As Rudolf Bultmann puts it, *Sitz im Leben* is "a typical situation or occupation in the life of a community."[8] The phrase "social context" better describes the underlying concept, but it is not com-monly used in form criticism.

As an example, a *Sitz im Leben*, or life setting, for one of the psalms might be the Festival of Booths or, more generally, worship at the temple. Recall that in form criticism *every* genre carries with it an implied life

---

7. John Barton, *Reading the Old Testament: Method in Biblical Study*, rev. and enlarged ed. (Louisville: Westminster John Knox, 1996), 32. Emphasis original.

8. Rudolf Bultmann, "The Study of the Synoptic Gospels," in *Form Criticism: Two Essays on New Testament Research*, trans. Frederick C. Grant (New York: Harper & Row, 1962), 4.

setting; therefore, it is part of the goal of form criticism to discover just what that life setting was.

4.2 DEVELOPMENT OF FORM CRITICISM

Like the literature it sought to describe, form criticism was a product of its sociocultural and historical environment. This section surveys its origins and development, with particular attention to its foremost proponents. However, this overview focuses primarily on the development of the "classic" version of form criticism—that is, the method associated with Gunkel and further developed by Bultmann, Dibelius, Mowinckel, von Rad, and others into the second half of the twentieth century. In the 1960s and 1970s, biblical scholarship began adopting ideas and methods from literary criticism. In 1969, James Muilenburg urged form critics to pay more attention to literary style, the use of rhetorical devices, and the artistry of literary composition.[9] While Muilenburg called his new methodology "rhetorical criticism," some scholars, such as Rolf Knierim, George Coats, and Marvin Sweeney, continued calling their method "form criticism," even while they transformed it into a more literary approach by incorporating aspects of redaction criticism, rhetorical criticism, structuralism, and literary criticism.[10]

4.2.1 DEVELOPMENT OF FORM CRITICISM
IN THE OLD TESTAMENT

As mentioned above, Hermann Gunkel (1862–1932) is credited with developing the methodology now called form criticism. His interest in classifying ancient literature stemmed from the work done by the Grimm brothers

---

9. James Muilenburg, "Form Criticism and Beyond," *JBL* 88 (1969): 1–18. This essay is also considered the founding statement for a new interpretive approach called rhetorical criticism. This renewed focus on literary artistry in biblical literature is covered in Douglas Mangum and Douglas Estes, eds., *Literary Approaches to the Bible*, Lexham Methods Series 4 (Bellingham, WA: Lexham Press, 2016).

10. The commentary series Forms of Old Testament Literature reflects this newer type of form criticism, which treats "form criticism" as both a literary and a sociohistorical method. The move toward transforming form criticism into a more literary method is evident in Rolf Knierim's essay "Old Testament Form Criticism Reconsidered," *Int* 27 (1973): 435–68. With regard to Muilenburg, Knierim clearly sees close study of literary composition as already a part of form criticism (458n91).

in classifying German fairy tales and folklore only a few decades earlier.[11] Their work was part of the nineteenth-century philosophical movement known as romanticism, which saw folktales and other such "popular" oral literature as representative of a nation's unique identity and tradition. Given the connection between a given society and its folklore, if, as Gunkel claimed, the biblical sources stemmed from folktales, deeper knowledge of their structure would lead to an increased understanding of the society within which they were developed and functioned.

At roughly the same time, the work of men such as Henry Rawlinson (1810–1895)—the first to decipher and translate cuneiform—allowed for the translation of major Mesopotamian literary works like Enuma Elish and the Epic of Gilgamesh. The biblical texts were no longer unique narratives from the ancient Near East; Israelite literature could now be compared and contrasted with the literature of its neighbors. Therefore, just as the Grimm brothers classified German folktales by their genre—saga, myth, etc.—the biblical texts could be so classified, especially in light of the newly discovered ancient Near Eastern parallels.

Gunkel began his work in the Pentateuch, which is natural given that early source criticism had also focused on these books. From 1901 to 1910, Gunkel published a three-volume commentary on Genesis, in which he outlined form criticism as his new methodology and applied it to the genres he perceived in Genesis. A pioneer of the discipline, Gunkel's greatest contributions were his commentaries on Genesis; on the Prophets (1917); and, especially, on Psalms (1926). Whether looking at prose or poetry, Gunkel sought to provide a description not only of the relevant genres but also of the place each genre had in the life of the people of Israel.

Sigmund Mowinckel (1884–1965), who had been influenced by Gunkel while studying in Germany, also applied form criticism to Psalms, but his approach was further informed by his interest in comparative religions.[12] This, in turn, led to Mowinckel's interest in the institutional cult of Israel

---

11. Gene M. Tucker, *Form Criticism of the Old Testament* (Philadelphia: Fortress, 1971), 5; Marvin Sweeney, "Form Criticism," in *To Each Its Own Meaning: An Introduction to Biblical Criticisms and Their Application*, ed. Steven L. McKenzie and Stephen R. Haynes, rev. and expanded ed. (Louisville: Westminster John Knox, 1999), 61.

12. Sweeney, "Form Criticism," 62.

as embodied in Psalms. In his seminal work, *The Psalms in Israel's Worship*, Mowinckel describes form criticism in Psalms:

> Religious experience and custom had long ago decided what details of content, what thoughts and formulas in the cult were "right" and "appropriate" in each type of psalm and situation in the cult. And these forms persist, even where the individual poet does not think consciously of a purpose any longer, or of gaining anything by this prayer. ... The realization of which elements of form normally belong to a certain type not only makes it possible to define the individual psalm and the cultic situation from which it originates, but is also of considerable importance for the exegesis, and for the interpretation of any obscure passage.[13]

Though clearly an heir of Gunkel's methodology, Mowinckel thought Gunkel was still too indebted to source criticism, at least in his approach to Psalms. Gunkel advocated for a division of Psalms based primarily on the use of the different names for Israel's deity. Psalms that used "Yahweh" were thus "Yahwist," and those that used "Elohim" were "Elohist," as in the Documentary Hypothesis. Additionally, Gunkel believed most of the psalms to be postexilic imitations of earlier psalms written by individual members of Israelite society rather than the actual cultic psalms used regularly in Israelite worship. They were "no real cult psalms; they were 'spiritualized' imitations of the old, now mostly lost, cultic psalm poetry."[14]

According to Mowinckel, Gunkel's approach to Psalms only went halfway. Mowinckel perceived Psalms in *entirely* cultic terms and went further than Gunkel in attempting to describe their cultic origins and setting. According to Mowinckel, the psalms are "with very few exceptions—real cult psalms, made for cultic use," rather than late imitations of even older forms, as Gunkel had claimed.[15] To argue for the antiquity of the forms or genres he proposed, Mowinckel even compared some of the biblical psalms to ancient Canaanite psalms that had been recently uncovered throughout the Levant, such as in Ugarit. More than any other, Mowinckel's

---

13. Sigmund Mowinckel, *The Psalms in Israel's Worship* (Grand Rapids: Eerdmans, 2004), 26.

14. Mowinckel, *Psalms in Israel's Worship*, 29.

15. Mowinckel, *Psalms in Israel's Worship*, 30.

form-critical work, especially his conceptualization of the psalmic genres, has influenced Psalms studies throughout subsequent generations.

Albrecht Alt (1883-1956) applied form criticism to the legal traditions in the Pentateuch, looking for a social setting for the origin of biblical law.[16] Alt argued that Israelite legal forms had been adopted from Canaanite ones.[17] He compared biblical laws with other ancient Near Eastern law codes, such as Hittite and Babylonian laws, but he recognized those materials were too distant to be the direct sources for Israel's law format. Examining the legal forms, Alt drew a distinction between casuistic laws, recognizable by their "if x, then y" structure, and apodictic (or apodeictic) laws, recognizable by their "you shall not x" structure. The former, he argued, evolved from Canaanite legal codes, since this pattern is common in ancient Near Eastern legal texts.[18] Although examples of Canaanite legal texts were lacking, Alt used the parallels with a wide range of ancient Near Eastern texts to argue for a "common legal culture that existed before the appearance of the Israelites."[19] However, he could not find any other ancient Near Eastern examples of the apodictic structure, so he posited that apodictic law was a unique development within Israel.[20] Furthermore, Alt speculated that these laws most likely originated in an annual covenant renewal ceremony, at which a tradition like the Ten Commandments would be recited and reaffirmed.[21]

Alt is also known for his work on patriarchal religion, titled *Der Gott der Väter* (i.e., *The God of the Fathers*), published in 1929.[22] In this work, he argues that the patriarchal period may be partially reconstructed, despite the extensive harmonization of the Genesis narratives. Behind this harmonization, he detects glimpses of the nature of Israelite religion before the

---

16. Sweeney, "Form Criticism," 62–63.

17. Albrecht Alt, *Essays on Old Testament History and Religion*, trans. R. A. Wilson (Oxford: Blackwell, 1966), 97. Alt uses the labels "Canaanite" and "Canaanites" with reference to "the inhabitants of Palestine before the Israelite settlement." He was aware that there was no single, homogeneous people known as Canaanites, but he uses the term as a convenient short-hand for the various groups inhabiting the region in the Late Bronze Age and early Iron Age.

18. Alt, *Essays*, 98.

19. Alt, *Essays*, 98.

20. Alt, *Essays*, 123–25.

21. Alt, *Essays*, 125–29.

22. An English translation of "The God of the Fathers" is included in Alt, *Essays*, 1–77.

adoption of exclusive Yahwism. According to Alt, the "God of the fathers" (e.g., Exod 3 and 6) was not equivalent to Yahweh as depicted in the narrative of Exod 3. Instead, multiple patron deities were associated with each of the individual patriarchs: the God of Abraham, the "Fear of Isaac" (Gen 31:42), and the "Mighty One of Jacob" (Gen 49:24). Therefore, each of the patriarchs worshiped a distinct patron deity—which explains the proliferation of cultic sites associated with the patriarchs. It was only later, Alt argues, that these three deities merged into "the God of the Fathers," and it is he who eventually came to be known as Yahweh when the twelve tribes of Israel decided to form a cohesive geopolitical entity.

With this project, Alt moved form criticism beyond the identification of genres and into the description of the history of Israel. Alt started with the assumption of oral genres in the Genesis narratives, dating to the patriarchal period, and drew conclusions regarding the nature of the religious atmosphere in which they arose. Alt's insights reflect the natural extension of form criticism into tradition-historical criticism.[23]

Two of Alt's students, Martin Noth and Gerhard von Rad, continued using form criticism and tradition history to attempt to explain Israel's development as a nation. However, they also became interested in applying notions of genre, not only to small units of text, but also to large-scale sections of biblical text like the Pentateuch, the Hexateuch (i.e., the Pentateuch plus Joshua), the Deuteronomistic History, and the work of the Chronicler.[24]

Continuing Alt's work in the Pentateuch, Martin Noth (1902–1968) was a historian who used form criticism to supplement the Documentary Hypothesis (i.e., source criticism). In his earliest work, Noth argued that the twelve tribes of Israel were originally disparate tribes that organized themselves around a single religious tradition of worshiping Yahweh, and

---

23. See chapter 5 on tradition-historical criticism for additional information.

24. Noth, particularly, was interested in explaining the formation of large literary collections. The Deuteronomistic History was Noth's label for the Former Prophets (Joshua, Judges, 1-2 Samuel, 1-2 Kings). Noth considered 1-2 Chronicles, Ezra, and Nehemiah to be the work of the Chronicler. Noth's approach to these historical books (both the Chronicler's History and the Deuteronomistic History) is characterized by his belief that they were the work of a single author/editor. See Martin Noth, *The Chronicler's History*, trans. H. G. M. Williamson (Sheffield: Sheffield Academic, 2001), 29.

that this arrangement was solidified by the covenant at Shechem (Josh 24).[25] Thus, the varied and disparate elements that make up the Pentateuch stem from oral traditions preserved among different tribes that only later (according to Noth, during the time of Ezra) became codified into a single narrative. Guided by the notion of oral traditions lying behind biblical texts, Noth distinguished several major historical experiences that formed the thematic core of the Pentateuch, including the exodus out of Egypt, the promise to the patriarchs, and the revelation at Sinai.[26] He also related the development and formation of these traditions to the development of the Israelite state.

Noth's most enduring legacy is undoubtedly his theory of the Deuteronomistic History. In his work *The Deuteronomistic History*, Noth argues that the redactions of the books of Joshua, Judges, Samuel, and Kings were the work of a single redactor working in the seventh–sixth centuries.[27] Since this redactor (or school of redactors) uses the language of Deuteronomy throughout their work, this redaction project is labeled "Deuteronomic" or "Deuteronomistic." Noth, like Alt, was using form criticism for tradition history. While Noth owed his insights to the assumption of oral traditions, he used the idea of genres to identify larger units and was increasingly interested in the role of redaction in the shaping of the oral traditions.

Gerhard von Rad (1901–1971), another pioneer of tradition-historical criticism, is also known for his application of form criticism to the Documentary Hypothesis. Von Rad was interested in the formation of the Hexateuch. He theorized that the core elements of the Hexateuch were oral credos (for example, Deut 26:5–9) that provided "brief summaries of YHWH's actions on behalf of Israel," which served as theological expressions of Israel's faith.[28] Von Rad identified the Yahwist (J, "Jahwist," in the classic Documentary Hypothesis), working during Solomon's reign, as the one responsible for combining this traditional material into a history of

---

25. Martin Noth, *Das System der zwölf Stämme Israels* (Stuttgart: Kohlhammer, 1930).

26. Martin Noth, *A History of Pentateuchal Traditions*, trans. Bernhard W. Anderson (Englewood Cliffs, NJ: Prentice-Hall, 1972).

27. Martin Noth, *The Deuteronomistic History*, 2nd ed. (Sheffield: JSOT Press, 1991).

28. Sweeney, "Form Criticism," 63.

the twelve tribes of Israel.[29] He argued that this text was used in Israel's covenant renewal ceremony at the Festival of Booths.[30] Eventually, von Rad developed his observations into a theological account outlining how the biblical text as a whole was a work of salvation history.[31] He saw the biblical text as revolving around the historical confessions of the Israelite community rather than its histories (in contrast to Noth or Alt) or its folktales (in contrast to Gunkel). Von Rad's greatest contribution to the discipline of form criticism was his observation that short genres may expand beyond a short pericope to encompass a larger genre and even influence the composition of the entire Bible.[32] With the work of von Rad, form criticism began to look beyond the earliest layers of traditions and became interested in the ongoing life of the traditions.

Although Gunkel and others had called attention to the oral history of the prophetic books, the foundational form-critical work on the Prophets was that of Claus Westermann (1909–2000). In his seminal work, *Basic Forms of Prophetic Speech* (1967), Westermann reviews the history of the study of prophetic speech forms in the twentieth century and provides a basic summary of these forms.[33] Although he admits that prophetic books include historical narratives and prayers, the core of most prophetic books is prophetic speech. At the heart of Westermann's book are studies of prophetic speech as messenger speech and the corresponding messenger formula—"thus says Yahweh"—utilized to introduce prophetic pronouncements, typically either of judgment or of salvation. It is important to note that for Westermann, though the surface structure of each type of pronouncements varies, their underlying deep structures are consistent throughout.[34]

While Westermann's key works appeared in the 1960s, 1970s, and 1980s, his form-critical method carried on the traditional approach of

---

29. Gerhard von Rad, *The Problem of the Hexateuch and Other Essays*, trans. E. W. Trueman Dicken (Edinburgh: Oliver & Boyd, 1966), 48–51, 69.

30. Von Rad, *Problem of the Hexateuch*, 35, 53.

31. Sweeney, "Form Criticism," 64.

32. Sweeney, "Form Criticism," 64.

33. Claus Westermann, *Basic Forms of Prophetic Speech*, trans. Hugh Clayton White (1967; repr., Louisville, KY: Westminster John Knox, 1991).

34. Sweeney, "Form Criticism," 65.

Gunkel, Noth, and von Rad, even while other form critics during this period were developing a form criticism more explicitly indebted to literary criticism. For that reason, Westermann can be considered one of the last form critics in the "classic" sense. Biblical criticism was changing as interest grew in the literary nature of the biblical text as it stands, rather than any idealized or theoretical "pure" forms that might lie behind the text. Interest was also growing in using the social sciences to better understand the social context of the people of Israel, under the assumption that their cultural worldviews and thought processes were reflected in the writings they preserved. Literary and social-scientific theories had a significant impact on the humanities in general. In biblical studies, they were at the heart of new methodological approaches such as rhetorical criticism, structuralist criticism, narrative criticism, and social-scientific criticism.

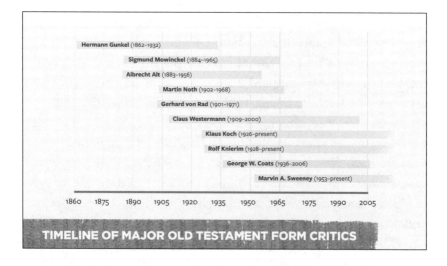

TIMELINE OF MAJOR OLD TESTAMENT FORM CRITICS

Instead of continuing their work under one of these new methodological labels, some form critics merely incorporated aspects of structuralism, narrative theory, or sociology into their form-critical work. For example, Klaus Koch applied the concepts of *langue and parole* from structural linguistics to form criticism. In linguistics, *langue* refers to the language system, while *parole* refers to the language in use. Koch revised the concepts for form criticism, making *langue* the form-critical genre that influenced the composition of the text and *parole* the actual literary structure of the text.[35] His most influential work, *The Growth of the Biblical Tradition*, outlines Koch's conceptualization of form criticism as a discipline.[36]

Rolf Knierim also incorporated structuralism into his form-critical method, arguing that literary and linguistic structures and conventions were already a part of form criticism.[37] Knierim also shifted emphasis from the study of the development of biblical texts over time to the study of the final form of the text. This shift made redaction criticism the first step in form criticism and tradition history.[38] Knierim argued that a student of the biblical text must first deal with the text present before them—one into which earlier text forms have been edited and possibly in a way that may have done damage to the original forms and genres. Like von Rad, Knierim noted that genres may encompass entire books, but unlike von Rad he argued that biblical texts must be examined at this level before one can discuss the possibility of smaller subunits.

Today's OT form criticism is exemplified by the commentaries published in The Forms of the Old Testament Literature series (FOTL). The form critics involved with that project, including Rolf Knierim, George Coats, and Marvin Sweeney, employ a method that attends to the text's literary structure; its message; and its social, historical setting.[39] These recent form critics clearly distinguish their goals from those of earlier form critics. Rather than attempting to reconstruct the social context and/or the history of Israel, they are concerned with the completed textual forms themselves, a more literary approach. In the opening section to his commentary on Genesis, Coats writes that "the value of the literary form resides in the form itself rather than in its contribution to a reconstruction of historical process."[40] In other words, historical issues are of lesser

---

35. Sweeney, "Form Criticism," 66.

36. Klaus Koch, *The Growth of the Biblical Tradition*, trans. S. M. Cupitt (New York: Scribner's, 1969).

37. Knierim, "Form Criticism Reconsidered," 439–43.

38. Sweeney, "Form Criticism," 67.

39. See George W. Coats, *Genesis: With an Introduction to Narrative Literature*, FOTL (Grand Rapids: Eerdmans, 1983); Marvin A. Sweeney, *Isaiah 1–39: With an Introduction to Prophetic Literature*, FOTL (Grand Rapids: Eerdmans, 1996); Rolf P. Knierim and George W. Coats, *Numbers*, FOTL (Grand Rapids: Eerdmans, 2005).

40. Coats, *Genesis*, 3.

concern than the texts' role as literature. Social context is directed toward a description of the genre rather than the other way around.

Thus, the task of the form critic is primarily descriptive rather than normative.[41] In the introduction to *Saga, Legend, Tale, Novella, Fable,* Coats takes to task those who would attempt to change the text to fit an idealized or theoretical form: "When a piece of art appears that does not match the ideal form of the genre, the interpreter has no right to reconstruct the piece according to a predetermined, ideal genre."[42] "Genre studies," as Coats calls form criticism, describes the text that exists rather than the text some say it should be. He is also careful to allow for texts functioning in ways outside their "normal"—i.e., typical—function. The goal of form criticism is to facilitate proper understanding and interpretation of the text by describing the formal structures within a text and their relation to other texts with similar structures, thereby allowing the interpreter to understand the function and intention of the text within its social context. In other words, the identity of a text can help scholars understand it better.

Marvin Sweeney's contribution to contemporary form-critical studies is his work on prophetic literature. Sweeney has written several commentaries on prophetic books utilizing form-critical methodology, as well as an introduction to prophetic literature and a book of essays about form criticism in the Prophets.[43] Like Coats, Sweeney starts from the perspective of large-scale genres (including whole books), yet he is also particularly interested in issues of intertextuality, i.e., how texts influence each other. In terms of form criticism, intertextuality moves beyond genres in isolation and discusses how various genres might influence each other, changing the structures, content, and intention of other texts due to their proximity to or influence from another text. Sweeney's interest in intertextuality points to a new and burgeoning aspect of biblical studies, one that form

---

41. George W. Coats, *Saga, Legend, Tale, Novella, Fable: Narrative Forms in the Old Testament Literature* (Sheffield, UK: JSOT Press, 1989), 7–15.

42. Coats, *Saga, Legend, Tale, Novella, Fable,* 11.

43. E.g., Marvin A. Sweeney, *The Twelve Prophets,* Berit Olam (Collegeville, MN: Liturgical Press, 2000); *Zephaniah: A Commentary,* Hermeneia (Minneapolis: Fortress, 2003); *The Prophetic Literature* (Nashville: Abingdon, 2005); *Form and Intertextuality in Prophetic and Apocalyptic Literature* (Tübingen: Mohr Siebeck, 2005); *Isaiah 40–66,* FOTL (Grand Rapids: Eerdmans, 2016).

criticism may interact with in productive ways.[44] As practiced today, form criticism is a multidimensional methodology that continues to bring new insights from other disciplines alongside it to supplement its traditional interest in the genre and life setting of the biblical text.

4.2.2 DEVELOPMENT OF FORM CRITICISM
IN THE NEW TESTAMENT

Form criticism, as it had been developed by Gunkel, began to be used by NT scholars within a decade of the completion of Gunkel's commentary on Genesis, though its use was initially confined to the Synoptic Gospels (Matthew, Mark, and Luke).[45] While there were prior studies concerned with literary form in the NT, the beginning of NT form criticism is frequently associated with the publication in 1919 of Martin Dibelius' *Die Formgeschichte des Evangeliums*.[46] Dibelius is also commonly credited with coining the term *Formgeschichte* ("form criticism"), which was quickly accepted as the name for this new methodology indebted to Gunkel. The rise of form criticism in NT scholarship is typically associated with three German scholars who had been influenced by Gunkel's approach to the OT—Dibelius, Karl Ludwig Schmidt, and Rudolf Bultmann.

At the beginning of the twentieth century, NT scholars were embroiled in a discussion of the life of Jesus as depicted in the Synoptics—the so-called Quest for the Historical Jesus. Although the first quest[47] ended

---

44. On the approach of intertextuality and its use in biblical studies, see Jeffery E. Leonard, "Inner-Biblical Exegesis and Intertextuality," in *Literary Approaches to the Bible*.

45. For a survey of form criticism as used in NT scholarship through much of the twentieth century, see Edgar V. McKnight, *What Is Form Criticism?* (Philadelphia: Fortress, 1969). While OT form criticism gradually evolved into more of a literary method in the last quarter of the twentieth century, NT form criticism became less influential as its concerns for literary form were taken up under explicitly literary approaches such as narrative criticism and structural criticism (see Mangum and Estes, *Literary Approaches to the Bible*).

46. Koch, *Growth of the Biblical Tradition*, 3. Ideas about literary form and oral tradition in the NT were evident long before Dibelius in the work of scholars such as Weizsäcker, Heinrici, Weiss, and Wendland (see Buss, *Biblical Form Criticism*, 263–68).

47. Within the field of Jesus research, three quests for the historical Jesus are recognized. The first quest lasted for almost the entire duration of the nineteenth century and consisted of the publication of various "Lives of Jesus," which were (often romanticized) attempts to harmonize the Synoptic Gospels into a true biography. It ended with Albert Schweitzer's *The Quest for the Historical Jesus* (2nd Eng. ed., London: Adam and Charles Black, 1911), in which he heavily criticized the biographies of Jesus that were being produced. The second quest began with Ernest Käsemann's 1953 lecture "The Problem of the Historical Jesus" and plateaued in

with Albert Schweitzer's 1906 critique of historical Jesus research, the life of Jesus and its depiction in the church's traditions (as embodied in the Gospels) was still very much at the forefront of NT studies. Moreover, as in OT studies, form criticism came swiftly on the heels of source criticism, which was applied to the NT in order to assess and delineate the sources lying behind the Synoptic Gospels (e.g., Q).

In 1919, Dibelius sought to introduce form-critical methodology to NT studies and establish it as *the* method of study. Dibelius argued that the Gospels were oral, "popular literature," and the so-called authors of the different books were simply the "collector[s] and editor[s]"[48] of those oral traditions. In other words, the content and style of the Synoptic Gospels has less to do with an individual person than with the way the early church passed down the stories about Jesus, which were already mostly fixed by the time the evangelists collated their manuscripts (c. 65–75). Dibelius also described the various genres utilized by these oral traditions—e.g., sermons, tales, legends, paradigms, the passion story—their defining features, and (briefly) their relationship to the social history of the early church. He was particularly interested in the role these stories played in shaping the ethics of the church.

Also in 1919, Karl Ludwig Schmidt published *Der Rahmen der Geschichte Jesu* (roughly translated "The Framework of the Life of Jesus"), which has not been translated into English. The major contribution of this work was to distinguish between the traditional, oral material and the editorial material—i.e., the material stemming from the Gospel writer himself.

In a later publication, Schmidt attempted to situate the Gospels in the wider history of literature,[49] classifying them as folklore and legend rather than as, say, Greek biography. Schmidt considers the Gospel writers to be relatively freehanded in their use of the traditional material. As one moves forward in time in the writing of the Gospels, "the constraint of the material, which is characteristic of all oral tradition, steadily declines, and the

---

the 1970s. The third quest has no defining beginning, but the 1980s saw new developments in the discipline that were retrospectively labeled as a third quest.

48. Martin Dibelius, *From Tradition to Gospel*, trans. Bertram Lee Woolf (New York: Scribner, 1965), 3. Although he is speaking regarding Luke vs. Acts, it applies more generally to the other Synoptics.

49. Karl Ludwig Schmidt, *The Place of the Gospels in the General History of Literature*, trans. Byron R. McCane (Columbia: University of South Carolina Press, 2002).

freedom of the authorial personality steadily increases."[50] Schmidt is thus willing to credit more to the mind of a specific Gospel writer than Dibelius is, though at the expense of the accuracy with which the Gospel writers handled the source material.

Rudolf Bultmann's earliest contributions to the field of biblical studies were his works on form criticism. Only a few years after Dibelius and Schmidt, he published his own magnum opus on form criticism, *The History of the Synoptic Tradition*, in which he quotes Dibelius in support of his claim that form criticism

> does not consist of identifying the individual units of the tradition according to their aesthetic or other characteristics and placing them in their various categories. It is much rather "to rediscover the origin and the history of the particular units and thereby to throw some light on the history of the tradition before it took literary form."[51]

Bultmann argued that form criticism not only allowed for the identification of the original form of a specific Gospel pericope but also made possible the identification of secondary additions and editorial flourishes. With these divisions in hand, a form critic would then be capable of tracing the history of the early church as it developed theologically and socially. Similar legends and folktales preserved in the rabbinic and (especially) Greek traditions were especially important for form critics as points of comparison.

The shining star of NT studies in the early twentieth century, form criticism shone brightly, but all too briefly. Bultmann's categorization of the Gospel texts into genres was so thorough and considered so definitive that it implied that there was very little else to accomplish. Moreover, others in the form-critical tradition, notably Vincent Taylor, held serious reservations regarding Bultmann's (and Dibelius' and Schmidt's) methodology. Taylor questioned the assumption that the oral traditions had no basis in the actual events of Jesus' life and criticized the extent to which form

---

50. Schmidt, *Place of the Gospels*, 83.

51. Rudolf Bultmann, *History of the Synoptic Tradition*, trans. John Marsh (New York: Harper & Row, 1963), 4. This quotation is from the 3rd rev. ed. of the German text, and so Bultmann here quotes an article published in 1929 by Dibelius.

criticism both ignored the role of eyewitness accounts and rejected the notion of an original structure/outline into which the units of tradition fit. To Taylor, Bultmann's method assumed that the early church was completely cut off from the disciples who founded the tradition and witnessed the events for themselves, an idea he found highly problematic. For Taylor, concern for community formation *and* the historical Jesus could coexist without the one completely overriding the other.[52]

As noted earlier with respect to OT form criticism, the rise of literary criticism after World War II prompted a shift in focus in biblical studies. In NT studies, the idea of the Gospel writers being mere collectors of oral tradition came under attack. Closer examination of the texts revealed that the Gospel writers had unique agendas in the way they arranged their materials, allowing them once again to be seen as theologians and editors in their own right.

Moreover, studies in rabbinic literature suggest that the assumed fluidity of the sources of the Gospels is more of an assumption than a reality. The closest parallel to the Gospel traditions are the early Jewish traditions, handed down at roughly the same era in history. The Dead Sea Scrolls, discovered in desert caves near Qumran in the mid-twentieth century, give scholars great insight into the preservation of ancient Jewish traditions. Unlike later, less literate folklore traditions in other countries, Jewish tradition was handled with care and a level of meticulousness for which form critics of the late nineteenth and early twentieth centuries did not account. Rather than being a fluid, ever-changing, and adapting tradition, the discoveries at Qumran exposed the strict nature of the keeping of oral traditions that lies behind Jewish and early Christian writings.

As with form criticism of the OT, NT form criticism evolved under influence from social-scientific and literary theories throughout the last quarter of the twentieth century. Today, form criticism is integrated with tradition history and redaction criticism as part of an approach to the biblical text that attempts to account for the development of NT material from oral traditions to written texts. This broad approach to NT interpretation has also incorporated social-scientific concepts and so has expanded

---

52. This summary of Taylor's view of form criticism is based on McKnight, *What Is Form Criticism?*, 47–50.

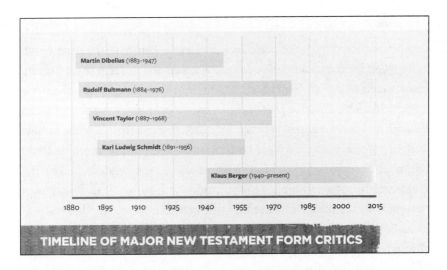

Martin Dibelius (1883–1947)

Rudolf Bultmann (1884–1976)

Vincent Taylor (1887–1968)

Karl Ludwig Schmidt (1891–1956)

Klaus Berger (1940–present)

| 1880 | 1895 | 1910 | 1925 | 1940 | 1955 | 1970 | 1985 | 2000 | 2015 |

TIMELINE OF MAJOR NEW TESTAMENT FORM CRITICS

into an interdisciplinary method not limited by the classic articulation of form criticism practiced by Bultmann, Dibelius, and others. For example, Richard Bauckham uses sociological and psychological insights to critique classic form-critical conclusions about the origin and transmission of the Gospels.[53] The work of James D. G. Dunn also illustrates how NT scholarship has moved beyond form criticism in its attempt to describe the development of the NT texts.[54]

4.3 APPLICATIONS OF FORM CRITICISM

Having outlined the methodology and history of form criticism, a few examples of how form criticism has been applied are in order. Due to the proliferation of genres within the biblical texts, as mentioned above, there is not space to discuss every genre that has been distinguished by form critics. Therefore, the following examples are limited to the most common areas of research—Pentateuch, Psalms, Prophets, and Gospels—and only the most important genre categories within them.

---

53. Richard Bauckham, *Jesus and the Eyewitnesses: The Gospels as Eyewitness Testimony* (Grand Rapids: Eerdmans, 2006).

54. See especially James D. G. Dunn, *Jesus Remembered* (Grand Rapids: Eerdmans, 2003); *The Oral Gospel Tradition* (Grand Rapids: Eerdmans, 2013); *Neither Jew nor Greek: A Contested Identity* (Grand Rapids: Eerdmans, 2015).

4.3.1 PENTATEUCH

One distinction that can be made in studying the genres of the Pentateuch is between legal and narrative texts. As noted above, legal texts may be categorized either as casuistic or apodictic.[55] According to Alt, apodictic law originated in Israel as part of the covenant-making ceremony between Yahweh and the Israelites (Josh 24). Alt noted that casuistic law was widely used in generating ancient Near Eastern legal codes like that of Hammurabi (eighteenth century BC). Thus, the genre was most likely adopted by the Israelites through common legal traditions. A form-critical comparison, however, shows that, while the life setting of this genre in other ancient Near Eastern cultures involved a king displaying wisdom and authority through the physical placement of law in the cities he controlled, in Israel the law originated with a *divine* king. Such a distinction points to how form criticism tries to uncover the purpose behind the use of different genres and show how different cultures can use the same genre to different effect.

Both forms of law may occur in longer, independent units (e.g., the Ten Commandments in Exod 20:1–17 and Deut 5:1–21), or mixed together (e.g., Exod 24:16–21). The free interchange between casuistic and apodictic laws in legal texts has complicated certain critical enterprises, but form criticism attempts to simply *describe* the phenomena under investigation. As recent scholars such as Knierim and Coats have pointed out, a particular example of a genre may not conform to the ideal genre, and one must be very careful before determining that the unique aspects are "unoriginal" because they do not fit an idealized type.

The distinction between casuistic and apodictic laws may then allow a form-critical scholar, at least in theory, to trace the formation of the original legal codes to which these laws belong. Once a specific code has been delineated based on form-critical criteria, early form criticism might attempt to determine the *Sitz im Leben* that may have produced the code; more recent form-critical enterprises might focus instead on synchronic and rhetorical analyses.

---

55. See the discussion of Albrecht Alt's work above in §4.2.1 Development of Form Criticism in the Old Testament. Casuistic law is conditional and describes hypothetical situations and their legal remedy ("if x, then y"). Apodictic laws are unconditional prohibitions ("you will not x").

CASUISTIC	APODICTIC
Conditional	Unconditional
Uses an "if x, then y" structure	Uses a "you shall not" structure

GENRES OF LAWS IN THE PENTATEUCH

An illustrative and brief example of how this process works comes from the "incest list" of Lev 18:6–17. A form critic might begin by noting that v. 6 appears to be a topic sentence, followed by a list of prohibitions beginning with the phrase "the nakedness of ... you shall not uncover," a formula that continues to v. 17. Verses 18–19 have similar wording (e.g., uncovering nakedness), but are not written in the exact same way as every other prohibition. On form-critical grounds, one might propose that the original list extends from vv. 6–17 and that vv. 18–19 were added on at a later date. Early form critics might then move on to discuss the life setting that would produce such a strong concern with incest. Perhaps it is a polemic against patriarchal marriage practices—Abraham married his half-sister (Gen 20:12), Jacob married sisters (Gen 29:15–30), and Isaac married his cousin (Gen 24), relationships that could be construed as forbidden based on a strict reading of the list. Form criticism as it is currently practiced might compare this to another, similar list of prohibitions found in Lev 20:11–20. Modern form critics might also discuss how the rhetoric of uncovering nakedness binds 18:6–19 together, despite the formal difference in wording, and how including a prohibition against sexually exposing a woman and her sister (v. 18) or a woman in her menstrual impurity (v. 19) in a list that otherwise seems to read against incest affects conclusions regarding authorial intention.

The first step in formal analysis of narrative texts, as with legal texts, is to determine genre. With respect to narrative genres, Gunkel's system

of classification has remained relatively stable throughout the history of
OT form criticism. The main genres to be considered are myth, folktale/
fable, saga, historical narrative, legend, and novella.

In the popular sense of the term, "myth" refers to unhistorical stories of
the gods, plural.[56] Since Israel held to the belief in only one God (or only one
supreme God),[57] there are no "authentic" myths preserved in the Hebrew
Bible. However, many biblical scholars have pointed out that depictions of
Yahweh often have many mythic elements[58] that approximate the myths
of Israel's neighbors, who were polytheistic. If one defines "myth" more
broadly—as Brevard Childs has done[59]—to include any action of a deity
that is preserved and understood by means of the ritual cult, then many
texts may be described as mythic that were not understood as such before,
such as Gen 1-2. The authors of narrative texts with mythic elements heavily adapted these elements to fit their own conception of reality and the
divine, often to great polemic effect.

Folktales and fables are similarly adapted and minimized in Israelite
storytelling. Traditionally, fables include an element of personification
of the natural world, which is preserved in such tales as that of Balaam's
donkey (Num 22:21-39) and Jotham's tale of the enthronement of various
trees (Judg 9:8-15). Narratives with magical elements like the Elijah/Elisha
cycle (1 Kgs 17-2 Kgs 13) and the exodus story (Exod 7-14) can be classified
as folktales.

---

56. The label "myth" commonly carries the connotation that the story is untrue or unhistorical, but the word has been used with several different meanings—not all of which necessarily exclude the possibility that the story is true or reliable. Buss identifies seven different,
but interrelated, meanings for "myth," ranging from just a word for stories to stories with
religious function (Buss, *Biblical Form Criticism*, 272). One problem with how the term gets used
in debates over biblical literature is the "assumption that a story cannot be both historical
(based on fact) and mythical (in its structure and role)" (Buss, *Biblical Form Criticism*, 273).

57. There is scholarly debate over whether Israelite religion should be considered monolatry or monotheism. Monolatry is the exclusive *worship* of a single deity, but it does not necessarily preclude the existence of others. Monotheism is the belief in the *existence* of only one
deity. For an introduction to this debate, see Mark S. Smith, *The Early History of God: Yahweh
and the Other Deities in Ancient Israel* (Grand Rapids: Eerdmans, 2002), 1-14.

58. Two good examples would be the "Yahweh as a divine warrior" motif (see Pss 7 and 98)
or the "Yahweh as a storm" motif (see Pss 18 and 29). Both of these are often found in psalms
celebrating Yahweh's victory over his enemies, but may also lie behind the way the story of
the exodus from Egypt is told, given that Yahweh controls the wind, appears in a cloud, and
is explicitly celebrated as a divine warrior in Exod 15.

59. Brevard S. Childs, *Myth and Reality in the Old Testament* (London: SCM, 1960), 29.

To tell tales of humankind, one turns to the genre of saga, by far the most common genre form critics use to describe narratives of the Pentateuch. Sagas often deal with great heroes of the past and often include "incredible" or miraculous elements and great deeds. They originate as oral tales and often have an element of the poetic; characterization is subordinate to plot, and characters often exist more as archetypes than as individuals. The stories presented in Gen 3–11, for all their mythic elements, are also great examples of saga; even Noah, despite being an important figure, is barely fleshed out, and what is told about him serves merely to further the plot. Gunkel further distinguished among three types of saga: *historical* (i.e., reflecting possibly real historical circumstances), *ethnographic* (i.e., interested in tribes and tribal relations), and *etiological* (i.e., interested in the origin of something). However, these categories have been questioned, especially the last, as it is not always apparent that etiology is the driving force of the narrative.

Westermann questioned Gunkel's use of the term "saga" to define the Genesis narratives at all.[60] Given that sagas are most often heroic tales of great deeds done to win honor—which he argued is lacking in the Genesis narratives—Westermann preferred the name "family narratives."[61] This term underscores the importance of the familial and tribal structures that lie behind this kind of storytelling. If one wishes to retain the saga terminology, one would have to adapt it to the specific concerns and *Sitz im Leben* of the Israelites.

Historical narratives, as defined by Gunkel, presuppose a modern notion of history. By "history," form critics are labeling a literary genre—not making a statement on whether the events actually occurred. Narratives labeled as "history" likely meet three qualifications: they are written, scientific, and public. "Written" refers to the notion that they were not preserved orally, but rather written down at the very outset; "scientific" means that they are systematic descriptions and explanations, "public" to the extent

---

60. Claus Westermann, *Genesis 12–36: A Continental Commentary*, trans. John J. Scullion (Minneapolis: Fortress, 1995), 49–54.

61. The only stories that come close to reflecting the traditional definition of saga are the judges narratives, especially that of Samson, who looks very much like a typical Homeric hero complete with supernatural strength, a weakness for women, and a keen mind for riddles and revenge.

that they are concerned with institutional affairs and nations. For example, Samuel, Kings, and Chronicles[62] are often classified as historical literature.

The final two categories considered here are the legend and the novella. Legends, like sagas, concern oral traditions of the past, but rather than focusing on heroes and heroic deeds legends typically revolve around holy men, holy places, or specific ceremonies. Although there are few "holy man" legends, one could place the Elisha cycle (2 Kgs 2–13) or the story of Samson in this category, though Samson does not quite fit the "holy man" label (Judg 13–16). As mentioned above, the biblical narratives are generally less interested in biographic material of individuals than they are in the history of the nation as a whole and God's interaction with his people via patriarchs, prophets, and kings. Examples of legends surrounding holy artifacts or locations include the ark narratives in 1 Sam 4–6 and the stories establishing the various holy cities—e.g., Bethel (Gen 28:10–19) and Gilgal (Josh 4:1–5:9).

MYTH	Stories of the gods.
FOLKTALE OR FABLE	Stories that personify the natural world.
SAGA	Stories of great heroes of the past, often in poetic form.
HISTORICAL NARRATIVE	Stories that are written, scientific, and public.
LEGEND	Stories that focus on holy men, holy places, or specific ceremonies.
NOVELLA	Fictional stories that usually are intended to make a point.

GENRES OF NARRATIVES IN THE PENTATEUCH

Novellas are "short fictitious stories with a plot and usually also a point."[63] The plot is generally better developed, with a climax, dénouement, and possibly subplots. It may also explore the deeper, psychological

---

62. Although clearly more theological in nature, Chronicles still represents a historical genre. The formal characteristics of its structure and purpose differ little from the Kings narratives and therefore must be classified, purely on formal grounds, as history.

63. Tucker, *Form Criticism*, 40.

aspects of a character. Generally, God is a minor character, if he is present at all in the narrative, preferring to act through indirect means rather than overt action. Ruth and the Joseph story are good examples of the novella. Once genre has been determined, the next step proceeds much as with legal texts: either a focus on life setting or a focus on rhetorical and synchronic analyses of the resulting narrative blocks.

4.3.2 PSALMS

Form-critical work on Psalms is still largely based on the early classifications of poetic genres identified by Gunkel and Mowinckel.[64] They identified important genres such as royal psalms (e.g., Psa 2), hymns of praise (e.g., Psa 149), enthronement psalms (e.g., Psa 47), national and personal lament psalms (e.g., Psa 80 and Psa 3, respectively), national and personal thanksgiving psalms (e.g., Psa 124 and Psa 18, respectively), cursing/imprecatory psalms (e.g., Psa 69), wisdom psalms (e.g., Psa 1), and hymns of Zion (e.g., Psa 87). Some psalms, such as Pss 9–10, did not fit their categorization in a straightforward way, so these are considered mixed-genre psalms. Their classifications emphasize the oral nature of the psalms

Royal	Wisdom	Lamentation
Ps 2	Ps 1	Pss 3, 80
Praise	**Zion**	**Thanksgiving**
Ps 149	Ps 87	Pss 18, 124
Imprecatory	**Mixed Genre**	**Enthronement**
Ps 69	Pss 9, 10	Ps 47

GENRES OF PSALMS

---

64. Hermann Gunkel, *Einleitung in die Psalmen: Die Gattungen der religiösen Lyrik Israels*, completed by J. Begrich (Göttingen: Vandenhoeck & Ruprecht, 1933), trans. into English as *Introduction to Psalms: The Genres of the Religious Lyric of Israel* (Macon, GA: Mercer University Press, 1998); *The Psalms: A Form-Critical Introduction* (Philadelphia: Fortress, 1967). Mowinckel's work appeared in English as *The Psalms in Israel's Worship*.

and hint at the religious purpose for the poetry. In fact, the most lasting contribution of form criticism of psalms is the recognition that they are texts for religious worship, not simply lyric poetry. In other words, they are "impersonal, stylized, multipurpose texts, reusable on many similar or even regularly recurring occasions."[65]

While some types of psalm are best categorized based on their content (e.g., royal or wisdom psalms), lament psalms have recognizable formal features and a typical pattern.[66] For example, the following features are associated with laments:

1. address to God

2. complaint

3. request for help

4. expression of confidence

5. assertion of innocence/confession of sin

6. expression of praise/vow of praise

The lament generally begins with a cry to God to draw his attention to the prayer. Then, the speaker may outline the complaint itself, explaining the difficult circumstances that require divine assistance. After explaining the situation, the speaker formally asks for God's help and often either protests his innocence or confesses his sin. A lament typically ends with the speaker anticipating divine deliverance and either praising God for it right then or promising to praise him when the deliverance comes. While these features are typical, the request for help is the key element that characterizes a psalm as a complaint. The table below shows how some of these elements are evident in Psa 13, an individual lament.[67]

---

65. Barton, *Reading the Old Testament*, 39.

66. On the structure and features of lament or complaint psalms, see Erhard S. Gerstenberger, *Psalms Part 1: With an Introduction to Cultic Poetry*, FOTL (Grand Rapids: Eerdmans, 1988), 11–14.

67. The biblical text is the NRSV.

Address to God	Psa 13:1–2	How long, O LORD? Will you forget me forever? How long will you hide your face from me? How long must I bear pain in my soul, and have sorrow in my heart all day long? How long shall my enemy be exalted over me?
Request for Help	Psa 13:3–4	Consider and answer me, O LORD my God! Give light to my eyes, or I will sleep the sleep of death, and my enemy will say, "I have prevailed"; my foes will rejoice because I am shaken.
Affirmation of Confidence	Psa 13:5	But I trusted in your steadfast love; my heart shall rejoice in your salvation.
Vow of Praise	Psa 13:6	I will sing to the LORD, because he has dealt bountifully with me.

Form criticism of the psalms had been heavily associated with the reconstruction of Israelite religious history due to early conclusions relating form and *Sitz im Leben*, especially Mowinckel's argument connecting some psalms with an annual Israelite enthronement festival celebrating Yahweh as king.[68] A contemporary form-critical analysis might focus on the formal distinctions among various psalms of a specific genre; how are the various royal psalms similar or different? How does their form relate to the form of enthronement psalms or hymns of Zion? What do these similarities and differences suggest about their use in liturgy and performance? These are the kinds of questions a form-critical analysis of Psalms might attempt to answer.

---

68. For an overview and critique of this idea, see Hans-Joachim Kraus, *Psalms 1–59: A Continental Commentary*, trans. Hilton C. Oswald (Minneapolis: Fortress, 1993), 86–89.

4.3.3 PROPHETS

As noted above, form-critical work on the prophetic books focuses on prophetic formulas or the similar patterns in prophetic messages.[69] Form critics emphasize that the traditional verse and chapter divisions in prophetic books do not always correspond to the actual shift in subject matter. Moreover, as with many narrative genres, prophetic literature was originally spoken, rather than written. It was only later, as prophecy evolved, that a preference for long, written speeches developed, as in Ezekiel and Isa 40–55.

Narrative units concerned with a prophet's activities are called prophetic accounts (for example, Isa 7:1–8:15). Prophetic literature may also include prayers directed to Yahweh (Hab 3). Addresses from the prophet to the people are called "speeches," but one must be careful to recall that these were probably not the pages-long addresses characteristic of prophetic literature in its present form, nor did the speeches originate with a written draft. They were practiced and delivered orally and were likely short. One can further define the speech genre as messenger speech (see above), and such speeches delivered either threats of judgment or promises of salvation (Hos 2:1–13; Amos 9:11–15). Other genres include vision reports, which report a special vision from Yahweh (Amos 7:1–6); vocational accounts, which detail how and when the prophet was called to be a prophet (Isa 6); and woe oracles, criticizing specific attitudes or actions (Isa 5:8–24). Again, the determination of genre in prophetic literature is a crucial first step in form-critical analysis. The next step is to discuss how genre might affect interpretation, why certain formal elements might be transformed or missing from a specific text, or how various oracles of a single type are related to each other.

4.3.4 GOSPELS

As with form-critical analyses of the OT, genre distinction is key in studies on the Gospels, leading to rhetorical, stylistic, or tradition-historical analyses. A few of the major genres are described here.[70]

---

69. For an overview of prophetic genres, see Sweeney, *Isaiah 1–39*, 15–30.

70. More detailed surveys of the main NT forms can be found in McKnight, *What Is Form Criticism?*, 21–33; Stephen H. Travis, "Form Criticism," in *New Testament Interpretation: Essays on Principles and Methods*, ed. I. Howard Marshall (Milton Keynes, UK; Waynesboro,

Pronouncement stories are brief, religious, well-rounded stories utilized for teaching or preaching purposes.[71] Some examples include the account of the rich young ruler (Mark 10:17–31) and that of Mary and Martha (Luke 10:38–42). These are stories with a didactic point toward which the entire narrative drives. Dibelius identified five characteristics of these accounts:[72]

1. They are brief, simple stories with little added detail.

2. They are self-contained, set off from the literary context.

3. They have a religious tone.

4. They have a didactic style, suitable for preaching.

5. They build toward a didactic point oriented around a word or action of Jesus.

Tales/miracle stories are stories that exalt a key, central figure. They are self-contained and descriptive and provide a detailed account of the malady with a note regarding the success of the healing and (perhaps) a reaction to it. They lack overtly religious language and, unlike the previous category, are not didactic.[73] Examples include the account of the healing of a leper (Mark 1:40–45) and the story of Jesus' stilling the storm (Mark 4:35–41).

The category of sayings/parables is the broadest, since it includes the sayings and teachings of Jesus that are not connected with a particular event (such as a miracle) and do not fit the characteristics of a pronouncement story.[74] There are many subgroups for this category, including maxims, metaphors, prophetic calls, short and long commands, and sermons. Many of Jesus' familiar statements and stories fall into this category (e.g., Mark 2:17; Luke 15:11–32).

GA: Paternoster, 1979), 153–62; and Darrell L. Bock, "Form Criticism," in *Interpreting the New Testament: Essays on Methods and Issues*, ed. David Alan Black and David S. Dockery (Nashville: Broadman & Holman, 2001), 106–24.

71. This form has also been called a "paradigm" (Dibelius) and an "apophthegm" (Bultmann), but Taylor's preference for "pronouncement story" has been commonly accepted by NT form critics (see Travis, "Form Criticism," 155–56).

72. McKnight, *What Is Form Criticism?*, 22; Bock, "Form Criticism," 112.

73. Travis, "Form Criticism," 156.

74. Bock, "Form Criticism," 114.

Legends/stories about Jesus are told to exalt him as a holy figure; however, these do not include any divine element, as do myths.[75] A legend is concerned with the person for his or her own sake, rather than as a vehicle to describe a particular saying or event. Stories like the triumphal entry (Mark 11) and the transfiguration (Mark 9) were considered legends by Bultmann.[76] Stories that are too supernaturally charged to be considered mere "tales," legends and stories where God or another divine being acts overtly or is directly experienced (like Jesus' baptism or the resurrection), are considered myths.[77]

Genre	Description
PRONOUNCEMENT STORIES	Brief, religious, well-rounded stories used for teaching or preaching
TALES / MIRACLE STORIES	Stories that exalt a key, central figure.
SAYINGS / PARABLES	All sayings or teachings of Jesus that are not specifically associated with a controversy or event.
LEGENDS / STORIES	Stories intended to exalt Jesus as a holy figure.

GENRES IN THE GOSPELS

4.4 LIMITATIONS OF FORM CRITICISM

Those seeking a more objective approach to biblical criticism could describe the defining feature of form criticism as a limitation, namely its primarily descriptive character.[78] Relying as it does on informed intuition rather

---

75. Bock, "Form Criticism," 115–16.

76. Bock, "Form Criticism," 116.

77. Bultmann did not make a distinction between "legend" and "myth," so he considered the transfiguration, for instance, to be a legend, despite its supernatural aspects. Dibelius separated "myth" from "legend," using "myth" for stories with supernatural aspects. As noted earlier, "myth," as used in form criticism, does not address the historicity of the event but rather merely indicates the involvement of supernatural beings in the action of the plot.

78. Practitioners of form criticism do not always follow the strictures of their own discipline. Indeed, some form critics go beyond the bounds of description to judge a given form on the basis of an idealized form. It is this very practice that Coats found so problematic about form criticism as it was practiced in the early twentieth century.

than proof, those of a more scientific bent might claim its conclusions are entirely arbitrary. Form criticism is also open to the criticism that it imposes modern genre categories on ancient materials. Modern scholars do not know enough about the genres of the ancient Near East to make comprehensive, definitive descriptions of them. Moreover, if knowledge of genre is critical to understanding a text, how does one deal with texts of ambiguous genre? One may go so far as to claim that since so little is known about the literary culture of Israel outside the biblical texts, next to nothing about the texts themselves can be said definitively. However, critical study of any kind of text rests on the assumption of some level of similarity between one culture and another—even one human mind and another—so the accusation of arbitrariness must be measured against the reality of imperfect knowledge.

Reliance on informed intuition, however, is less easily explained away, as is the thorny issue of texts with ambiguous genre. Literary classifications are always less strict than some would prefer because, as Coats and others point out, texts are the product of human minds and human creativity. Informed intuition *must* be the foundation of genre studies because humans rarely create a piece of art that is exactly according to the "ideal" type, even when such a type exists.

However, the inability to distinguish between an idealized form and reality is an ongoing limitation of the form-critical methodology. In its earliest days, form critics took great pains to determine the "original" form of a pericope, with an eye toward being able to extricate any later, extraneous elements once the original form was detected. This fixation with an idealized, original form fails to take into account the nature of human creativity; humans rarely stay within fixed boundaries of artistic expression, even in literature. Post–World War II, this approach was questioned; form critics were forced by the reactions of rhetorical and literary criticism to admit that the process of assigning genre was not always cut-and-dried. Linguistic categories, such as deep structure and surface structure, have allowed genre critics to distinguish between the underlying elements that are required by a genre and the many different ways in which they are adapted and modified to suit the needs of the speaker/author and the audience. Thus, contemporary form criticism, especially of the OT, has moved toward a solution to one of the limitations that have plagued form criticism since its inception.

In reaction to these limitations, some form critics err on the side of being overly precise. As a result, form critics can become atomistic, readily multiplying theoretical genre forms. This leads to confusion and may be overwhelming, especially since form critics have no standardized method of categorizing genres. What one form critic calls a "nature miracle" in the Gospels, another might call a "gift miracle" or even a "commission account." At times, it seems this distinction of naming is done merely on principle, so that a scholar can have his own name for a story rather than that which is already in use. In other words, form critics do not always follow the adage "quality over quantity."

One final limitation of form criticism lies in the perceived relationship between genre and life setting. The assumption that a genre developed in a specific life setting and can therefore be used as evidence of that life setting is circular reasoning. For example, if Psalms *are* the original psalms used in Israelite worship, then they are evidence for the original religious setting, a conclusion that can be used as evidence that they are the original psalms, which can be used as evidence for the nature of Israelite worship, and so forth.

The close association between early form criticism and tradition-historical criticism has also been perceived as a weakness, though one that has been overcome in recent years. Form critics such as Noth and von Rad became so fixated on reconstructing the history of the nation of Israel that concern for the genre and its features became secondary. Moreover, too heavy an emphasis on social context neglects the literary elements of the story for the sake of its utility in reconstructing history. In other words, form critics have often viewed texts in almost exclusively utilitarian terms, ignoring their artistry. Although the emphasis has shifted in form criticism away from reconstructing the nature of Israelite life and religion, scholars must still be aware of this problem and seek to minimize its effects as much as possible.

4.5 CONTEMPORARY INFLUENCE OF FORM CRITICISM

In OT studies, form criticism is still very much an actively used methodology, though it has changed shape in recent decades to become more closely associated with rhetorical and literary criticisms. Form criticism still retains its usefulness as a descriptive discipline when used alongside other critical methodologies. It is still a discipline that enjoys respect and utility in contemporary OT studies, albeit in a less dominant role than in the early twentieth century.

In NT studies, on the other hand, much form-critical methodology has fallen out of favor. Given its association with the quest for the historical Jesus and its subsequent critiques, this was inevitable. As noted above, NT studies appear to have moved beyond form criticism, whereas in OT studies form criticism was able to adapt and evolve to suit the changing interests of biblical scholars.

4.6 RESOURCES FOR FURTHER STUDY

The Forms of the Old Testament Literature Series

> This commentary series is dedicated to applying form criticism to the OT. A number of volumes in the series provide general introductions to the major types of OT literature—e.g., narrative (Genesis), prophetic (Isa 1–39), apocalyptic (Daniel), history (1 Kings), wisdom (Wisdom literature), and religious poetry (Psalms, Part 1). Each volume also includes a glossary that defines and offers examples of the major literary forms for that type of literature.

Bock, Darrell L. "Form Criticism." In *Interpreting the New Testament: Essays on Methods and Issues,* edited by David Alan Black and David S. Dockery, 106–24. Nashville, TN: Broadman & Holman, 2001.

> Bock provides a helpful introduction to NT form criticism with more detailed explanations and examples related to the various genres.

Bultmann, Rudolf. *The History of the Synoptic Tradition.* Translated by John Marsh. New York: Harper & Row, 1963.

> New Testament scholars still interact with and build on Bultmann's classification of the genres in the Gospels, which he lays out in detail in this book.

Coats, George W. *Genesis: With an Introduction to Narrative Literature.* The Forms of the Old Testament Literature Series 1. Grand Rapids:

Eerdmans, 1983; *Saga, Legend, Tale, Novella, Fable: Narrative Forms in the Old Testament Literature.* Sheffield: JSOT Press, 1989.

Coats' commentary on Genesis also provides a general introduction to the form-critical approach to biblical narrative literature. His *Saga, Legend, Tale, Novella, Fable* is a good book to read to get a basic understanding of later developments in form criticism, especially as they pertain to narrative genres. The introduction provides a good summary of Coats' views on the purpose of form criticism.

Dibelius, Martin. *From Tradition to Gospel.* Translated by Bertram Lee Woolf. New York: Scribner, 1965.

While NT interpretation has moved beyond the early form criticism of Dibelius, his work is still widely discussed, along with that of Bultmann (listed above) and Schmidt (listed below).

Gunkel, Hermann. *Genesis.* Translated by Mark E. Biddle. Macon, GA: Mercer University Press, 1997; *The Psalms: A Form-Critical Introduction.* Translated by Thomas M. Horner. Philadelphia: Fortress, 1967.

Gunkel's commentary on Genesis is widely considered the starting point for biblical form criticism. Gunkel is most known for his application of form criticism to Genesis and to the book of Psalms. His classification of types of psalms is still a fundamental part of Psalms research.

Schmidt, Karl Ludwig. *The Place of the Gospels in the General History of Literature.* Translated by Byron R. McCane. Columbia, SC: University of South Carolina Press, 2002.

Alongside Dibelius and Bultmann, Schmidt is one of the key figures for studying early form criticism of the NT.

Tucker, Gene M. *Form Criticism of the Old Testament.* Guides to Biblical Scholarship. Old Testament Series. Philadelphia: Fortress, 1971.

A bit dated, this is still a useful little introduction to form criticism, though one should note that he writes from the perspective of one who agrees wholeheartedly with the methodology and so should not be read if one is looking for an understanding of its weaknesses and limitations.

5

TRADITION-HISTORICAL CRITICISM

Gretchen Ellis

5.1 DEFINITION AND GOAL OF THE METHOD

The approach to biblical interpretation that we refer to as tradition-historical criticism is also known as "tradition history," "tradition criticism," or "traditio-historical criticism." The goal of tradition-historical analysis is to reconstruct how biblical traditions were transformed from oral traditions into written texts. More than other types of biblical criticism, tradition history depends on the findings of other methodologies, especially source criticism and form criticism.[1]

5.1.1 RELATION TO FORM CRITICISM

Not long after form criticism became the dominant methodology, some of its practitioners, such as Martin Noth and Gerhard von Rad, became convinced that they could study more than the oral origins of the biblical texts. According to these scholars, the entire history of the biblical texts could

---

1. Robert A. Di Vito, "Tradition-Historical Criticism," in *To Each Its Own Meaning: An Introduction to Biblical Criticisms and Their Application*, ed. Steven L. McKenzie and Stephen R. Haynes (Louisville, KY: Westminster John Knox, 1999), 90–91. The interrelationship of source criticism, form criticism, and tradition criticism led Klaus Koch to treat both source and tradition criticism as tools under the umbrella of form criticism (see Klaus Koch, *The Growth of the Biblical Tradition*, trans. S. M. Cupitt [New York: Scribner's, 1969], 53, 77–78).

be discerned—from initial oral traditions to the final written state, and everything in between. Concern for the entire growth of the text, as well as the communities and methods employed in this process, is the central focus of tradition-historical criticism.

Tradition-historical criticism stood on the shoulders of its predecessors—namely, source criticism and form criticism. Source criticism, as it was practiced in the nineteenth and early twentieth centuries, assumed that the biblical texts were the result of the compilation and editing of various written source documents into the final compositional whole that exists today. Form criticism argued that the biblical texts in fact had an oral prehistory prior to their assemblage in written form, shifting focus from the final form to its preliterary stages.[2] Tradition-historical criticism combined these focuses. Tradition-historical critics were concerned with the *entire* history of the biblical text, from the original oral form to the final edited text and all the stages in between.

As with form criticism, this methodology was concerned with studying more than the texts themselves. Interest in the life setting (called the *Sitz im Leben* in form criticism) of the communities in which the text developed grew into an interest in how these communities both preserved and changed the traditions they received from their forebears. Moreover, the increased concern with specific communities of tradition led to an interest in how geographical differences influenced what traditions were preserved and why. Initially fostered by the proponents of form criticism, this new methodology quickly outgrew its origins and became something broader and more complex.

Tradition-historical criticism has a more complicated relationship with the rest of the biblical-critical methodologies than does any other methodology. Over the years, scholars have viewed it from a variety of perspectives: as equivalent to form criticism (Gerhard von Rad), as an extension of form criticism (Klaus Koch), as reliant on the work of both source criticism and form criticism (Martin Noth), and as antithetical to source criticism (Ivan Engnell).[3] Still other scholars propose that tradition-historical criticism

---

2. Note that this one-sided emphasis on the original forms of the oral texts shifted after WWII.

3. Von Rad's tradition-historical interpretation of the Hexateuch was laid out in an essay titled "The Form-Critical Problem of the Hexateuch." Koch's approach is outlined in his *The*

is unique and distinct from all the rest—i.e., form criticism, source criticism,[4] textual criticism, and redaction criticism—(Wolfgang Richter), or that it is a kind of hybrid of them all (Magne Saebø).[5] Similar perspectives on the overlap and interaction among source criticism, form criticism, tradition history, and redaction criticism are found in NT studies.[6] Many works surveying method in NT interpretation do not even cover NT tradition-historical criticism independently of discussions of source, form, or redaction criticism.[7] However, this is largely due to the view that "tradition history" covers the entire enterprise of diachronic investigation of the NT text and involves the interaction of source criticism, form criticism, and redaction criticism.[8] In his foreword to Rast's *Tradition History and the Old Testament*, J. Coert Rylaarsdam equates OT tradition history with NT redaction criticism.[9] This view of tradition history as a method closely integrated with both form and redaction criticism is explicit in the work of Klaus Koch, who applies the same approach to both OT and NT texts.[10] For Koch, a form-critical approach culminates in a return to careful study

---

Growth of the Biblical Tradition. For summary and evaluation of the methods of Noth and Engnell, see R. N. Whybray, *The Making of the Pentateuch: A Methodological Study* (Sheffield: Sheffield Academic, 1994), 185–201.

4. Source criticism was called "literary criticism" in biblical scholarship well into the twentieth century. As biblical scholarship drew more broadly from the study of literature in general in the last half of the twentieth century, the use of the label "literary criticism" was no longer a clear reference to source criticism. For the sake of clarity, this chapter uses the term "source criticism" when referring to this discipline. However, older works of biblical scholarship may refer to source criticism as literary criticism.

5. Richter's method is laid out in his *Exegese als Literaturwissenschaft* (Göttingen: Vandenhoeck & Ruprecht, 1971). Magne Saebø's approach to tradition history is exemplified by his commentary on Deutero-Zechariah: *Sacharja 9-14: Untersuchungen von Text und Form* (Neukirchen-Vluyn: Neukirchener Verlag, 1969). For a summary of his conclusions, see Michael Floyd, *Minor Prophets: Part 2* (Grand Rapids: Eerdmans, 2000), 444–46.

6. See David R. Catchpole, "Tradition History," in *New Testament Interpretation*, ed. I. Howard Marshall (Milton Keynes, UK: Paternoster, 1977), 165–66.

7. For example, David Alan Black and David S. Dockery, eds., *Interpreting the New Testament: Essays on Methods and Issues* (Nashville: Broadman & Holman, 2001); Stanley E. Porter and David Tombs, eds., *Approaches to New Testament Study* (Sheffield: Sheffield Academic, 1995); Stanley Porter, ed., *Handbook to Exegesis of the New Testament* (Leiden: Brill, 1997).

8. David R. Catchpole, "Source, Form and Redaction Criticism of the New Testament," in *Handbook to Exegesis of the New Testament*, 167–88. By contrast, Catchpole's 1977 essay introducing the method was called "Tradition History."

9. J. Coert Rylaarsdam, editor's foreword to *Tradition History and the Old Testament*, by Walter E. Rast (Philadelphia: Fortress, 1972), vii.

10. Koch, *Growth of the Biblical Tradition*.

of the final form of the text after the various stages of transmission have been studied.[11] This may seem to be a rather bewildering array of opinions. To better understand why any and all of these opinions have arisen, one must understand the goals and history of tradition-historical criticism.

5.1.2 UNDERLYING ASSUMPTIONS

As with other criticisms, tradition-historical criticism is based on several basic assumptions. From source and form criticism, tradition-historical critics[12] inherited the assumption of composite biblical texts. Due to their close association with form criticism, tradition-historical critics assume that the original layers of the biblical texts were oral. However, unlike form critics—who are primarily interested in the original oral form behind the text—tradition critics are interested in both the original form and the subsequent stages the text underwent as it developed into the present written form. They are interested in the entire history of the tradition, not just in its original shape.

Above all, tradition-historical critics assume that the stages of development from the original form of the text to the present one can be distinguished and described using the text itself. According to Martin Noth,

> The growth and formation of the large body of traditions now found in the extensive and complicated literary structure of the Pentateuch was a long process, nourished by many roots and influenced by manifold interests and tendencies. In the course of this development, traditions which doubtless were circulated and transmitted orally at first were probably written down in time, for reasons that are no longer known to us and to an extent that can no longer be determined with certainty. In any event, later on they were brought together in large literary works and these in turn, through the purely literary labors of the so-called redactors, were finally compiled into the large corpus of the transmitted Pentateuch.

---

11. Koch, *Growth of the Biblical Tradition*, 57.

12. For a description of the most formative tradition-historical critics and their contributions to the discipline, see §5.2 Development of Tradition-Historical Criticism.

It is the task of a "history of Pentateuchal traditions" to investigate this whole process from beginning to end.[13]

Thus, tradition-historical critics go beyond form criticism and attempt to explain far more than do even the earliest form critics. A form critic, for example, would be content with determining which features of a text were "original" based on genre recognition and social context. Tradition-historical critics hold that once this original form is determined, they can trace when and how various other elements were added. In this way, it is easy to see why some view tradition criticism as an amalgam of source, form, and redaction criticisms. Tracing the growth and development of a specific tradition in the text naturally requires that one deal with the possibility of both written and oral sources, as well as how they were compiled and edited into the final form of the text; tradition-historical critics assume that such a process of excavating the compositional layers of the text is both desirable and possible.

The close connection between tradition-historical criticism and form criticism means that there is a great deal of crossover in terms of their underlying assumptions. Both assume that the religious background and social setting of the text can be determined based on a close reading of the text. The text is therefore a source of information about more than just the text itself; it provides a window into the religious views of the communities that preserved it. One can, for example, determine the various cultic settings of the psalms and their original context (e.g., festival or pilgrimage) by simply reading the psalms themselves.

This assumption is more comprehensive than that of form criticism. Form critics hold that they can recover the original social context of the oral texts based on their genre characteristics. Tradition-historical critics go one step further and assume that they can *also* recover a broader understanding of the religious themes and movements reflected in the text. This is due, in part, to their interest not only in the tradition itself but also in the "streams of tradition" to which different groupings of text belong.

---

13. Martin Noth, *A History of Pentateuchal Traditions*, trans. Bernhard W. Anderson (Englewood Cliffs, NJ: Prentice-Hall, 1972), 1.

Moreover, tradition-historical critics assume that their approach allows them to describe the religious history of the Israelites. Indeed, tradition-historical criticism is often associated with the so-called history of religions school.[14] This dovetails nicely with their interest in the history of transmission of the biblical text more broadly. In the same way that an original form can illuminate the social context that gave rise to it, the different stages in the development of the text provide insight into how the religion of Israel grew and developed over time. Each stage in the transmission process is a window into the religious milieu of the time at which the change happened. Think, for example, of a diary. Each entry in the diary provides the reader with insight into what the writer was thinking, experiencing, and doing at the time it was written. Only in this case, the "diary entries" are texts that are handed down from generation to generation and added to, modified, annotated, and reinterpreted based on the atmosphere in which the carriers of the tradition lived.

Although similar in many ways to other criticisms, tradition-historical criticism goes beyond its parent disciplines in scope and detail. Rather than focusing primarily on the original form of the texts, tradition-historical criticism seeks to describe the entire history of the tradition from its oral origins to its final literary, redacted form in the present text. Consequently, tradition-historical critics are interested in far more than the social context of the oral text. Their reconstruction of the history of the text is used to explain movements within Israelite religion at the time the text was created, as well as how it changed over time. In sum, OT tradition-historical criticism seeks to define the origin and development of both the texts preserved in the OT and the movements within Israelite religious history that affected what, how, when, where, and why people preserved these specific texts. For the NT, tradition-historical criticism explores the development

---

14. Called *Religionsgeschichtliche Schule* in German. This school is most often associated with scholars such as Herman Gunkel, Albert Eichhorn, and Hugo Gressman—i.e., German scholars at the turn of the twentieth century and the decades immediately after. Members of this school of thought were interested in more than tradition history; indeed, their interests were broader even than specifically Israelite religious history. The association between the two is mentioned here because tradition-historical critics hold that the results of the tradition-historical enterprise may be used to understand Israelite religious history, as it would have been studied in the history of religion school. (All dates are AD unless otherwise noted.—Eds.)

of Gospel traditions and looks for the possible use of traditional material within NT texts such as Christian hymns or creedal statements in Paul's letters (e.g., Phil 2:6–11; 1 Tim 3:16).

5.1.3 KEY CONCEPTS

Tradition-historical criticism lacks the kind of specialized German vocabulary that characterizes some other types of criticism. However, there are several important concepts that shape and define the approach.

5.1.3.a Traditio and Traditum[15]

In his book on the history of OT tradition-historical criticism, Douglas Knight divides what he calls "the phenomenon of oral tradition" into two distinct but closely related components.[16] The most familiar one is the *traditum*, the traditional material itself. From the outset, this would appear to be the logical topic of inquiry for the tradition-historical critic. However, as Knight points out, studying the history of a tradition requires knowledge of more than just the traditions themselves; one must also understand *how* the traditions were preserved, i.e., the *traditio*. The *traditio* is, in Knight's words, "the process (in its totality and in its details) whereby traditional material is passed from one generation to the next."[17] Knight is careful to note that methods of transmission may vary both with and within each generation. Sometimes the tradition is rigidly and painstakingly handed down in all its minutiae. At other times, that very same tradition may be passed on with changes of various kinds—additions, alterations, deletions, variations in wording, etc.—that are either intentional or unintentional. The tradition critic's goal is to understand not only the tradition itself but also the mechanism by which the communities that preserved the tradition handed it down. However, even the most important scholars of tradition-historical criticism generally do not make this distinction explicitly; yet the distinction between *traditio* and *traditum* is still a useful tool for explaining the methodology's twofold interest.

---

15. For a full treatment, see Douglas A. Knight, *Rediscovering the Traditions of Israel*, 3rd ed. (Atlanta: Society of Biblical Literature, 2006), 5–16.

16. Knight, *Rediscovering the Traditions of Israel*, 5.

17. Knight, *Rediscovering the Traditions of Israel*, 5.

5.1.3.b Traditionists and Streams of Tradition

As mentioned above, the tradition-historical critic's interest goes beyond the tradition itself to include the people groups that preserve and pass on traditions. These people groups are sometimes referred to as "traditionists." This interest is motivated by the belief that the "who" of tradition history makes a great deal of difference in how one interprets the tradition.[18]

For example, the same liturgical texts—that is, texts used in religious worship—can exist in slightly different versions based on the community using the text. A traditional Christian hymn may have many different wordings and even accompanying tunes in different churches. One denomination may have decided to make the language more gender inclusive by replacing "men" with "all" or "them"; another may have decided to update archaic language or change a word or two to allude to another, similar hymn in the same hymnal. Or the hymn may have originally been in a different language (with its own history in that language) and have several different translations. Knowing which groups of people were involved in this process may help illuminate why they made the changes they did and determine what may have been the "original" text of the hymn.

Another, related term used by tradition-historical scholars is "stream of tradition." This term refers to the body of traditions inherited by those who preserved some of its components and that were shaped by the socioreligious environments of that specific time and place.[19] Rather than referring to the traditionists themselves, "stream of tradition" refers to those traditions informed by the traditionists' context: ideological commitments, religious or cultural values, political affiliations, archetypes, etc. In the hymnal example, this might refer to the denomination's core beliefs, ethical and social commitments, political or social standing, relationship to broader society, or any other information that may illuminate a more thorough interpretation.

---

18. Those involved in preserving and passing on traditional material are sometimes also called tradents.

19. Knight, *Rediscovering the Traditions of Israel*, 14.

5.1.3.c Localization of Tradition

Related to the tradition-historical critic's interest in the specific communities that preserved and changed traditions is an interest in where these specific groups were located geographically and culturally. The process by which a tradition becomes associated with a specific location is called localization and may occur at various geographic levels—from as specific as a single city, like Beth-El, to as general as the entire northern kingdom of Israel after the divided monarchy. Tradition-historical critics argue that physical location affects how a story is told and why it was preserved. This may be especially true for etiologies (origin stories) that describe why a city has a particular name or how a tribe came to settle in a particular area. The Genesis narratives are full of such stories (e.g., Gen 11), and it is thought that many of them were handed down by people who lived in that area, or perhaps they were later adapted to fit the Israelite religious context.

According to tradition-historical critics, localization need not be limited to etiologies; localization may also occur when a significant thematic element becomes associated with a particular site. Sigmund Mowinckel, for example, claims that traditions with royal or cultic significance were most likely preserved by elite social circles in Jerusalem due to the city's significance as the center of royal and religious activity.[20] Traditions might also be assigned to a specific location because an important person or event is linked with a specific site. For example, the city of Shechem was strongly associated with the establishment of the covenant in Deut 27 and Josh 24. Tradition-historical critics, therefore, consider it likely that these covenant traditions were preserved and transmitted in and around Shechem. Localization may also occur at a wider geographic level than that of a city, as regional geography and concerns may also be significant in determining where a tradition originates. The Elijah/Elisha cycle (1–2 Kings), for example, would most likely have been preserved in the northern kingdom of Israel, given that it centers on northern kings.

This second example highlights another aspect of localization with which tradition-historical critics must grapple: the transfer of a tradition from one location to another. When Israel fell to the Assyrians in 722 BC,

---

20. See Sigmund Mowinckel, *Psalmenstudien II: Das Thronbesteigungsfest Jahwas und der Ursprung der Eschatologie* (Kristiania: A. W. Brøggers Bogtrykkeri, 1922).

most of the stories preserved by northern traditionists may have been transferred to southern circles for preservation. This raises the question of how this geographical move might have affected how these stories were told as they were integrated into a new socioreligious context.

5.2 DEVELOPMENT OF TRADITION-HISTORICAL CRITICISM

Although it arose shortly after form criticism became the dominant methodology in biblical criticism, tradition-historical criticism soon took on a life of its own. Many of the names found below are also associated with other forms of biblical criticism, and each of these scholars continued to utilize aspects of source and form criticism as part of their tradition-historical approach. Their work in tradition-historical criticism, however, led them to conclusions that they likely would not have reached through source or form criticism alone.

5.2.1 OLD TESTAMENT

Hermann Gunkel (1862–1932), the father of form criticism, was not technically a tradition-historical critic. However, his insights into the importance of understanding the oral history of texts paved the way for this methodology to develop. In his groundbreaking commentary on Genesis, he proposes that behind the written texts lay oral sources and that "at the time when they were written down the legends were already very old and had already a long history behind them."[21] Gunkel further theorizes that the earliest, oral stages of development had the greatest creative impact on how the stories were told; he also emphasizes the relationship between these traditions and Israel's neighbors, such as Babylon, Phoenicia, and Egypt. Studying the adaptation of such traditions into the Israelite context and their mode of transmission in its earliest stages was central to Gunkel's work,[22] as was attempting to discern how the sources[23] used in the Pentateuch might have collected these traditions.[24] His interest in the

---

21. Hermann Gunkel, *The Legends of Genesis*, trans. W. H. Carruth (Chicago: Open Court Publishing, 1901), 88.

22. Gunkel, *Legends of Genesis*, 88–122.

23. i.e., the J, E, D, and P of the classic Documentary Hypothesis.

24. Gunkel, *Legends of Genesis*, 123–60.

earliest stages of the oral text, how it was collected, and how it related to other ancient Near Eastern literature shaped tradition-historical criticism in the years subsequent to his work.

Sigmund Mowinckel (1884–1965), an important early form critic, is also an important figure in the development of tradition history. Given his interest in the Psalms and Prophets, Mowinckel's greatest contributions lie in his research on cultic traditions and their localization in and around Jerusalem. According to his analysis, many psalms were originally part of a yearly celebration of the kingship of Yahweh, called an enthronement festival. The most important psalms for this festival included such thematic elements as Yahweh's kingship and the preeminence of the temple and Mount Zion. Since these psalms also often mention Yahweh's supreme lordship and his role as creator of the universe, Mowinckel enfolded these themes into the celebration of Yahweh's enthronement.

Altogether, these various motifs form a core of traditions that Mowinckel associates with the southern kingdom of Judah and its capital city of Jerusalem. In other words, he uses the psalms to propose a stream of tradition that extended beyond the psalms themselves, united primarily by their thematic similarity. In such a schema, even larger traditions, such as the Genesis creation account, could be localized in the south due to thematic similarity with the creation motifs found in the psalms. If true, the confluence of these themes had a significant impact in the shaping of prophetic traditions, such as Isaiah, that are also associated with Jerusalem and may have even had a significant role in the final redaction of the entire biblical corpus, including the northern traditions that were integrated into the text around 722 BC. Thus, in his discussion of the psalmic and prophetic traditions of the south, Mowinckel established an important theory for the preservation of specific traditions originating around Jerusalem.

In the 1930s, Martin Noth (1902–1968) and Gerhard von Rad (1901–1971)—form critics and pioneers of tradition-historical criticism—changed the face of biblical criticism through their extensive interest in the history of biblical traditions and their transmission. Their studies paved the way for deeper interest in tradition history. In order to fully comprehend tradition-historical criticism, we must establish an understanding of their contributions to the methodology.

Martin Noth is well known for developing the concept of the Deuteronomistic History—the hypothesis that the books of Joshua, Judges, Samuel, and Kings were the work of a single author/editor. Central to Noth's investigation into this phenomenon is his interest in how older blocks of material are redacted into a final form. Having accepted the oral prehistory of the biblical text, Noth became increasingly interested in how these originally oral sources became finalized in their present, written form.

His pursuits raised the question of whether the redactional stage is a legitimate stage of inquiry for the tradition-historical critic. Prior to Noth and von Rad, interest in the traditions that lay behind the biblical text had been primarily focused on their original, oral stages. This fixation on the original stages meant that the final form of the text was being neglected in favor of an idealized form not actually present in the text. Unwilling to completely abandon the final, redacted stage of the text, Noth argued that tradition history must also encompass the redactional stage or stages. This was especially useful in situations where the redactor was also an author, which Noth argued was true for the Deuteronomistic Historian.[25] Noth argued that, rather than being merely a collator and organizer of biblical tradition, the Deuteronomistic Historian had a measure of creative control over not just what was included but also how and why it was included. He believed the Deuteromistic History reflected "such a unity of perspective and such a linguistic homogeneity that we must be in the presence of a real *author*."[26] Noth's concern with multiple stages of the text carried over into his other scholarly work, providing the basis for tradition-historical research.

---

25. The "Deuteronomistic Historian" (or the "Deuteronomist") is a shorthand label for the person responsible for the composition of the Deuteronomistic History. While Noth argued for the Deuteronomistic History as the work of a single person, later scholars posited the existence of a "school," "circle," or "movement" of like-minded people involved in Deuteronomic redaction of the historical books and possibly other parts of the OT. For further discussion, see Norbert F. Lohfink, "Was There a Deuteronomistic Movement?" in *Those Elusive Deuteronomists: The Phenomenon of Pan-Deuteronomism*, ed. Linda S. Schearing and Steven L. McKenzie (Sheffield: Sheffield Academic, 1999), 36–66.

26. Thomas Römer and Albert de Pury, "Deuteronomistic Historiography (DH): History of Research and Debated Issues," in *Israel Constructs Its History: Deuteronomistic Historiography in Recent Research*, ed. Albert de Pury, Thomas Römer, and Jean-Daniel Macchi (Sheffield: Sheffield Academic, 2000), 49, italics original.

In his work on the Pentateuch, *A History of Pentateuchal Traditions*, Noth displays an interest not only in the individual units of tradition—as had been the purview of form critics—but also in the thematic elements that lay behind these oral traditions, the incorporation of these themes into preserved textual units, and how these texts were redacted into their final form.[27] Noth's work led to the conclusion that the biblical text began not with a specific text but with a thematic framework that was later filled out with individual traditions that fit with each particular theme.

Another of Martin Noth's lasting contributions is the concept of the Israelite amphictyony, an association of neighboring states organized around a common center—in Israel's case, Jerusalem.[28] In his 1930 publication *Das System der zwölf Stämme Israels* ("The System of the Twelve Tribes of Israel"), Martin Noth first applied the concept of amphictyony to the formation of the twelve tribes of Israel.[29] According to Noth, prior to the development of the Israelite monarchy the twelve tribes listed in Gen 49[30] united as a single group due to their mutual allegiance to Yahweh. Thus, the so-called nation of Israel was originally a conglomeration of tribes devoted to the sole worship of Yahweh rather than a familial one. This tribal league, according to Noth, was solidified during the covenant renewal ceremony at Shechem (see Josh 24) and developed during the time of the Judges (1200–1000 BC). Centralization of worship and the institution of the monarchy developed as a natural outgrowth of the initial impulse to unite around a single deity and religious site.[31] For Noth, investigation

---

27. Noth's interest in tradition history encompassed every layer of transmission history, from its earliest form to its final form. Thus the birth of tradition-historical criticism is associated with his work and that of von Rad.

28. This concept is most commonly associated with ancient Greek city-states. The Delphic Amphictyony, for example, was a league of people groups formed to support and protect the ancient temples to Apollo and Demeter founded after the Trojan War. Members of such amphictyonies aided one another in war, and eventually the system developed political overtones in addition to the religious ones present from the beginning.

29. Martin Noth, *Das System der zwölf Stämme Israels* (Stuttgart: Kohlhammer, 1930).

30. The hypothesis was also derived from Num 1; 26.

31. The idea of an Israelite amphictyony was heavily challenged and has been all but discarded in recent years. The concept of amphictyony is not native to the ancient Near East, as it was used primarily in relation to Greek city-states. The argument goes that Greek city-states developed in different ways than did the polities in the ancient Levant and Mesopotamia; therefore, one cannot use a concept from one cultural context to explain the other. Another argument against the amphictyony model is the lack of archaeological support: no central shrine dating to the period of the judges has been found. Since this was one of

into the traditions of Israel and their transmission led naturally into a discussion of their socioreligious history and development. In other words, tradition history led to religious history.

In each of his formative works, Noth helped to define the research interest of tradition-historical criticism: (1) the *entire* history of a tradition, including thematic, oral, and redactional stages; and (2) the religious and social history of the nation of Israel, which gave birth to these traditions.

Gerhard von Rad was another founder of tradition-historical criticism, but rather than starting with a thematic framework, as Noth did, von Rad proposed that the core of the Pentateuch was an ancient confession of faith, or credo, found in Deut 26:5-9.[32] According to von Rad, this credo represents the earliest declaration of the mighty acts of Yahweh on behalf of his people and serves as the organizing principle of the Hexateuch (Genesis-Joshua), which ought to be studied form critically and in its entirety. Like Mowinckel before him, von Rad was interested in the social context that gave rise to the credo, which he believed to be the covenant renewal ceremony celebrated during the Feast of Booths.[33] Such a renewal ceremony was, theoretically, designed to unite and solidify the nation of Israel under the monarchy by way of common religious confession. In the same way that many elementary schools today begin the day by reciting the pledge of allegiance in order to create a sense of unity and commitment to the good of the nation, so von Rad's credo functioned to create a sense of national religious identity.

Von Rad moved from text to theme rather than vice versa, as Noth had done. Given the content of what von Rad considered to be the oldest historical creeds, he separated the story of the exodus (Exod 1-15) from the story of the revelation at Sinai (Exod 19-Num 10). Von Rad argued that these traditions were originally separate, with distinct interests, intentions,

---

the fundamental presuppositions of Noth's hypothesis, the lack of a centralized sanctuary challenges his hypothesis. Overall, the notion was criticized and rejected for a complete lack of supporting evidence (see Christopher Levin, "Das System Der Zwölf Stämme Israels," in *Congress Volume Paris 1992*, ed. J. A. Emerton [Leiden: Brill, 1995], 163-78).

32. See also Deut 6:20-24 and Josh 24:2b-13. Von Rad believed that the form found in Deut 26 was the oldest.

33. Gerhard von Rad, *The Problem of the Hexateuch and Other Essays*, trans. E. W. Trueman Dicken (Edinburgh: Oliver & Boyd, 1966), 35-39. The connection of covenant renewal with the observance of the Feast of Booths derives from Deut 31:10-11.

and cultic settings. The exodus narrative is more properly "redemptive history" in that it deals with Yahweh's saving actions on behalf of his people, and the Sinai narrative is a revelation of God's justice, what von Rad calls "apodeictic law."[34] However, similar to Noth, von Rad argues that these two traditions were creatively unified by the Yahwist, whose contributions are not those of an editor but those of an author who creatively interwove originally disparate traditions. Moreover, von Rad utilized this tradition-historical framework—the development of the Hexateuch around the original credo—to describe the development of Israelite theology from its incipient stages in the confession of Yahweh's mighty deeds to its full form as expressed in the entire biblical text. For von Rad, tradition history allowed the scholar to trace not only the social and religious history of Israel but also its theological history.

Scandinavian scholar Ivan Engnell (1906–1964) was known for his vociferous disagreement with the methodology employed by Noth and von Rad. In the aftermath of World War II, scholars became skeptical of the possibility of reconstructing an oral or idealized early form of the text with any degree of certainty. The waning influence of German scholarship also prompted reevaluation and sometimes rejection of those contributions made by prominent German scholars of the late nineteenth and early twentieth centuries. The widening philosophical interests in rhetorical criticism and sociology led to an increased focus on the present form of texts and how they related to different sociological contexts. Engnell's work reflects those specific movements.[35]

According to Engnell, it is not possible to recover the original wording of any of the traditions preserved in the biblical text, nor is it possible to discern any specific stages in the process of transmission.[36] The only written record of the text's stages is the present, finalized form; therefore, any investigation into the stages predating this one is doomed to failure. One cannot reconstruct a fundamentally oral enterprise because there is no evidence available to prove or disprove one's findings. According to Engnell,

---

34. Von Rad, *Problem of the Hexateuch*, 19; see 18–20 for the entire discussion.

35. For a detailed overview of Engnell's contributions related to tradition-historical criticism, see Knight, *Rediscovering the Traditions of Israel*, 197–220.

36. Magne Sæbø, *On the Way to Canon: Creative Tradition History in the Old Testament* (Sheffield: Sheffield Academic, 1998), 31.

the correct focus of tradition-historical study is the present form of the text, including its compositional techniques, motifs, structures, themes, and intentions. Although Engnell was willing to investigate small units of text, he insisted that each unit needs to be constantly related to its context within the wider composition. Moreover, Engnell emphasized the importance of other kinds of relevant data, including sociology, literary analysis, psychology, and cultural anthropology, for understanding biblical traditions.

Engnell also disagreed with Noth and von Rad as to the nature of the traditionists preserving the texts. Where Noth favored a singular Deuteronomistic Historian, Engnell preferred the idea of a school or community of people with similar ideological commitments.[37] These circles of tradition continued across generations, and, during that time period, the traditions were created and creatively joined with other traditions into the present form of the text. In prophetic literature, for example, the words of the prophet would have been orally handed down and circulated among his disciples for decades or longer prior to their written form. According to Engnell, the fundamentally communal nature of a text's production and transmission is essential to understanding the text itself.

Each of the scholars associated with tradition-historical criticism has their own unique take on the purposes of this method. To Gunkel and Mowinckel, tradition-historical criticism was not yet a fully formed discipline; however, they each utilized some of its basic assumptions to study the forms of the earliest oral sources of the Pentateuch (Gunkel) and the religious traditions of Jerusalem (Mowinckel). For Noth, tradition history served as a fundamental prerequisite to writing a history of Israel, whereas for von Rad it provided the basis for discussing the development of Israelite theology. Engnell used tradition-historical analysis to investigate the motifs and themes of the present form of the text, bringing into the foreground elements that had subsidiary function in earlier tradition-historical investigations.

---

37. Walter E. Rast, *Tradition History and the Old Testament* (Philadelphia: Fortress, 1972), 12.

5.2.2 NEW TESTAMENT

Tradition history is also part of a broad approach to studying NT biblical traditions and their development from oral stages to written texts that includes source, form, and redaction criticism. The same underlying assumptions and key concepts that informed the development of tradition history for the OT are brought to a tradition-historical study of a NT text. Charting the development of tradition history as a distinct NT method is not really possible due to its deep integration with NT form and redaction criticism.[38] However, the study of the origin and development of traditions behind NT texts has begun to move beyond both form criticism and redaction criticism by incorporating insights from social-scientific research.[39] The study of NT traditions, therefore, has moved toward more interdisciplinary models built from orality studies, media criticism, and other social sciences.[40]

5.3 APPLICATIONS OF TRADITION-HISTORICAL CRITICISM

Although we have already discussed certain aspects of the application of this methodology to the OT, we must bring these discrete elements together in order to get a better understanding of how certain texts have been handled in tradition-historical criticism.

5.3.1 PENTATEUCH/HEXATEUCH

As with source and form criticism, tradition-historical criticism began with a focus on the Pentateuch (or, in von Rad's case, the Hexateuch) with the goal of determining the nature of its original core and how it developed into the present form of the text.

---

38. Its origins for NT study are based in the development of form criticism. For an overview, see §4.2.2 Development of Form Criticism in the New Testament. NT redaction criticism also grew out of form criticism. For a discussion of the development of the discipline, see Maegan C. M. Gilliland, "Redaction Criticism, New Testament," in *The Lexham Bible Dictionary*, ed. John D. Barry (Bellingham, WA: Lexham Press, 2016).

39. See chap. 7 on social-scientific criticism. For a recent survey of these developments in NT scholarship, see Eric Eve, *Behind the Gospels: Understanding the Oral Tradition* (London: SPCK, 2013).

40. For a concise overview, see Rafael Rodríguez, *Oral Tradition and the New Testament: A Guide for the Perplexed* (London: Bloomsbury, 2014), 33–52.

According to von Rad, the center of the Hexateuch is a historical credo confessing the mighty acts of Yahweh in bringing his people out of Egypt. Recited yearly at a covenant renewal ceremony, this credo formed the original nucleus of Israelite socioreligious consciousness, defining Israel's people as those committed to the worship of Yahweh alone. As might be expected of a tradition-historical critic, von Rad went on to describe how other traditions became attached to this credo, fleshing out in detail the fundamental principles of how Yahweh, the God of Israel, relates to his people. Although many streams of tradition may have led to the development of the entire biblical corpus, for von Rad the core is Israel's confession, and this single tradition shaped the development of the rest. Thus, von Rad's primary contribution to Hexateuchal research is, in Douglas Knight's words, "in directing attention to the living process which brought individual, independent traditions together to form the Hexateuch as we know it."[41]

Due to the broad definition of "tradition," tradition-historical critics are equipped to discuss not only how specific texts may have developed but also how themes and motifs in the biblical texts were expanded and reinvented in the process of transmission. Tradition-historical critics recognize that sometimes a concept shapes the way a story is told rather than vice versa. According to Martin Noth, the center of the Pentateuch is not a specific text but rather a series of themes: (1) the deliverance from Egypt, (2) the settlement in the land, (3) the promise to the patriarchs, (4) the leadership in the wilderness, and (5) the revelation at Sinai.[42] Each of these traditions had its own history and development, distinct from the others, prior to being integrated into the Pentateuch. According to Noth, preservation of these traditions was due primarily to the dominance of a particular theme rather than the importance of one specific text. Texts were consolidated around these themes and preserved among the various tribes; only later, when Israel joined together as a single amphictyony, did these themes become interconnected and reinterpreted in light of the others.

The proposed reconstruction of the history of biblical tradition shapes how tradition-historical scholars interpret the Pentateuch/Hexateuch. For example, von Rad's commitment to an original credo led him to pit

---

41. Knight, *Rediscovering the Traditions of Israel*, 87.

42. Noth, *History of Pentateuchal Traditions*, 46–62.

the redemptive-historical themes related to the exodus over against the Sinai revelation because what he assumes to be Israel's original credo (Deut 26:5–9) lacks mention of Sinai. Furthermore, Noth's preference for thematic centrality over against a single textual core dovetails nicely with his historical reconstruction of the Israelite amphictyony. In short, von Rad started with a core and explained how other themes became attached to it, but Noth started with multiple independent cores and explained how they became interwoven. Both are representative of the project of tradition-historical criticism.

5.3.2 PSALMS

The most significant name in tradition-historical criticism on the book of Psalms is that of Mowinckel, whose most important contribution is his description of the annual enthronement festival and its relationship to the preservation of religious traditions in Jerusalem. Unlike Gunkel, Mowinckel assumed that the psalms preserved in the biblical text were the original psalms used by the people of Israel in their various religious activities. At the time when Mowinckel wrote, it had been discovered that the Enuma Elish[43] was recited during the Babylonian new year festival in praise of the supremacy of Marduk. The notion of a Babylonian enthronement festival for Marduk carried over into OT scholarship. Mowinckel terms the psalms praising the kingship of Yahweh (such as Pss 47; 93; 95–100) as "enthronement psalms" and argues that they stemmed from a similar sociocultural context as the Enuma Elish. Based on the parallels from Babylonian literature, the enthronement festival was an annual event—most likely occurring during the springtime feast of the new agricultural year—that celebrated the supremacy of Yahweh, his sole kingship, and his provision. The celebration of such an important festival explains the dominance of certain themes in the so-called enthronement psalms: Yahweh's kingship,

---

43. This classic work of ancient Mesopotamian epic poetry details the creation of the world and humanity, ending with the coronation of Marduk in honor of his work of bringing order to chaos. The story originally functioned to depict the supremacy of Marduk over the other gods in the Babylonian pantheon.

his supremacy as creator and judge of the universe, the subjugation of the nations to him, and the cultic centrality of Zion.[44]

As mentioned above, Mowinckel used his theory of the centrality of Jerusalem to go beyond the psalmic traditions and to explain the entire complex of thematic elements, which he localized in Jerusalem, in light of his work on the psalms. Nevertheless, Mowinckel's development of important thematic elements in the Jerusalem circle is due primarily to his interest in the cult, especially the yearly enthronement festival of Yahweh in Jerusalem. Thus, tradition-historical analysis moved Mowinckel's scholarship beyond analyzing the original forms of the psalms to proposing a history of Jerusalem's traditions, founded on his reconstruction of the practices of Israelite worship, which were themselves derived from his analysis of the psalms.

5.3.3 NEW TESTAMENT

The study of NT traditions and their development predominantly focuses on the Gospels. This is due in part to the prominence of historical Jesus research in the twentieth century. One goal of historical Jesus research had been determining the authenticity of sayings that occurred in different versions in different Gospels. While current studies of the oral traditions behind the Gospels do not have the same goal, the various versions of Jesus' sayings offer a simple example of the sort of evidence used in tradition history of the NT.

All four Gospels recount Peter's confession of his knowledge of Jesus' true identity, but the accounts differ in key details (Matt 16:13–16; Mark 8:27–30; Luke 9:18–20; John 6:66–69). For example, Matthew and

---

44. Mowinckel enfolded a vast number of psalms into the cultic setting of the enthronement festival that most readers would not initially identify as particularly relevant to that setting. Psalms of ascent, such as Pss 15 and 24, are related to the festival because they describe an ascent into Zion consistent with a procession leading up to the actual pronouncement of Yahweh's enthronement. Since the enthronement psalms mention the subjugation of the nations under Yahweh, other psalms with this theme (e.g., Psa 66:1–12) are included as well. Other thematic elements consistent with Yahweh's kingship, such as Yahweh's judgment of Israel and the other nations (Pss 50; 75), Yahweh's residence in Zion (Psa 76), and Yahweh's control over creation (Psa 8) and fertility (Psa 65), are also declared part of the enthronement celebration. Thus, Mowinckel assigns almost a full third of the book of Psalms (about 45 psalms) specifically to the celebration of the annual enthronement festival, all due to his commitment to the religious experience lying behind the biblical texts.

Mark both place the event in the vicinity of Caesarea Philippi, while John appears to put it in the context of Jesus' teaching at Capernaum (John 6:59). Luke does not explicitly identify where the event took place, but he adds the detail that Jesus raised the topic of his identity with his disciples "while he was praying alone" (Luke 9:18).[45] In the three Synoptic Gospels, the scenario is essentially the same: Jesus asks his disciples what rumors they have heard about his identity, they answer, and when he presses them on who *they* think he is, Peter confesses his belief in Jesus as the Messiah. In John, Peter volunteers his assessment in response to a different question (John 6:67). However, the exact wording of the exchange between Jesus and the disciples is different in each of the Synoptics. There are three different versions of Jesus' question:

- Mark 8:27—"Who do **people** say that **I** am?"

- Matthew 16:13—"Who do **people** say that the **Son of Man** is?"

- Luke 9:18—"Who do the **crowds** say that **I** am?"

The content is the same, but the wording Jesus uses to refer to himself and the people differs. Interestingly, while Mark and Luke both have Jesus refer to himself in the first person, they differ in the word used to describe the people. There are also three different versions of the answer he receives from the disciples:

- Mark 8:28—"And they told him, saying, 'John the Baptist, and others Elijah, and others that you are one of the prophets.'"

- Matthew 16:14—"And they said, Some say John the Baptist, but others Elijah, and others **Jeremiah** or one of the prophets."

- Luke 9:19—"And they answered and said, 'John the Baptist, but others, Elijah, and others, that one of the **ancient** prophets **has risen**.'"

---

45. Biblical quotations in this section are from the LEB.

Again, the gist of their answer is the same, but there are notable differences, such as Matthew's addition of Jeremiah as one of the figures with whom Jesus was associated. Luke makes explicit the implications of the idea that Jesus is "one of the prophets" by adding that the people think "one of the ancient prophets has risen." Finally, Peter's confession itself is phrased four different ways, including the statement in John 6:69. While John 6:69 could be explained as a different event, Raymond Brown identifies it as the "Johannine parallel to the Synoptic scene at Caesarea Philippi."[46]

- Mark 8:29—"You are the Christ!"

- Matthew 16:16—"You are the Christ, the Son of the living God!"

- Luke 9:20—"The Christ of God."

- John 6:69—"You are the Holy One of God."

For the tradition-historical critic, these differences potentially reflect various stages in the development of the tradition. Building on the conclusions of source criticism about the relationships among the Gospels, a tradition critic would likely conclude that Mark contains the earliest version of the tradition and that Matthew and Luke added small details enhancing their view of Jesus' identity.[47] John's version is the most transformed, as he has more extensively reworked earlier traditions into his own account.

5.4 LIMITATIONS OF TRADITION-HISTORICAL CRITICISM

One of the greatest weaknesses of tradition-historical analysis is how easily it may be overextended. The task of learning the history of traditions and their transmission is a legitimate field of research, but one whose conclusions cannot be proven, only theorized (albeit convincingly). Reconstructing history is difficult and problematic, even in the presence of documents and traditions. Tradition-historical critics sometimes attempt to make the method do and say more than it actually is capable of.

---

46. Raymond E. Brown, *The Gospel according to John I–XII* (Garden City, NY: Doubleday, 1966), 301.

47. Catchpole, "Tradition History," 167.

Attempting to recreate the history and development of Israel and Israelite theology or early Christianity and early Christian theology solely from analyzing the biblical text is beyond the bounds of tradition-historical inquiry; other sources and means of knowledge of the ancient past must also be considered. Like trying to use only astronomy to explain the origin of life on earth, tradition-historical criticism—like all other biblical criticisms—simply does not explain everything about the history and development of Israel and its texts.

One logical corollary to this critique is the notion that the results of tradition-historical work are implausible. In other words, the results are too detailed and precise to possibly be accurate, given the limitations of the method. Noth, in particular, is often criticized for the comprehensiveness and decisiveness with which he reconstructs the history of the text. After reading Noth's work, some are left wondering how it is possible for him to be so definitive about something that has little archaeological or historical evidence. Engnell goes so far as to argue that the task of attempting to reconstruct any stage of the text other than the present one is hopeless. Although one may rightly criticize Engnell for being *overly* critical of the contributions of tradition-historical criticism, his critique rightly points out that tradition-historical work can easily become too confident in its own conclusions.

Engnell also accused tradition-historical criticism of being overly dependent on modern preconceptions about ancient life and religion. He argued that Noth and von Rad relied too much on written transmission in their reconstruction of tradition. Indeed, Engnell's fixation on the oral nature of Israelite transmission stemmed from his position that tradition-historical criticism had not accepted that ancient Near Eastern peoples did not transmit their stories the same way modern Europeans do.

This raises the question of the relationship between oral and written texts—an important area of contemporary research. How can one tell the difference between a written text that reflects an original oral source and one that was originally written? Is it possible to determine the relationship between spoken and written Hebrew when there are no recordings of the former? How one answers these questions determines whether one thinks tradition-historical work is even possible.

Furthermore, recent studies in orality, literacy, and the process of transmission have raised questions regarding how one might classify the faithfulness of a tradition to the Bible's "original" wording and phrasing.[48] Much like the questions being posed in translation theory, contemporary discussions of tradition-historical criticism revolve around the very process of transmission itself, including how one can determine which process is more faithful than another, or even whether "faithful" is a good word to use.

Finally, tradition-historical criticism, as it was commonly practiced in its early years, requires a fundamental trust in the authenticity of the stories present in the text—a trust that many contemporary scholars are unwilling to grant.

Tradition-historical critics often assume that behind the biblical traditions are recollections of actual historical events, events that may not have actually happened as described, if at all. In other words, tradition-historical criticism sometimes fails to distinguish between the history of traditions and their historicity and relies too much on the criteria of historicity and authenticity in attempting to discern which elements are most important for study. Modern scholarship emphasizes the difficulty of truly discerning the age of various elements in a tradition, casting a shadow on the entire tradition-historical method.

5.5 CONTEMPORARY INFLUENCE OF TRADITION-HISTORICAL CRITICISM

Despite the many critiques of tradition-historical criticism, there is no outright rejection of the method in modern scholarship. The general opinion is that, while the techniques and interests of tradition-historical criticism are useful, and its conclusions may be helpful for exegesis and historiography, it is not to be pursued for its own sake or in isolation from other relevant methods. Nevertheless, the lack of precise methodological procedures and criteria for the analysis of specific texts has made this field less popular than other forms of biblical scholarship. This has yielded an

---

48. For example, the essays collected in *Performing the Gospel: Orality, Memory, and Mark*, ed. Richard A. Horsley, Jonathan A. Draper, and John Miles Foley (Minneapolis: Fortress, 2006); see also James D. G. Dunn, *The Oral Gospel Tradition* (Grand Rapids: Eerdmans, 2013).

array of opinions regarding the rightful place and relationship between tradition-historical criticism and other methods.

That various questions are still being posed regarding the reliability and nature of tradition-historical criticism testifies to its ongoing importance in biblical criticism. Were it entirely problematic, it would be rejected out of hand. Whether it *continues* to have a place in biblical criticism depends on how one answers the objections and criticisms leveled above.

5.6 RESOURCES FOR FURTHER STUDY

Gunkel, Hermann. *Genesis*. Translated from the 1910 3rd ed. by Mark E. Biddle. Macon, GA: Mercer University Press, 1997.

> This text not only began the study of form criticism, but it also influenced what later became tradition-historical criticism. It contains many useful remarks regarding Gunkel's reconstruction of the history of the Pentateuchal traditions in Genesis.

Knight, Douglas A. *Rediscovering the Traditions of Israel*. 3rd ed. Society of Biblical Literature Studies in Biblical Literature 16. Atlanta: Society of Biblical Literature, 2006.

> Knight's book is a thorough and comprehensive discussion of the development of tradition-historical criticism in biblical studies. Knight provides a complete treatment of how this discipline developed; his analysis of the strengths and weaknesses of each of the scholars discussed briefly above is quite excellent.

Koch, Klaus. *The Growth of the Biblical Tradition: The Form Critical Method*. Translated from the 2nd German ed. by S. M. Cupitt. New York: Charles Scribner's Sons, 1969.

> Although the title suggests an interest primarily in form criticism, Koch discusses all areas of analysis, including tradition-historical criticism, which he considers to be an extension of the form-critical method.

Niditch, Susan. *Oral World and Written Word: Ancient Israelite Literature*. Philadelphia: Westminster John Knox, 1996.

Niditch's work is an excellent modern introduction to the issues and concerns of oral tradition in Israelite literature. She is quite readable to a nonscholarly audience.

Noth, Martin. *A History of Pentateuchal Traditions*. Translated by Bernhard W. Anderson. Englewood Cliffs, NJ: Prentice-Hall, 1972; *The Deuteronomistic History*. Sheffield: Sheffield Academic, 1981.

These two books present Noth's approach to tradition-historical criticism of the Pentateuch and the Deuteronomistic History, respectively.

von Rad, Gerhard. *The Problem of the Hexateuch and Other Essays*. Translated by E. W. Trueman Dicken. Edinburgh and London: Oliver & Boyd, 1966; *Genesis: A Commentary*. Rev. ed. Translated by John H. Marks. Philadelphia: Westminster, 1972.

The first essay in *The Problem of the Hexateuch* expounds von Rad's theory of the historical credo and the covenant-renewal ceremony associated with it. It also discusses his reconstruction of the various traditions in the Hexateuch and how they were added to the credo by the various editors of the ot. His Genesis commentary reveals his methodology in practice, especially as it relates to a deeper understanding of his commitment to the theology of Genesis, as well as its form and tradition-historical criticism.

Rast, Walter E. *Tradition History and the Old Testament*. Guides to Biblical Scholarship. Philadelphia: Fortress, 1972.

Though this text is a bit dated, it is still an excellent introduction to tradition-historical criticism. His discussion of the Scandinavian school is quite useful for explaining its differences from the German scholars, and he includes a nice overview of tradition-historical criticism of the Prophets.

6

REDACTION CRITICISM

Jeffery Leonard

After spending two and a half chapters charting the rise and fall of Jeroboam in the northern kingdom of Israel, the book of Kings devotes a scant eleven verses to Solomon's heir in the southern kingdom of Judah, Rehoboam. Only two features of Rehoboam's reign capture the author's attention: illicit worship practices deemed to have provoked YHWH to anger (1 Kgs 14:22–24) and a humiliating military defeat suffered by the Judean monarch:

> In the fifth year of King Rehoboam, King Shishak of Egypt came up against Jerusalem; he took away the treasures of the house of the Lord and the treasures of the king's house; he took everything. He also took away all the shields of gold that Solomon had made; so King Rehoboam made shields of bronze instead, and committed them to the hands of the officers of the guard, who kept the door of the king's house. (1 Kgs 14:25–27)[1]

While the author, often labeled the Deuteronomist or Deuteronomistic Historian, recounts this sin and defeat in succession, he never specifically links one with the other, nor does he suggest Rehoboam himself was involved, either as leader or as participant, in the nation's illicit worship. These sins are laid at the feet of "Judah" and "they," never "Rehoboam" or

---

1. Unless otherwise noted, all translations are from the New Revised Standard Version (NRSV).

"he." What is left as a matter of speculation in Kings, however, is spelled out clearly in Chronicles:

> When the rule of Rehoboam was established and he grew strong, *he abandoned the law of the Lord*, he and all Israel with him. In the fifth year of King Rehoboam, *because they had been unfaithful to the Lord*, King Shishak of Egypt came up against Jerusalem. (2 Chr 12:1–2, emphasis added)

That Chronicles used the narrative in Kings as a historical source is clear from its verbatim repetition of the Deuteronomist's account (note especially 1 Kgs 14:25–28; 2 Chr 12:9–11). But the Chronicler has not simply duplicated the Deuteronomistic material; he has augmented it, specifying that Rehoboam had abandoned the law of YHWH and that Shishak's invasion was a direct result of the people's infidelity.

A similar situation is seen in Chronicles' description of the leprosy that afflicted King Uzziah. The book of Kings notes only:

> *The Lord struck the king*, so that he was leprous to the day of his death and lived in a separate house. Jotham the king's son was in charge of the palace, governing the people of the land. (2 Kgs 15:5. emphasis added)

The Chronicler offers a more expansive account, tracing the king's growing pride until it culminates in his presumptuous entry into the temple to "make offering on the altar of incense" (2 Chr 26:16). When the priests rebuke Uzziah for his error, the Chronicler records:

> *Now he had a censer in his hand to make offering, and when he became angry with the priests a leprous disease broke out on his forehead, in the presence of the priests in the house of the Lord, by the altar of incense. When the chief priest Azariah, and all the priests, looked at him, he was leprous in his forehead. They hurried him out, and he himself hurried to get out, because the Lord had struck him.* King Uzziah was leprous to the day of his death, and being leprous lived in a separate house, for he was excluded from the house of the Lord. His son Jotham was in charge of the palace of the king, governing the people of the land. (2 Chr 26:19b–21, emphasis added)

Again, the accounts overlap sufficiently to establish that the Chronicler depends directly on the Deuteronomist, but the Chronicler does more than parrot the Deuteronomist's account; he expands and clarifies it, tracing Uzziah's leprosy to a specific moment of royal transgression.

The Chronicler's expansions are not always negative. His treatment of the reign of Manasseh, for example, stands as one of the greatest stories of repentance in all of the Bible. Like Kings, Chronicles describes in detail the "evil in the sight of YHWH" that Manasseh did and the "abominable practices of the nations" that he followed (2 Chr 33:1–9; 2 Kgs 21:1–9). At the conclusion of this indictment, though, the Chronicler's narrative parts ways with the Deuteronomist's. Whereas Kings goes on only to specify that Manasseh's sins would be to blame for the exile, Chronicles charts a series of events that lead to the monarch's dramatic turnaround:

> Therefore the LORD brought against them the commanders of the army of the king of Assyria, who took Manasseh captive in manacles, bound him with fetters, and brought him to Babylon. While he was in distress he entreated the favor of the LORD his God and humbled himself greatly before the God of his ancestors. He prayed to him, and God received his entreaty, heard his plea, and restored him again to Jerusalem and to his kingdom. Then Manasseh knew that the LORD indeed was God. ... He took away the foreign gods and the idol from the house of the LORD, and all the altars that he had built on the mountain of the house of the LORD and in Jerusalem, and he threw them out of the city. He also restored the altar of the LORD and offered on it sacrifices of well-being and of thanksgiving; and he commanded Judah to serve the LORD the God of Israel. (2 Chr 33:11–16)

Scholars remain divided over the historical value of Chronicles' expansions of the narrative shared with Kings. Some of the Chronicler's additions may well represent genuine historical traditions that the Deuteronomist opted not to include. In many cases, though, historical concerns take a backseat to ideology as the Chronicler attempts to press the nation's history into a particular theological mold. Each of the examples cited above—and other cases that could be cited as well—reflect a concern over the immediate exercise of divine justice. From the Chronicler's perspective, Rehoboam does not just lose a battle; he loses a battle because he abandoned the law.

Uzziah does not just contract leprosy; he does so at a particular moment because he acted arrogantly and angrily toward the priests. In the case of Manasseh, it must have seemed impossible to the Chronicler that a king as irredeemably wicked as the Deuteronomist suggests could enjoy a stable reign of fifty-five years. The difference between the long reign of Manasseh and the short reign of his successor, Amon, must surely be that the father repented, while the son did not (2 Chr 33:23).

While the value of Chronicles' additions to Kings may be difficult to judge from a historical perspective, there is little question concerning their value for understanding the Chronicler's own values and beliefs. It is precisely at the point that the Chronicler edits and supplements his earlier sources that he casts light on his own historical situation and theological concerns. What is true in Chronicles is true elsewhere in the Bible as well. In texts ranging from the Pentateuch to the Deuteronomistic History to the Prophets and the Synoptic Gospels, editors or "redactors" shaped the sources they inherited as they passed them along to future generations. The branch of biblical scholarship that examines this editorial shaping is known as redaction criticism.

6.1 DEFINITION AND GOAL OF THE METHOD

Redaction criticism is the method of biblical interpretation that focuses directly on the editorial or redactional process whereby the texts of the Bible came to achieve their present form. The primary goal of redaction criticism is to understand better the beliefs, values, practices, and intentions of the redactor or redactors responsible for molding a text into a coherent whole. As the examples from Chronicles above demonstrate, it is in the redactional shaping of the traditions inherited from Kings that the Chronicler's own beliefs move most clearly to the fore. For the author of the Deuteronomistic History (or at least for the author of the preexilic version, labeled Dtr[1]), Josiah was a second Moses, a king whose reforms held out the promise of delivering the nation from exile and whose death at the hands of Pharaoh Neco was a devastating and inexplicable tragedy. Chronicles' handling of the Josianic material reveals that the Chronicler did not regard Josiah in the same light. While Josiah's reforms may have been important, according to the Chronicler, those of Hezekiah were just as important. While Josiah's death may have been tragic, the Chronicler contends it was the result of the king's failure to listen to the divine command uttered through Neco (2 Chr 35:22). The interpretive method that focuses squarely on the significance of these editorial changes is redaction criticism.

A secondary goal of redaction criticism is to shed light on the character of the underlying source materials used by a given redactor. Examples of this sort of approach abound. For instance, based on an analysis of Chronicles, Baruch Halpern posits the existence of an independent Deuteronomistic work on which both Kings and Chronicles relied.[2] Expanding on a thesis first advanced by Frank Moore Cross, Steven McKenzie argues that the first version of Chronicles (Cross' Chr[1], thought to have extended from 1 Chr 10 to Ezra 3:13) knew the Deuteronomistic History only in its preexilic version (Dtr[1]), not in its final form.[3] Menachem Haran analyzes redactional language in Kings to suggest the literary character of "the Book of the Chronicles of the Kings of Judah" and "the Book of the Chronicles of the Kings of Israel," two sources cited by the Deuteronomist.[4]

Studies in a similar vein venture beyond the Former Prophets. An analysis of Psa 78's use of earlier source material suggests that the author knew the historical traditions of JE (the Yahwistic and Elohistic parts of the Pentateuch) at a time prior to their connection with D or P (the Deuteronomistic and Priestly parts of the Pentateuch), and that he relied on a version of the ark narrative in which 2 Sam 6 had not yet been separated from 1 Sam 4–6.[5] In the NT, James Dunn argues that the use of Mark in Matthew and Luke suggests the Markan tradition had not reached a fixed literary form when Matthew and Luke drew on it.[6] As these uses of redaction criticism suggest, this method overlaps considerably with source criticism.

---

2. Baruch Halpern, "Sacred History and Ideology: Chronicles' Thematic Structure: Indications of an Earlier Source," in *The Creation of Sacred Literature: Composition and Redaction of the Biblical Text*, ed. Richard Elliott Friedman (Berkeley: University of California Press, 1981), 35–54.

3. Steven L. McKenzie, *The Chronicler's Use of the Deuteronomistic History* (Atlanta: Scholars Press, 1985).

4. Menachem Haran, "The Books of the Chronicles 'of the Kings of Judah' and 'of the Kings of Israel': What Sort of Books Were They?," VT 49, no. 2 (1999): 156–64.

5. Jeffery M. Leonard, "Historical Traditions in Psalm 78," PhD diss., Brandeis University, 2006.

6. James D. G. Dunn, *A New Perspective on Jesus: What the Quest for the Historical Jesus Missed* (Grand Rapids: Baker, 2005), 35–56.

6.1.1 RELATIONSHIP TO SOURCE AND FORM CRITICISM

The nature of redaction criticism can be further defined by comparing it to other, similar interpretive methods. Three such methods—source criticism, form criticism, and innerbiblical interpretation—are particularly important for understanding and distinguishing redaction criticism.

6.1.1.a Source Criticism

Source criticism developed as an attempt to account for the various duplications, differences, and contradictions found within biblical texts.[7] In the Pentateuch, for example, increasingly rigorous examination of its text in the wake of the Renaissance and Reformation yielded a growing catalog of internal inconsistencies. Legal corpora, especially, were observed to treat the same subject in contradictory ways. For example, in one text female Hebrew slaves were to be released at the end of six years of service, just as male Hebrew slaves were (Deut 15:12); in another, they were not to be released (Exod 21:7). One text treats all slaughter, including slaughter to secure meat, as a sacrifice that must be performed at the tabernacle (Lev 17:1–5); another text treats slaughter for meat as common and allows it to be performed anywhere (Deut 12:15).

Readers also began to notice that narrative texts sometimes preserve two (or even three) versions of a story. Thus, Beersheba is so named twice (Gen 21:31; 26:33), Jacob's name is changed to Israel twice (Gen 32:28; 35:10), Moses strikes the rock to produce water at Meribah twice (Exod 17:5–7; Num 20:7–13), and a patriarch passes his wife off as his sister before a foreign king three times (Gen 12:10–20; 20:1–18; 26:6–14). In stories such as Noah's flood (Gen 6–8); Joseph's sale as a slave (Gen 37); and the punishment of Korah, Dathan, and Abiram (Num 16), internal tensions suggest two versions of a story have actually been woven together into one. The names used in the Pentateuch for God (Elohim, YHWH), specific humans (Abram/Abraham, Jacob/Israel, Jethro/Reuel), and even places (Sinai/Horeb) differ from one group of texts to another. Even the values and concerns of the text vary dramatically. From Exodus 25 to Numbers 10, for example, issues of ritual sanctity loom large, the tabernacle (or "tent of meeting") is mentioned more than two hundred times, and Aaron—mentioned more than

---

7. See chap. 3 of this volume on source criticism.

one hundred and fifty times—is a constant focus of attention. Deuteronomy, on the other hand, places far more emphasis on centralization than sanctity (Deut 12:5–14; 16:6) and mentions the tabernacle only once (31:14–15) and Aaron just three times (9:20; 10:6; 32:50).

The solution source criticism offers to this state of affairs is to suggest that the Pentateuch, as it now stands, is a compilation of materials derived from various earlier sources. The nature of these sources and the manner of their combination has been the subject of considerable scholarly debate. As the identity of the Pentateuchal sources was refined over the course of the eighteenth and nineteenth centuries, scholars gradually shifted away from the notion that the text had been formed by stringing together fragments of tradition and moved instead toward the idea that longer documentary sources underlay the text. Presented in its most influential form by Julius Wellhausen, this Documentary Hypothesis eventually suggested that four long literary sources—distinguished by the labels J, E, D, and P (designating the Yahwist, Elohist, Deuteronomist, and Priestly sources, respectively)—had been woven together to form the final Pentateuch.

The overlap between redaction criticism and source criticism is substantial. In that redaction criticism considers the manner in which a redactor shapes earlier sources, it builds on a foundation laid by source-critical work. When the character of a redactor's source material is not as straightforwardly evident as it is in Chronicles' use of Kings or in Matthew and Luke's use of Mark, the line between source and redaction can be exceedingly difficult to determine. Indeed, at the heart of many of the most contentious debates in the study of the composition of the Pentateuch lies the issue of distinguishing source from redaction.

6.1.1.b Form and Tradition Criticism

Form criticism emerged, at least in part, as a corrective to what was thought to be an excessively literary focus in source criticism.[8] Source critics, both before and after Wellhausen, focus on the development and compilation of *written* traditions. With the publication of his Genesis commentary in 1901, Hermann Gunkel made the case that too little emphasis had been placed on

---

8. For further discussion, see chap. 4 on form criticism in the present volume.

the development of traditions in their pre-literary or oral stage.[9] Gunkel emphasized the oral genres or forms (German, *Gattungen*) of traditions and the original *Sitz im Leben* or "life setting" from which they would have emerged. In a work like Psalms, Gunkel demonstrated that the individual hymns, laments, and other forms were not the literary products of individuals but liturgical pieces intended for oral performance by the community.[10] Elsewhere, form criticism was used with great effect for shedding light on the background of Israelite law, the messages of the prophets, and even the Gospels.

The challenge form criticism presents for source criticism and, by implication, redaction criticism, lies in its contention that much of the development of the biblical traditions took place *prior to* their being written. Indeed, various Scandinavian scholars, such as Johannes Pedersen and Ivan Engnell, placed such heavy emphasis on the oral development of traditions that they rejected outright the literary model associated with Wellhausen.[11] While most have stopped short of the conclusions reached by the so-called Scandinavian school, it remains the case that "tradition history" (*Überlieferungsgeschichte*), another method that developed out of form criticism, attributes to the oral phase of a tradition's development much of the shaping and supplementation that redaction criticism would regard as a literary enterprise.[12]

9. Hermann Gunkel, *Genesis übersetzt und erklärt* (3rd ed.; Göttingen: Vandenhoeck & Ruprecht, 1910). The first and second German editions appeared in 1901 and 1902, respectively. The third edition has been translated into English: *Genesis* (Macon, GA: Mercer University Press, 1997). Gunkel's views on Genesis became more widely known during this time, primarily due to the publication of an English translation of the introduction from the 1901 edition of the commentary that appeared as *The Legends of Genesis*, trans. W. H. Carruth (Chicago: The Open Court Publishing Co., 1901).

10. Hermann Gunkel and Joachim Begrich, *Introduction to the Psalms: The Genres of Religious Lyric of Israel*, trans. James D. Nogalski (Macon, GA: Mercer University Press, 1998).

11. Ivan Engnell, *Gamla Testamentet: En traditionshistorisk inledning*, vol. 1 (Stockholm: Svenska Kyrkans Diakonistyrelses Bokförlag, 1945).

12. On the development of tradition history and its relationship to form criticism, see chap. 5 of the present volume on tradition-historical criticism.

6.1.1.c Innerbiblical Interpretation

Redaction criticism and innerbiblical interpretation overlap in important respects.[13] The two disciplines are alike in their sensitivity to the presence of interpretive and explanatory comments from later preservers of tradition. Indeed, many of the examples of innerbiblical exegesis grouped by Michael Fishbane under the heading of "scribal comments and corrections" could just as readily be treated as redactional activity.[14] Where redaction criticism and innerbiblical interpretation tend to part company is in the role they cast for the interpreter. In redaction criticism, the interpreter serves as editor. In this role, the redactor may arrange and rearrange, or comment and expand on, the traditions he has inherited. Ultimately, though, the form of the composition remains the responsibility of earlier tradents[15] who passed the materials down to the redactor. By contrast, in innerbiblical interpretation the interpreter serves as author. Like the redactor, the innerbiblical exegete draws on earlier materials. He does so, however, through echo, allusion, and quotation, activating the older text in *his own* composition rather than injecting his interpretive work into another author's composition. However, the differences between redaction criticism and innerbiblical interpretation are fluid and differ both from one text to another and from one interpreter to another.

6.1.2 UNDERLYING ASSUMPTIONS

Redaction criticism proceeds from a number of guiding assumptions. First, the final form of nearly all biblical texts stands as the end result of a process of editing together earlier literary traditions. Second, behind this process of editing together earlier literary traditions lies a redactor (or redactors) whose editorial hand can be identified. Third, the manner in which a redactor shapes the inherited tradition sheds light on the redactor's own beliefs, values, theology, and historical circumstances.

---

13. On the method of innerbiblical interpretation, see Jeffery Leonard, "Inner-Biblical Interpretation and Intertextuality," in *Literary Approaches to the Bible*, ed. Douglas Mangum and Douglas Estes (Bellingham, WA: Lexham Press, 2016).

14. Michael A. Fishbane, *Biblical Interpretation in Ancient Israel* (Oxford: Clarendon, 1985), 23–88.

15. A "tradent" is someone involved in preserving and passing on traditional teachings or beliefs.—Eds.

6.1.2.a Biblical Books Developed through the Editing of Literary Traditions

With the advent of form criticism and tradition history, the burden of proof has shifted onto source and redaction critics to demonstrate that significant shaping of biblical traditions took place at a literary, and not just an oral, stage. Redaction criticism's case for such literary development begins with an obvious but also quite important point: the Bible as it stands is a collection of literary works. Whatever its preliterary shape may have been, in its final form the Bible is a library of texts.

Moving backward from this fixed point, there is abundant evidence that the Bible's preliterary traditions did not coalesce into written books in one fell swoop. The famous "Scroll of 605 BC" described in Jer 36 provides a vivid example of growth and development in compositions already in written form. This scroll, dictated by Jeremiah, recorded and read aloud by Baruch, and then burned piece by piece by Jehoiakim, is dictated again by the prophet and supplemented in the process: "Then Jeremiah took another scroll and gave it to the secretary Baruch son of Neriah, who wrote on it at Jeremiah's dictation all the words of the scroll that King Jehoiakim of Judah had burned in the fire; *and many similar words were added to them*" (Jer 36:32, emphasis added). That this now already edited literary piece was subject to even further editorial activity is evident from how it has been fully incorporated into the larger book of Jeremiah and can no longer be definitively isolated.

Other examples of this sort of development on a literary level could be cited as well. There is widespread scholarly agreement that the scroll presented to Josiah in 2 Kgs 22, whatever the actual circumstances of its composition and discovery, was a form of the law code found in Deut 12–26. As such, it represents a text—already in written form—that would go on to be incorporated into a larger literary work. Similarly, the repeated uses of the term *sēper* (סֵפֶר), meaning "scroll" or "book," in Deuteronomy to refer to the book of Deuteronomy specifically and not the Pentateuch as a whole attest to the book's independent literary existence, which preceded its incorporation into the larger written Pentateuch (see Deut 28:58, 61; 29:20, 21, 27 [Heb., 19, 20, 26]; 30:10; 31:24, 26).

Finally, numerous biblical works are straightforward in their admission that they were built on earlier, written sources. The most famous of these are, of course, the references in Kings to "the Book of the Acts of Solomon" (1 Kgs 11:41), "the Book of the Annals of the Kings of Israel" (e.g., 1 Kgs 14:19), and "the Book of the Annals of the Kings of Judah" (e.g., 1 Kgs 14:29), and in Chronicles to "the Book of the Kings of Judah and Israel" (2 Chr 16:11) and even "the Commentary on the Book of Kings" (2 Chr 24:27). Elsewhere, references are also made to "the Book of the Wars of YHWH" (Num 21:14–15) and "the Book of Jashar" (Josh 10:13; 2 Sam 1:18). Even the many descriptions of characters' preserving records on scrolls—whatever the historical value of any particular narrative of this sort—attest to a widespread and ancient recognition that larger written works were built on smaller ones (e.g., Exod 17:14; 24:7; 1 Sam 10:25; Neh 7:5, etc.).

6.1.2.b The Editorial Work of Biblical Redactors Can Be Identified

The examples cited above point to a pattern of dependence by later biblical texts on earlier literary traditions. Chronicles' use of Kings suggests that one of the most important clues for identifying redactional activity is a sudden and unexpected change in a narrative's direction, tone, or genre. These shifts are to be expected as the by-product of a redactor having juxtaposed materials from quite different sources. The Chronicler's remarkable word of praise for Manasseh's repentance in the midst of an otherwise scathing indictment of the Judean king (2 Chr 33), the incongruous condemnation of Josiah after two chapters of sustained praise (2 Chr 34–35), the abrupt interruption of Hezekiah's story for a lengthy description of the reorganization of the priests and Levites (2 Chr 31)—all of these raise suspicions that a redactor's hand is at work, supplementing old material with new and sometimes adding transitional phrases in between.

Another key assumption of redaction criticism is that the conclusions reached by comparing texts such as Chronicles and Kings may also apply to other texts. The Deuteronomistic History (DtrH; i.e., Joshua, Judges, Samuel, and Kings), the very work on which the Chronicler relied, also bears the marks of redactional activity. Much of DtrH is quite confident about the future of Judah and its capital, Jerusalem, conceding that, while part of the kingdom may be torn away because of a monarch's sins, the kingdom will never fall completely "for the sake of my servant David" (see 1 Kgs 11:12–13, 32, 34–36; 15:4; 2 Kgs 8:19; 19:34; 20:6). As the oracle to Jeroboam in 1 Kgs 11:34–36 insists:

Nevertheless I will not take the whole kingdom away from him [Solomon] but will make him ruler all the days of his life, for the sake of my servant David whom I chose and who did keep my commandments and my statutes; but I will take the kingdom away from his son and give it to you—that is, the ten tribes. Yet to his son I will give one tribe, so that my servant David may always have a lamp before me in Jerusalem, the city where I have chosen to put my name.

There is, of course, ample warning about disobedience, but the punishment for this disobedience revolves around the provocation of divine anger and the withdrawal of divine blessing on the land (see, e.g., Deut 28:15–48). Intruding on these passages, though, are quite specific threats, not just of divine cursing but of a national destruction and exile that cannot be avoided and that negates the repeated dynastic promises to David and his heirs. The most detailed (and most terrifying) of these threats is found in Deut 28:49–68, which warns of attack by a "grim-faced nation" that will lay siege to the nation's towns until the people are reduced to cannibalism before being scattered to the nations with no hope of return. Numerous other, similar passages are scattered throughout DtrH (e.g., Deut 4:27–31; 29:28 [Heb., 29:27]; Josh 23:11–13, 15–16; 2 Kgs 17:19; 20:17–19), as are passages such as 1 Kgs 2:4 that transform the unconditional promises to David into promises contingent on the nation's continued obedience (cf. also 1 Kgs 6:11–13; 8:25b, 46–53): "Then the Lord will establish his word that he spoke concerning me: 'If your heirs take heed to their way, to walk before me in faithfulness with all their heart and with all their soul, there shall not fail you a successor on the throne of Israel.'"

One explanation for these contradictory promises concerning the future of the Davidic dynasty is that of Frank Cross, who argues that DtrH was produced in two editions.[16] The first edition, which Cross maintains was written before the exile to support Josiah's reforms, culminated in 2 Kgs 23:25a: "Before him [Josiah] there was no king like him, who turned

---

16. Frank Moore Cross, *Canaanite Myth and Hebrew Epic: Essays in the History of the Religion of Israel* (Cambridge, MA: Harvard University Press, 1973), 274–89.

to the LORD with all his heart, with all his soul, and with all his might, according to all the law of Moses."

But when Josiah died tragically by Neco's arrow and subsequent kings allowed his reforms to flounder, the Davidic dynasty was crushed, and the nation went into exile. It was in exile, Cross argues, that a redactor updated the first edition of the Deuteronomistic History (Dtr¹), expanding earlier warnings to encompass the dynasty's fall and the nation's destruction and thus producing a second version of the history (Dtr²).

6.1.2.c Editorial Work Reflects the Redactor's
Own Beliefs and Circumstances

In the case of minor insertions intended only to introduce collections of materials or link together earlier sources, little information can be gleaned about the redactor's own perspective. In examples such as those previously cited for Chronicles and the Deuteronomistic History, however, the redactor's voice is more easily heard. In the redactor's treatment of the underlying Kings narrative, Chronicles' concern for Levitical matters, the southern kingdom, and the immediate exercise of divine judgment shine through most clearly. Similarly, in the redactor's editing and updating of Dtr¹ this exilic Deuteronomist's concern to explain the fall of the Davidic monarchy and Judah is most evident.

Such insights are, of course, not limited to the Hebrew Bible. The redactional activity present in the Synoptic Gospels especially reveals similar patterns. Most scholars would accept the notion that Matthew (and Luke) relied on Mark as a literary source for the life and teachings of Jesus. But Matthew's handling of the Markan material he inherits reveals important facets of his own theological concerns. This is evident, for example, in the case Matthew makes for the continued relevance of the law. As Mark recounts the tale of the Pharisees' chastising Jesus for allowing his disciples to eat with unwashed hands, Mark notes that Jesus said: "Do you also fail to understand? Do you not see that whatever goes into a person from the outside cannot defile, since it enters, not the heart but the stomach, and goes out into the sewer?" (Mark 7:18b–19a). Mark draws a very specific conclusion from this statement, namely, "Thus he declared all foods clean" (v. 19b).

While Matthew recounts the same encounter in his Gospel, his version of Jesus' statement is somewhat different. In Matthew, Jesus instructs: "Are you also still without understanding? Do you not see that whatever goes into the mouth enters the stomach, and goes out into the sewer? But what comes out of the mouth proceeds from the heart, and this is what defiles" (Matt 15:16–18). Matthew concedes only that what goes out of the mouth is what defiles, not that what goes into the mouth cannot defile. Further, Matthew omits entirely Mark's comment, "Thus, he declared all foods clean." For Matthew, the food laws have not been rendered obsolete, as they have been in Mark.

In a second example, Mark 13:18 records a warning from Jesus concerning desperate times that lie ahead. In this warning, Jesus is said to have told the audience, "Pray that it may not be in winter." Matthew copies this same section, but his version reads, "Pray that your flight may not be in winter or on a Sabbath" (Matt 24:20). Matthew's addition (or even restoration) of the reference to the Sabbath highlights his belief that the Sabbath remains a living observance for his community.

In both of the aforementioned cases, it is Matthew's redaction of the underlying Markan source material that throws into sharp relief his continued commitment to even the ritual aspects of the Torah. The insights gleaned from Matthew's redactional activity further clarify themes that run throughout the evangelist's Gospel (e.g., Matt 5:17–20, 23–24; 23:23).

6.1.3 KEY CONCEPTS

Redaction criticism uses many of the concepts and categories introduced by source and form criticism. For example, the idea that biblical books were edited together from various written sources is a fundamental concept for source criticism.[17] The terms "redactor" and "redaction" are commonly used in source criticism. Redaction could apply to the editing process as a whole or to a particular editorial layer added to the literary tradition by a redactor. The redactor, for both source and redaction criticism, is the person responsible for editing and supplementing earlier literary traditions. In many cases, it is likely that the redactor was not a single individual but

---

17. See §3.1.2 Underlying Assumptions and §3.1.3 Key Concepts for more background on source criticism.

a succession or "school" of related tradents who shaped a source. Often "redactor" and "editor" are used interchangeably, though some distinguish the two by using "editor" to refer to persons who introduce minor corrections and additions to texts, reserving "redactor" for those responsible for larger-scale adaptation and supplementation of earlier materials. Source and redaction critics may use the letter "R" as an abbreviation for "Redactor." Both also make use of the common source critical abbreviations J, E, D, and P for the Pentateuchal sources.[18] They add J, E, and P to R to label the different redactors of the Pentateuch—e.g., R^{JE} for the "Redactor of JE" who first linked the Yahwistic and Elohistic sources of the Torah together, and R^{JEP} for the "Redactor of JE and P" who added P to J and E. Some use "R" alone to refer to the final redactor of the Pentateuch as a whole. Redaction criticism may also incorporate terminology from form criticism, such as *Sitz im Leben* ("life setting") or *Gattung* ("genre").[19] While redaction criticism builds on aspects of source and form criticism, redaction critics are less interested in the origins of the discrete parts of the text and more interested in what the final form of the text means and what significance is held by the selection and arrangement of material.

6.2 DEVELOPMENT OF REDACTION CRITICISM

While source criticism began in earnest in the eighteenth century and was a thriving enterprise by the nineteenth, biblical scholars were quite slow to turn their attention from differentiating the writings of the Yahwist, Elohist, Deuteronomist, and Priestly authors to examining the contribution of the redactor(s) who edited their works together. In a discussion of inner-biblical exegesis, James Kugel attributes this delay to the largely Protestant origins of critical biblical scholarship.[20] Much of early Protestant biblical interpretation was keenly interested in stripping away what it considered to be centuries of "Church-sponsored misinterpretation or willful

---

18. J = the Yahwist; E = the Elohist; D = the Deuteronomic source; P = the Priestly source (see §3.1.3 Key Concepts).—Eds.

19. See §4.1.4 Key Concepts for discussion of the terms *Sitz im Leben* and *Gattung*.

20. James R. Kugel, "The Bible's Earliest Interpreters," review of *Biblical Interpretation in Ancient Israel*, by Michael Fishbane, *Prooftexts: A Journal of Jewish Literary History* 7 (1987): 269–83.

obfuscation."[21] As a result, Kugel argues, it set up "a general opposition between the 'biblical' (good) and anything that was 'postbiblical' (bad, because a corruption of the biblical)."[22] As this tendency was extended into the Bible itself, early materials were generally treated as better than later materials, the work of the earlier prophets as of a more noble spirit than the work of later priests, the precise words of the prophets as more authentic than the later reports of their messages, and so forth.[23] The contribution of redactors to a work could easily be regarded in the same light as the layers of church tradition that filter the reader's understanding of the biblical text.[24] Thus, Kugel observes:

> And so the Protestant task (and consequently that of modern biblical scholarship) has always been to cast such interlopers out, to recover the authentic (or "most authentic") text, oracle, event, and throw the rest away. Little wonder, then, that the biblical text that seeks to interpret or elaborate upon an earlier biblical text has been viewed ipso facto as of secondary importance, and that the processes of interpretation and assimilation that underlie such acts were for some time generally judged unworthy of scrutiny.[25]

Kugel notes that this pattern began to change, ironically, as the Protestant search for the authentic words of the prophets required an ever more attentive consideration of redactors' work, even "if only the better to separate chaff from wheat."[26]

The beginnings of redaction criticism are found in the mid-twentieth century in the studies of Gerhard von Rad and Martin Noth.[27] Influenced by form criticism's attempt to trace biblical traditions back to their earliest

---

21. Kugel, "Bible's Earliest Interpreters," 270.
22. Kugel, "Bible's Earliest Interpreters," 270.
23. Kugel, "Bible's Earliest Interpreters," 270.
24. Kugel, "Bible's Earliest Interpreters," 270.
25. Kugel, "Bible's Earliest Interpreters," 270.
26. Kugel, "Bible's Earliest Interpreters," 270.
27. In the twentieth century, the study of the Pentateuch and the Former Prophets was a seedbed for methodological innovation in biblical research. Noth and von Rad were at the forefront of these innovations, introducing ideas that extended, modified, and integrated aspects of source criticism, form criticism, tradition-historical criticism, and redaction criticism. In a sense, redaction criticism is the culmination of a research trajectory that began seeking the origins of biblical texts in written sources, moved to considering oral tradition

forms, von Rad and Noth sought to apply redaction criticism to the composition of the Pentateuch (or, in von Rad's case, the Hexateuch) as a whole. This involved bringing together what today would be described as tradition-historical criticism, in the case of the traditions' preliterary phase, and source criticism, in the traditions' further development as literary works.

Von Rad's approach, outlined in his lengthy essay "The Form-Critical Problem of the Hexateuch," began with the identification of several Hexateuchal texts that he regarded as ancient Israelite creedal statements (Deut 26:5–9; 6:20–24; and Josh 24:2–13).[28] These texts, he argued, preserve a "Settlement Tradition" outlining the basic events of the nation's redemptive history: "the humble beginnings of Israel in the patriarchal age, the oppression in Egypt, the deliverance by Yahweh and his bringing them into the promised land."[29] In von Rad's estimation, the pivotal first step in the development of the Hexateuch occurred when the Yahwist source, using the Settlement Tradition as an outline, edited together a variety of early traditions ranging from local cultic legends to the Sinai pericope and primeval history to form his own foundational work. The Yahwist could thus be regarded as a "great collector and editor," in essence the Hexateuch's first redactor.[30] For von Rad, it was this first redactional move that gave the Hexateuch its definitive form. And while he credited the Elohist and Priestly writer with "admittedly great theological originality," he insisted, "Their writings are no more than variations upon the massive theme of the Yahwist's conception."[31] Von Rad attributed the final combination of the Hexateuchal traditions to redactors; however, he regarded these redactors as bound, to some degree, by the documents they inherited.[32]

Extending and, in some cases, challenging von Rad's work, Martin Noth envisioned "the task of a 'history of traditions'" as one in which the traditions' development was traced from first step to last:

---

and social context, and then returned to examining the final written texts in light of what had been learned about literary composition and oral tradition.—Eds.

28. Gerhard von Rad, *The Problem of the Hexateuch and Other Essays*, trans. E. W. Trueman Dicken (Edinburgh: Oliver & Boyd, 1966), 1–78.

29. Von Rad, *Problem of the Hexateuch*, 5.

30. Von Rad, *Problem of the Hexateuch*, 51.

31. Von Rad, *Problem of the Hexateuch*, 74.

32. Von Rad, *Problem of the Hexateuch*, 77.

In the course of this development, traditions which doubtless were circulated and transmitted orally at first were probably written down in time, for reasons that are no longer known to us and to an extent that can no longer be determined with certainty. In any event, later on they were brought together in large literary works and these in turn, through the purely literary labors of so-called redactors, were finally compiled into the large corpus of the transmitted Pentateuch.[33]

Noth viewed the pre-Yahwistic, and thus preliterary, stage of the Pentateuchal traditions as one in which a number of key themes were joined to form a common source document or *Grundlage* (G), on which the Yahwist and Elohist relied independently of one another.[34] Noth regarded the combination of J and E as the work of a redactor, R[JE], who used J as the primary source into which E was incorporated.[35] In perhaps his most important contribution, Noth argued that J, E, and P do not extend into Deuteronomy or, as in the case of von Rad, through the Hexateuch. Instead, Noth insisted that Deuteronomy originally existed independently of the other Pentateuchal sources as the first part of the Deuteronomistic History (Deuteronomy, Joshua, Judges, Samuel, Kings). With Deuteronomy thus separated, Noth argued that a redactor had integrated JE into the literary framework of P to form a Tetrateuch (Genesis–Numbers), ending with the Priestly account of the death of Moses (R[JEP]). Only once this work was connected to the Deuteronomist's was the Priestly account of Moses' death moved to its current place in Deut 34, thereby creating the Pentateuch as we know it.[36]

Recent decades have seen a dramatic reconceptualization of the process by which the Pentateuchal sources were redacted together. In the

---

33. Martin Noth, *A History of Pentateuchal Traditions*, trans. Bernhard W. Anderson (Englewood Cliffs, NJ: Prentice-Hall, 1972), 1.

34. Noth, *History of Pentateuchal Traditions*, 39.

35. Noth, *History of Pentateuchal Traditions*, 25–27.

36. Noth, *History of Pentateuchal Traditions*, 32n126, 160, 170–72. Noth's deliberate use of the term "Pentateuch" to refer only to Genesis–Numbers plus parts of Deut 34 is prone to generate confusion (see *History of Pentateuchal Traditions*, 6).

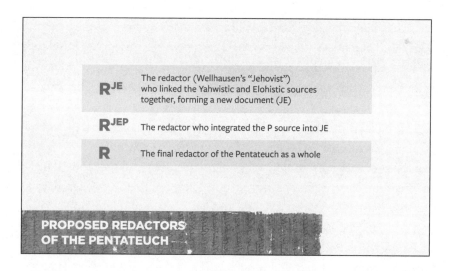

R^JE The redactor (Wellhausen's "Jehovist") who linked the Yahwistic and Elohistic sources together, forming a new document (JE)

R^JEP The redactor who integrated the P source into JE

R The final redactor of the Pentateuch as a whole

PROPOSED REDACTORS OF THE PENTATEUCH

wake of Rolf Rendtorff's criticisms of the Documentary Hypothesis,[37] there has been a decided move away from the notion of a Yahwist as the first assembler of the Pentateuchal themes (von Rad) or first inheritor of those themes from the *Grundlage* (Noth). In place of the continuous sources of the Documentary Hypothesis—whether Yahwist (J), Elohist (E), or Jehovist (JE)—it is now frequently suggested that the major themes of the Torah remained independent and fragmentary until they were joined together by a Deuteronomistic or Priestly redactor working at a date much later than traditional source critics would have imagined.[38]

Though built largely on a foundation laid in Pentateuchal research, redaction criticism has by no means been limited to this section of Bible. Noth himself produced important analyses of the redactional activities of the Deuteronomistic History and the Chronicler's work, for example,[39] and other scholars have applied the tools of redaction criticism to explain matters such as the compilation of the prophetic books. In the NT, redaction

---

37. Rolf Rendtorff, *Das überlieferungsgeschichtliche Problem des Pentateuch* (Berlin: de Gruyter, 1976), 1–28. English translation: Rolf Rendtorff, *The Problem of the Process of Transmission in the Pentateuch*, trans. John J. Scullion (Sheffield: Sheffield Academic, 1990), 11–42.

38. The various influential studies of H. H. Schmid, Erhard Blum, Martin Rose, and others are considered in Thomas B. Dozeman and Konrad Schmid, eds., *A Farewell to the Yahwist? The Composition of the Pentateuch in Recent European Interpretation* (Atlanta: Society of Biblical Literature, 2006).

39. Martin Noth, *The Deuteronomistic History*, 2nd ed. (Sheffield: Sheffield Academic, 1991); *The Chronicler's History*, trans. H. G. M. Williamson (Sheffield: JSOT Press, 1987).

criticism has been particularly well suited to the analysis of the Synoptic Gospels. Thus, as early as the 1950s Hans Conzelmann used the techniques of redaction criticism to consider the theology of Luke, and Willi Marxsen did the same in Mark.[40] Countless studies have followed in the wake of these first forays.

6.3 APPLICATIONS OF REDACTION CRITICISM

As the preceding discussion suggests, redactional influence on literary sources can vary dramatically from one text to another. Headings, textual linkages, explanatory comments, and large-scale supplementation and reconfiguration are all potential contributions from a redactor. Indeed, the range of potential modifications is so great that some have advocated for a distinction between "editors," who largely leave their source material intact, and "redactors," who subject it to more thorough revision.[41] However, there remains no formal attempt to distinguish between these two types of activity.

6.3.1 HEADINGS

Among the most obvious insertions in a text are the headings that introduce passages, especially in the prophetic books. These headings range from the very brief introduction to Obadiah, "The Vision of Obadiah," to the much more expansive opening to Amos: "The words of Amos, who was among the shepherds of Tekoa, which he saw concerning Israel in the days of King Uzziah of Judah and in the days of King Jeroboam son of Joash of Israel, two years before the earthquake" (1:1).

With the exception of Ezekiel, each of these headings in the prophetic books is composed in the third person and stands outside the prophet's oracles as a marker of the collection that follows. Similar sorts of headings are interspersed throughout the prophetic books, introducing even single oracles with language such as "The word that Isaiah son of Amoz

---

40. Hans Conzelmann, *Die Mitte der Zeit: Studien zur Theologie des Kukas* (Tübingen: J. C. B. Mohr, 1954); Willi Marxen, *Der Evangelist Markus: Studien zur Redaktionsgeschichte des Evangeliums* (Göttingen: Gütersloh Mohn, 1956), 67.

41. This issue is addressed in Jean-Louis Ska, "A Plea on Behalf of the Biblical Redactors," *Studia Theologica* 59 (2005): 4–5.

saw concerning Judah and Jerusalem" (Isa 2:1) or "The word that came to Jeremiah from the LORD" (Jer 11:1).

Outside the prophets, perhaps the most famous of these headings are the generational formulae (variations of "these are the generations of so-and-so") that head sections of the book of Genesis (2:4; 5:1; 6:9; 10:1; 11:10, 27; 25:12, 19; 36:1; 37:2). The ten occurrences of the formula provide the book with an overall structure, signaling to the reader what comes next.

6.3.2 TEXTUAL LINKAGES

Faced with the task of joining together sources that are not always harmonious, redactors often insert comments to smooth over textual disjunctures. A common form of this kind of textual linkage is repetitive resumption (also called *Wiederaufnahme*). For example, once Joseph is sold into slavery (Gen 37) the story does not immediately turn to his travails in Egypt. Instead, what follows is a lengthy account of Judah's ill-treatment of his daughter-in-law, Tamar. The result of this insertion is a disruption of Joseph's story. Thus, at the beginning of Gen 39 the redactor reminds the reader, "Now Joseph was taken down to Egypt, and Potiphar, an officer of Pharaoh, the captain of the guard, an Egyptian, bought him from the Ishmaelites who had brought him down there."[42] The repetition of information from Gen 37:36 signals the resumption of the story.

Similar patterns are found elsewhere. For example, after Moses' failed first encounter with Pharaoh in Exod 5, the text goes on to recount a word of divine encouragement to Moses (Exod 6:1–9). The section concludes with a renewed divine commission and a subsequent word of protest from Moses: "Then the LORD spoke to Moses, 'Go and tell Pharaoh king of Egypt to let the Israelites go out of his land.' But Moses spoke to the LORD, 'The Israelites have not listened to me; how then shall Pharaoh listen to me,

---

42. Internal tensions and contradictions in the account of Joseph's sale into slavery (Gen 37) suggest two different versions of the story have been woven together. This is particularly evident in that two different brothers, Reuben (vv. 21–22, 29–30) and Judah (vv. 26–27), try to preserve Joseph's life, and two different bands of people, Midianites (vv. 28a, 36) and Ishmaelites (vv. 25, 27, 28b), take Joseph to Egypt. Most source critics would label the account in which Judah advocates selling Joseph to the Ishmaelites rather than killing him as J, and the account in which Midianites capture Joseph after Reuben has him thrown into a pit as E. The repetitive resumption in Gen 39:1, which refers to Ishmaelites, only appears to know J's account. This may bolster a position like that of von Rad, who regarded even the Yahwist as a redactor of earlier, pre-Yahwistic traditions.

poor speaker that I am?'" (Exod 6:10–12). Interestingly, this exchange is repeated in almost the exact same wording later in the chapter: "On the day when the LORD spoke to Moses in the land of Egypt, he said to him, 'I am the LORD; tell Pharaoh king of Egypt all that I am speaking to you.' But Moses said in the LORD's presence, 'Since I am a poor speaker, why would Pharaoh listen to me?'" (vv. 28–30).

A logical suggestion for this duplication is not difficult to find. On the heels of the first exchange, a long Levitical genealogy has been inserted in the text (Exod 6:14–27), and this insertion brings the larger narrative to a halt. Thus, the redactor uses resumptive repetition to pick up where the story left off. This suggestion assumes that the redactor responsible for the duplicate inherited a text that had already been redacted at least once, when what is now Exod 6:10–12 and 6:13–27 were placed together.

6.3.3 EXPLANATORY COMMENTS

Alongside their role in linking together texts from different sources and, sometimes, genres, redactional insertions also eliminate narrative tensions and contradictions. Genesis 26 opens with a phrase heard often in the patriarchal narratives, "Now there was a famine in the land." When the narrative proceeds to recount the story of a patriarch who, driven to a foreign land by famine, unsuccessfully attempts to pass off his wife as his sister to the foreign king, a reader might reasonably wonder whether he or she had not heard this story (twice!) before (Gen 12:10–20; 20:1–18). As if to allay any concerns that this might be the case, the redactor helpfully supplements "Now there was a famine in the land" with "besides the former famine that had occurred in the days of Abraham" (Gen 26:1b).

A similar case is found in Exodus' description of the hail plague. As has long been recognized, the order of the plagues in the present form of Exodus presents certain logical difficulties. For example, Exodus attributes to the seventh plague, hail, such a destructive force that it wipes out "all the plants of the field in the land of Egypt" (Exod 9:22), "all the plants of the field," and "every tree in the field" (Exod 9:25). Were this the case, there would be nothing left for the locusts, the eighth plague, whose ravenous appetites are described in even greater detail. "They covered the surface of the whole land, so that the land was black; and they ate all the plants in the land and all the fruit of the trees that the hail had left; nothing green was left, no tree, no plant in the field, in all the land of Egypt" (Exod 10:15). Had the hail plague caused the sort of damage the story describes, there ought to have been no plants left for the locusts to eat. A redactional insertion following the hail plague provides the solution: "Now the flax and the barley were ruined, for the barley was in the ear and the flax was in bud. But the wheat and the spelt were not ruined, for they are late in coming up" (Exod 9:31–32). The insertion explains that, while the flax and barley may have been ruined by the hail, the wheat and spelt did not bloom until just before the plague of locusts.[43]

An additional example of this kind of explanatory redactional editing is found in the account of David's defeat of Goliath. Although rightly treasured as one of the most famous biblical narratives, the account of David's battle against the Philistine champion contains some of the Bible's thorniest text-critical problems. A comparison of the ancient versions of 1 Sam 17–18 reveals that the traditional Hebrew text of the Bible, the Masoretic Text (MT), differs quite radically from the Septuagint's version of these chapters as preserved in Codex Vaticanus (known as LXX[B]). In 1 Sam 17, vv. 12–31, 41, 48b, 50, and 55–58 are all present in the Hebrew text, but missing in the Greek translation. While it may be tempting to imagine that the Septuagint has abbreviated the longer narrative, the more likely suggestion is that additional materials were joined to the Hebrew after its translation into Greek.[44] If that is the case, the Septuagint represents an older Hebrew version of the narrative that lacked the additional verses now found in the MT.

The effect of these additions on the larger narrative is profound. In the older version of the narrative, David is said to be "a man of valor, a warrior" (1 Sam 16:18) who enters Saul's service as a musician and soon leaves his father's household altogether to be Saul's armor bearer (v. 21). As the Israelite and Philistine armies array against one another, David is, as one would expect, already there serving the king. When Goliath's taunts go unanswered by Saul's troops, David steps forward to meet the challenge, and while the offer of Saul's armor proves to be of no value to David since

---

43. Note that Psa 78:46–48 charts a different strategy for resolving this difficulty, namely the reversal of the hail and locust plagues.

44. Note the discussion in Steven L. McKenzie, *David: A Biography* (Oxford: Oxford University Press, 2000).

he is unaccustomed to such gear, it is only his training, not his stature, that is called into question.

In the additional verses found in the MT of 1 Sam 17, a much different picture of the future king emerges. In this account, David still lives with his father and is only sent to the front to check on his brothers (vv. 17–18); he is certainly not the king's armor bearer. When David asks why no one responds to the challenges uttered by Goliath, he is rebuked by Eliab in the manner of an elder brother speaking to a young child. When David finally defeats the Philistine champion, Saul (and Abner) are quite mystified as to who the young man is (vv. 55–58).

Joining these two divergent narratives together was no small feat. To accomplish this task, the redactor regularly intersperses comments that knit the two together. As explanation for how David could be both shepherd for his father and servant to Saul, the redactor adds in 1 Sam 17:14b–15, "The three eldest followed Saul, but David went back and forth from Saul to feed his father's sheep at Bethlehem." In the older narrative, Goliath utters his challenge to the Israelites only once, decreasing the chances that the itinerant David of the later version would have been there to hear him. To resolve this difficulty, the redactor adds, "For forty days the Philistine came forward and took his stand, morning and evening" (v. 16) and later, "he spoke the same words as before" (v. 23), giving David opportunity to hear the Philistine's bluster when he arrived later. To explain David's audience with Saul—in the older tradition David already had access to the king as his armor bearer—the redactor suggests, "When the words that David spoke were heard, they repeated them before Saul, and he sent for him" (v. 31). Despite the redactor's explanatory comments, sufficient tension remains in the narrative to identify sources even apart from the chapter's text-critical difficulties. The redactor's work has served to smooth out some of the text's disjunctures and to allow quite different traditions to be read together.

6.3.4 RECONFIGURATION

When one source is joined to another, its original meaning is inevitably altered. It is entirely possible that the Yahwist regarded the questions to the hiding Adam in Gen 3:9–11—Where are you? Who told you you were naked? Did you eat of the fruit?—as straightforward requests for information from a deity who did not yet know the answers. But once Genesis 1 and its account of a God so exalted and powerful that he creates the world merely by speaking has been set in front of this narrative, this reading of the questions is no longer viable. Whatever the questions may originally have meant, in the present context they can no longer mean God did not know.

In many cases, such a reconfiguration of a text's original meaning is more than an incidental by-product of joining sources together. On the contrary, it is a deliberate shaping of the tradition by a redactor whose intentions differed from those of the sources they inherited. The numerous examples from Chronicles cited thus far vividly illustrate this point. While the Deuteronomistic History may have been written to lend support to Josiah's reforms (in the case of Dtr[1]) or to account for the disaster of exile (Dtr[2]), in the hands of the Chronicler the Deuteronomists' traditions are used for entirely different purposes. As Chronicles adapts the Deuteronomistic traditions to suit its own goals, the traditions that are carried over into Chronicles are naturally reconfigured.

One arena in which this reconfiguration of earlier traditions is most vividly seen is in the Synoptic Gospels. Matthew, Mark, and Luke are well-known for their extensive literary overlap. This overlap is commonly explained as Mark having served as a source for Matthew and Luke.[45] As these later Gospels draw on Mark, they do much more than simply duplicate Mark's text. They edit, augment, and reconfigure Mark's material to fit within their own Gospel accounts. As they do so, their own historical and theological concerns come to the fore.

In the so-called Markan Apocalypse in Mark 13, the evangelist presents his readers with a lengthy sermon from Jesus on the imminent arrival of the end times. In this sermon, Jesus warns the disciples of terrible days of judgment that lie ahead. He cautions the disciples not to let anyone lead them astray, telling them, "Many will come in my name and say, 'I am he!'" (vv. 5–6). Jesus warns, "Nation will rise against nation, and kingdom against kingdom; there will be earthquakes in various places; there will be famines," and cautions, "This is but the beginning of the birth pangs" (v. 8). Jesus envisions calamities attending these events that will shake the very fabric of the cosmos: "The sun will be darkened, and the moon will not give its light, and the stars will be falling from heaven" (vv. 24–25). The

---

45. See §3.3.3 Gospels in this volume's chapter on source criticism for more information.

only salvation for God's elect, Jesus consoles, will lie in that God will cut short those days (vv. 18–20).

In chapter 21 of his own Gospel, Luke draws extensively on Mark's version of Jesus' sermon. As he does so, he introduces a number of redactional changes into the text. In Luke, Jesus warns the disciples not only against those who would say, "I am he!" but also against those who say, "The time is near!" (v. 8). Luke repeats Jesus' warning of wars, earthquakes, and famines verbatim but, strikingly, omits Mark's reference to these being the beginning of birth pangs (vv. 10–11). Jesus mentions sun, moon, and stars in Luke, just as he does in Mark, but his language is that of signs and portents, not cosmological collapse: "There will be signs in the sun, the moon, and the stars" (v. 25). Perhaps most significantly, Jesus does not suggest in Luke that these days of trouble will be short. On the contrary, Jesus warns of a time of trouble that will span an entire era of Gentile domination: "There will be great distress on the earth and wrath against this people; they will fall by the edge of the sword and be taken away as captives among all nations; and Jerusalem will be trampled on by the Gentiles, until the times of the Gentiles are fulfilled" (vv. 23–24).

The cumulative effect of Luke's editing of the Markan Apocalypse is readily apparent. Whereas Mark envisions the imminent arrival of a brief but intense period of suffering followed by the return of Jesus, Luke argues Jesus' return will be delayed. For Luke, it is now a false prophecy to claim "The time is near!" He does not mention birth pangs because these signal the onset of labor and promise that the time of travail will soon be past. Instead, Luke observes that Jerusalem lies fallen and that the times of the Gentiles must be endured before the end will come.

6.3.5 NARRATIVE EXPANSION

In many cases, redactors exercise only a light touch as they pass along the materials they have inherited, sometimes leaving a transition that is quite jarring for the reader. This is the case, for example, in parts of the book of Numbers, as the text moves unpredictably from one subject and genre to another.[46] When a text lacks a narrative thread to give the material coher-

---

46. Note, for example, the difficult shifts from one sort of text to another in Num 14–21.

ence—a situation common in the prophetic books—these difficulties are even more pronounced.

Elsewhere, redactors set to their task with a somewhat heavier hand, not only connecting source materials but also supplying them with linking and explanatory comments that cement them together and resolve tensions created by their union. As redactors continue along this path, they increasingly blur the lines between redactor and author.[47] In a provocative reconsideration of the Pentateuch's priestly materials, Frank Cross makes the case that P "never existed as an independent narrative document" and should instead be regarded as an expansion of the underlying JE narrative rather than as an independent literary source.[48] In essence, Cross treats P as a redactor who reworks JE, supplementing it with other written and oral traditions to form the Tetrateuch.[49] This sort of redactional activity is also witnessed in the extensive reworking and supplementation evident in the Chronicler's use of Kings and in the later Synoptics' use of Mark.

6.4 LIMITATIONS OF REDACTION CRITICISM

As with all interpretive methods, redaction criticism is not without its limitations and its detractors. The most vocal opposition to redaction criticism has come from John Van Seters.[50] Van Seters contends that the very notion of editors and editions, redactors and redaction, developed only in the print and book culture that grew out of the Renaissance. As a result, he regards the application of these terms and the modern ideas they thus import into the biblical world as grossly anachronistic. Van Seters insists biblical writers must be treated solely as authors and not as redactors. As

---

47. As von Rad notes, distinguishing author from collector is by no means a new difficulty (von Rad, *Problem of the Hexateuch*, 50–51).

48. Cross, *Canaanite Myth and Hebrew Epic*, 324. Cross notes that Mowinckel regarded P in a similar light, though without denying its traditional status as an independent documentary source.

49. Cross, *Canaanite Myth and Hebrew Epic*, 320. In a consideration of the plagues in Exod 7–11, Bénédicte Lemmelijn argues that the Priestly contribution to these chapters is such that the line between redactor and author may have been drawn too sharply and should perhaps be reconsidered altogether (Bénédicte Lemmelijn, "The So-Called 'Priestly' Layer in Exod 7,14-11,10: 'Source' and/or/nor 'Redaction'?," *RB* 109 [2002]).

50. Note, for example, John Van Seters, "The Redactor in Biblical Studies," *JNSL* 29 (2003): 1–19; *The Edited Bible: The Curious History of the "Editor" in Biblical Criticism* (Winona Lake, IN: Eisenbrauns, 2006).

authors, these writers may have drawn on earlier materials, but they did so in such a way that those materials are entirely subverted to the purposes of the new work. Thus, Van Seters would argue the Yahwist is no more an editor or redactor than is Homer or Herodotus—authors surely—who nevertheless draw on earlier source material.

While Van Seters' objections have not been successful in putting an end to redaction criticism, they have forced critics to address various methodological issues that had not been explored prior. Some scholars have responded to Van Seters' critique by arguing it is not the notion of redactor that is anachronistic but that of author. Jean-Louis Ska, for example, maintains, "The problematic notion, in my opinion, is not exactly that of the editor or redactor, but the very notion of 'author' in ancient times, both in Greece and in Israel."[51] Ska insists it was the ancient writer's job to interpret and "actualize" in a new setting the traditions that were already the "common possession of all the members of the community." He continues:

> This is the basic reason why there is 'editorial,' 'redactional' or 'compositional' activity in antiquity. The ancient writers were not later editors of ancient authors, but living channels of transmission of ancient—mostly anonymous—and collective traditions; their task was to 'actualize,' to give new life, to these traditions.[52]

In this role, Ska argues, the modern notion of "author" is even less helpful than the terms "editor" and "redactor" that Van Seters criticizes.[53]

The challenge of distinguishing author from redactor arises in a different way, even for those unconvinced by Van Seters' accusations of anachronism. In a discussion of redaction criticism, John Barton raises the issue of the "disappearing redactor," the redactor whose work is so successful that it can no longer be confidently identified.[54] Key to redaction

---

51. Ska, "Plea on Behalf of the Biblical Redactors," 7.

52. Ska, "Plea on Behalf of the Biblical Redactors," 7.

53. Ska, "Plea on Behalf of the Biblical Redactors," 15. Note also the contribution of Karel van der Toorn (*Scribal Culture and the Making of the Hebrew Bible* [Cambridge, MA: Harvard University Press, 2007]), which elicited a lengthy response from Van Seters (see John van Seters, "The Role of the Scribe in the Making of the Hebrew Bible," *Journal of Ancient Near Eastern Religions* 8 [2008]: 99–129).

54. John Barton, *Reading the Old Testament: Method in Biblical Study*, rev. and enl. ed. (Louisville: Westminster John Knox, 1996). On the background of the term "disappearing

criticism is the notion that some secondarily linked texts were originally so divergent that only a redactor's skillful hand could allow them to be read harmoniously. However, if a redactor succeeds in editing the texts together well enough to allow them to be read as a unity, does this not throw doubt onto the original premise that the texts were originally divergent? As Barton summarizes:

> The more impressive the critic makes the redactor's work appear, the more he succeeds in showing that the redactor has, by subtle and delicate artistry, produced a simple and coherent text out of the diverse materials before him; the more also he reduces the evidence on which the existence of those sources was established in the first place.[55]

On one level, the essence of Barton's argument must be conceded. To the degree that a text reads harmoniously, any potential redactional shaping it may have experienced will be difficult to discern. A redactor who redacts skillfully may indeed leave a redaction too subtle to identify. On the other hand, none of the examples Barton puts forward as candidates for such a dilemma actually prove convincing. The redactor may have made a reasonable attempt to produce one creation story from two (Gen 1–2) or to craft one flood story from two (Gen 6–8), yet the lingering internal tensions and redactional seams in the stories are so obvious that the redactor is in no danger of slipping into obscurity.

6.5 CONTEMPORARY INFLUENCE OF REDACTION CRITICISM

Redaction criticism began with the efforts of von Rad and Noth to trace from first step to last the development of the Bible's major blocks of narrative literature. With their predecessor, Gunkel, the pendulum of biblical research had swung from source criticism to an examination of the oral traditions that lay in the preliterary phase of the Bible's development. With von Rad and Noth, the pendulum shifted in the opposite direction, to a consideration of the redactor's role in the shaping of the final form

---

redactor," see 254n24.

55. Barton, *Reading the Old Testament*, 57.

of the text. It is in this concern for the text's final form and the redactors/ authors who put the text in that form that the impact of redaction criticism is most keenly felt in modern research.

In Pentateuchal studies, this emphasis has been particularly evident in the growing number of scholars who reject outright the source-critical approach associated with Wellhausen and move instead toward fragmentary or supplementary approaches heavily dependent on the redactor's role. Although the documentary approach to the Pentateuch's composition was never without its critics, this particular challenge to the hypothesis began with von Rad's successor at the University of Heidelberg, Rolf Rendtorff. Rendtorff argues that source criticism offers no convincing explanation for bridging the gap between the oral traditions identified by form criticism and the lengthy literary documents proposed by source critics. He argued instead that the bulk of the Tetrateuch developed as small units or cycles of tradition (a Jacob-Esau cycle, a Jacob-Laban cycle, etc.) that were joined to form larger narrative complexes and that these complexes remained independent until a Deuteronomistic redactor "clamped together all the Pentateuchal traditions under one embracing theme."[56] The effect of this move was to give tremendous weight to the role of the redactor in bringing the Pentateuch into existence. The continued influence of Rendtorff's proposal is evident in the numerous studies that have followed and advanced the path he set. H. H. Schmid, Erhard Blum, Martin Rose, and a host of others have increasingly emphasized the role of Deuteronomic/ Deuteronomistic or Priestly redactors in the Pentateuch's formation, generally at the expense of the earlier Yahwistic and Elohistic contributions.[57] The irony that a redactor first proposed by source critics to explain the Documentary Hypothesis would be the one who now threatens to undermine the hypothesis itself has not gone unnoticed.[58]

Redaction criticism's emphasis on the manner in which biblical texts reached their final form has also helped pave the way for the many "new" forms of literary criticism that take the final form of the text as their

---

56. Rendtorff, *Das überlieferungsgeschichtliche Problem*, 79.

57. The views of these authors are addressed in Dozeman and Schmid, *Farewell to the Yahwist?*

58. John Van Seters, "An Ironic Circle: Wellhausen and the Rise of Redaction Criticism," *ZAW* 115 (2003): 487–500.

starting point. While structuralist and reader-response approaches ulti-mately share little in common with redaction criticism, there can be little doubt that the move from the increasingly atomistic proposals of source and form criticism to the ultimate form of the text passed on by the redac-tor aided their development.

6.6 RESOURCES FOR FURTHER STUDY

Barton, John. *Reading the Old Testament: Method in Biblical Study*. Rev. and enl. ed. Louisville: Westminster John Knox, 1996.

> Barton's book is an invaluable guide to numerous methods used in biblical interpretation. His concerns about redaction criticism are worth consideration.

Cross, Frank Moore. *Canaanite Myth and Hebrew Epic: Essays in the History of the Religion of Israel*. Cambridge, MA: Harvard University Press, 1973.

> Cross' work addresses, among other topics, the dual redaction of the Deuteronomistic History and the nature of the Priestly contribution to the Pentateuch (that is, whether it was an independent source or redaction).

Dozeman, Thomas B., and Konrad Schmid, eds. *A Farewell to the Yahwist? The Composition of the Pentateuch in Recent European Interpretation*. Atlanta: Society of Biblical Literature, 2006.

> An important compilation of recent developments in Pentateuchal scholarship (especially in Europe) on the composition of the Pentateuch.

Fishbane, Michael A. *Biblical Interpretation in Ancient Israel*. Oxford: Clarendon, 1985.

> The techniques raised in Fishbane's seminal volume on innerbiblical exegesis often bear directly on redaction criticism.

Noth, Martin. *The Chronicler's History*. Translated by H. G. M. Williamson. Sheffield: JSOT Press, 1987.

———. *The Deuteronomistic History*. 2nd ed. Sheffield: Sheffield Academic, 1991.

————. *A History of Pentateuchal Traditions*. Translated by Bernhard W. Anderson. Englewood Cliffs, NJ: Prentice-Hall, 1972.

In these three books, Noth explores the formation of the Pentateuch, the Former Prophets, 1–2 Chronicles, and Ezra–Nehemiah. He seeks to give an account for how various layers of biblical tradition had come to be combined into larger literary compositions.

von Rad, Gerhard. *The Problem of the Hexateuch and Other Essays*. Translated by E. W. Trueman Dicken. Edinburgh: Oliver & Boyd, 1966.

Von Rad's seminal essay "The Form-Critical Problem of the Hexateuch" (1938) is translated in this volume. Von Rad combines the source- and form-critical approaches to analyze the Hexateuch's composition. He emphasizes the role of the Yahwist in giving the Pentateuch its definitive character.

Rendtorff, Rolf. *Das überlieferungsgeschichtliche Problem des Pentateuch*. Berlin: de Gruyter, 1976.

Rendtorff was a major force in the development of redaction criticism. His dissatisfaction with both source criticism and form criticism (or the traditio-historical method) led him to consider how Pentateuchal narratives had been collected and arranged into larger units. By shifting focus to the formation of larger textual units, he drew attention to the role played by the redactor.

7

SOCIAL-SCIENTIFIC CRITICISM

Coleman Baker & Amy Balogh

Since the emergence of critical biblical interpretation in the nineteenth century, scholars have used countless interpretative methods to better understand the ancient texts and the worlds from which those texts emerged. The methods explored in this volume describe both historical and literary approaches that have significantly improved our understanding of the biblical texts. This chapter adds to this rich discussion by exploring social-scientific interpretation, an array of methods adopted by biblical studies in the latter part of the twentieth century that continues to expand today. This chapter defines the social-scientific method and its central objectives, gives a brief history of its development, and then introduces a few case studies that illustrate the utility of social-scientific criticism for understanding the Bible.

7.1 DEFINITION AND GOAL OF METHOD

Since the academic category "social sciences" includes numerous disciplines, each with its own set of methods from which to choose, there is much debate about how to define social-scientific interpretation as a whole. Perhaps the most comprehensive definition of the methodology, or range of methodologies, is that of John H. Elliott:

> Social-scientific criticism of the Bible is that phase of the exegetical task which analyzes the social and cultural dimensions of the text and of its environmental context through the utilization of the

perspectives, theory, models, and research of the social sciences. As a component of the historical-critical method of exegesis, social-scientific criticism investigates biblical texts as meaningful configurations of language intended to communicate between composers and audiences.[1]

In other words, the social sciences offer modern biblical interpreters a set of tools that, when used properly, are capable of yielding insight into the cultural background that informed and affected both the authors of the Bible and their respective audiences. Elliott later adds that this approach "studies the text as both a reflection of and a response to the social and cultural settings in which the text was produced"; its goal is to aid in determining the "meaning(s) explicit and implicit in the text, meanings made possible and shaped by the social and cultural systems inhabited by both authors and intended audiences."[2] Among social-scientific critics of the Bible, the primary objective is to understand the nature and content of the reciprocal relationship between culture, author, and audience, illuminating the biblical text through the lens of extrabiblical texts, artifacts, and cultures contemporaneous with the period under investigation.

7.1.1 RELATIONSHIP TO OTHER APPROACHES

As Elliott mentions in his definition, social-scientific interpretation is "a phase of the exegetical task" or "a component of the historical-critical method of exegesis."[3] That is, when interpreting ancient texts, the "perspectives, theory, models, and research of the social sciences" cannot stand alone. Rather, they are part of a larger interpretive framework that includes other methods explored in this volume, such as historical and source-critical methods.[4] Social-scientific interpretation is thus linked with these other methodological approaches and complements them by means of the second component of Elliott's definition, namely that social-scientific interpretation "analyzes the social and cultural dimensions of the texts."

---

1. John H. Elliott, *What Is Social-Scientific Criticism?* (Minneapolis: Fortress, 1993), 7.

2. Elliott, *What Is Social-Scientific Criticism?*, 8.

3. Elliott, *What Is Social-Scientific Criticism?*, 7.

4. See chap. 2 for more information on the historical-grammatical method and chap. 3 for a discussion of source-critical methodology.

The vast historical and cultural gap between modern readers and the ancient authors necessitates this step of the exegetical process, a step that requires the interpreter to understand the broad sweep of historical events during which the biblical material was written and edited, where the biblical text under investigation falls within the timeline of historical events, and the cultural systems that were operative at the time(s) and place(s) in which that text was written. This task requires the interpreter to be attentive to the social, cultural, and environmental dimensions of ancient life in order to determine where the text's author engages those dimensions, both explicitly and implicitly.

7.1.2 UNDERLYING ASSUMPTIONS

Like any other form of interpretation, there are certain assumptions one must hold in order to work with social-scientific criticism. First, those using social-scientific methods in the study of the Bible assume that modern modes of studying social groups and societal systems may be successfully applied to the study of the ancient world.[5] In the early years of modern biblical studies, this assumption yielded many problematic uses of data and comparison, which then yielded problematic interpretations of the Bible. In more recent decades, with the reemergence of social-scientific criticism in biblical studies, scholars have become more mindful of the challenges an interpreter faces when applying modern language and frameworks to ancient phenomena.

The second assumption stems from the first: models and methods borrowed from the social sciences are tools for understanding rather than concrete frameworks on which to hang the biblical text.[6] The goal of social-scientific interpretation is not to describe exactly how things were conceived of in the ancient world, but to offer insight into how we, the modern readers, might better understand the background of the Bible in modern terms. Since the gap between antiquity and today limits the number and quality of resources available for the study of the ancient world, while also removing the possibility of performing fieldwork, this

---

5. Naomi Steinberg, "Social-Scientific Criticism," in *Methods of Biblical Interpretation*, ed. John H. Hayes (Nashville, TN: Abingdon, 2004), 275.

6. Philip F. Esler, "Social-Scientific Approaches," in *Dictionary of Biblical Criticism and Interpretation*, ed. Stanley E. Porter (New York: Routledge, 2007), 339.

assumption reduces the danger of imposing our worldview and our language onto ancient communities.

Finally, social-scientific criticism (broadly speaking, but especially of the Bible) assumes that members of a particular culture are socialized to accept its values, institutions, systems, and structures as normative.[7] This is especially evident in societies that are group oriented and have limited resources, especially if there is an emphasis on honor/shame or individual/ collective responsibility. Individuals or groups may, of course, deviate from what they inherit socially, but generally they do not. In instances where people do diverge from the norm, such divergence can only be gauged by understanding what they are diverging *from*.[8]

7.1.3 KEY CONCEPTS

One point of debate among those who utilize social-scientific approaches is exactly what constitutes social-scientific interpretation. There is little agreement as to the extent to which the perspectives, theories, models, and findings of the social sciences must inform an interpreter's work in order for it to be considered social-scientific. Dale Martin refers to the wide array of positions on the issue as "a spectrum of opinion about what precisely a social-scientific method should be," noting that the issue centers on whether the scholar uses models of research that have been tried and tested in the social sciences.[9] If the scholar is researching a society using traditional historical-critical modes of inquiry, such as those described in earlier chapters of this book, and does not explicitly use a model or theory from the social sciences to inform his or her work, then the scholar may be considered a "social historian" rather than a social scientist.[10]

While defining what social-scientific interpretation entails is somewhat contentious, there are three major objectives on which most social-

---

7. Esler, "Social-Scientific Approaches," 339.

8. Esler, "Social-Scientific Approaches," 339.

9. Dale Martin, "Social-Scientific Criticism," in *To Each Its Own Meaning: An Introduction to Biblical Criticisms and Their Application*, ed. S. L. McKenzie and S. R. Hayes (Louisville: Westminster John Knox, 1999), 129.

10. Martin, "Social-Scientific Criticism," 125. For more on the debate over the labels "social historian" or "social scientist," see David Horrell, "Models and Methods in Social-Scientific Interpretation: A Response to Philip Esler," *JSNT* 78 (2000): 84.

scientific interpreters of the Bible agree. First, social-scientific scholarship of the Bible seeks to further understand the cultural world of the biblical writings by employing perspectives and theories offered by the social sciences, such as anthropology, sociology, economics, psychology, geography, political science, and history. The most popular fields from which biblical scholars draw are sociology and anthropology, especially the subfield of archaeology, which scholars often employ in concert with more traditional forms of biblical criticism (e.g., redaction, source, and form).

The second objective of social-scientific interpretation is to analyze biblical texts in light of available knowledge pertaining to the social and cultural conditions of the ancient world. In order to adequately understand the biblical text, one must understand the broad historical and cultural contexts in which the writings emerged, as well as the texts themselves. Thus, many factors are taken into consideration, such as long-standing social structures and environmental conditions; the activities and policies of imperial forces; cooperation between imperial forces and local elites; the matrix of politics, family, and religion; and the tendency toward group identity. This aspect of social-scientific interpretation requires not only a general knowledge of the ancient historical framework under consideration, but also deep familiarity with the social constructs in place during that historical period.

Finally, social-scientific interpretation seeks to illuminate the ways in which the biblical text is both a reflection of and a response to the historical and social contexts from which it emerged. The biblical texts did not emerge out of a cultural vacuum but were shaped by the authors' historically and culturally informed perspectives. In this respect, the biblical texts reflect the cultural constructs of the ancient people who wrote, read, and heard them, even if, at times, their perspectives reflect an aversion to certain aspects of these cultural constructs. The prophets, for example, spoke against the political and economic injustices of their day; Jesus, likewise, stood against political and economic injustices while advocating for a model of society based on the kingdom of God rather than the Roman Empire. In this respect, the biblical texts respond to the cultural world in which they were written, and it is the work of social-scientific interpretation to reveal those responses.

7.2 DEVELOPMENT OF SOCIAL-
SCIENTIFIC CRITICISM

Social-scientific biblical interpretation did not become a distinct discipline until the latter part of the twentieth century, but its predecessors may be traced as far back as the medieval period. While early uses of social-scientific criticism were usually based on problematic generalizations and comparisons, early scholars argued that a literal understanding of the text ought to come before spiritual interpretation. Among these interpretative pioneers was Rabbi Jonathan, whose work on the compositional order of the three biblical books traditionally attributed to Solomon (i.e., Proverbs, Ecclesiastes, Song of Songs) represents one of the first attempts to understand the social factors that influenced the biblical writers.[11] However, since the social sciences were not yet developed, scholars of the medieval era did not have social-scientific tools available and were therefore limited in terms of method.

This concern for sociohistorical understanding of the biblical text was occasional throughout the medieval period but emerged again as the social sciences themselves became distinct disciplines in the eighteenth and nineteenth centuries.[12] The increasing attention to the historical gap between the ancient cultures of the Bible and the more modern cultures of the post-Renaissance period urged biblical scholars of the seventeenth and eighteenth centuries toward the use of comparative approaches that would eventually come to characterize the social-scientific method.

The increasing dominance of the natural sciences in academic circles was a primary cause for the emergence of the social sciences. According to Robert Wilson, those interested in the study of society "believed that the methods of the natural sciences could be transferred to sociological research," providing "the objectivity necessary for their discipline's

---

11. According to Robert Wilson, Rabbi Jonathan's argument was that Solomon wrote "Song of Songs in the passion of his youth, Proverbs in the wisdom of his middle years, and Ecclesiastes in the cynicism of his old age" (Robert R. Wilson, *Sociological Approaches to the Old Testament* [Philadelphia: Fortress, 1984], 2).

12. For an excellent survey of the sociohistorical concern during the middle period, see Beryl Smalley, *The Study of the Bible in the Middle Ages* (New York: Philosophical Library, 1952); and Susan Boynton and Diane J. Reilly, eds., *The Practice of the Bible in the Middle Ages: Production, Reception, and Performance in Western Christianity* (New York: Columbia University Press, 2011).

academic respectability."[13] As Wilson also notes, the social sciences may be divided into three broad categories: sociology, anthropology, and psychology. Of these three, sociology and anthropology have had the most impact on biblical scholarship, as scholars were eager to undertake social-scientific modes of investigation soon after such models and theories began to arise in the late nineteenth century.[14]

Sociology may be defined as the study of society and of human social interaction and values that employs various research techniques and typically focuses on complex, large-scale, modern societies.[15] One major development in the field of sociology stems from two of the field's early representatives, Auguste Comte and Max Weber.

Auguste Comte, who coined the term "sociology," asserted that societal disorder could be understood historically and overcome in the future by "using the same methods of inquiry ... that had proved so successful in the natural sciences."[16] Comte argued that social life could be understood according to what he called "social laws." The development and understanding of these social laws by which social order is maintained would bring about the betterment of humankind.[17] By contrast, in his work on the sociology of religion, Max Weber emphasized that "generalized theoretical categories are as essential to the proof of causal relationships in the human and cultural field as they are in the natural sciences."[18] Thus, Weber's attempt to bridge the gap between the natural sciences and the study of society focused strongly on the role of theory in illuminating the

---

13. Wilson, *Sociological Approaches*, 11.

14. Wilson, *Sociological Approaches*, 22.

15. Josep R. Llobera, *An Invitation to Anthropology: The Structure, Evolution, and Cultural Identity of Human Societies* (New York: Berghahn Books, 2003), 13.

16. Philip Esler, ed., *Ancient Israel: The Old Testament in Its Social Context* (Minneapolis: Fortress, 2006), 4.

17. For an overview of Comte's writings, see Gertrud Lenzer, ed., *Auguste Comte and Positivism: The Essential Writings* (New Brunswick: Transaction, 1998).

18. Max Weber, *The Theory of Social and Economic Organization*, trans. A. M. Henderson and Talcott Parsons (New York: Free Press, 1964), 88. Weber's other works on the sociology of religion include Max Weber, *The Sociology of Religion*, trans. Ephraim Fischoff (Boston: Beacon, 1963); *The Religion of China: Confucianism and Taoism*, trans. and ed. Hans H. Gerth (New York: Free Press, 1951); *The Religion of India: the Sociology of Hinduism and Buddhism*, trans. and ed. Hans H. Gerth and Don Martindale (New York: Free Press, 1958); and *Ancient Judaism*, trans. and ed. Hans H. Gerth and Don Martindale (New York: Free Press, 1952).

human condition more than on the role of individual "laws" or causes and effects.

While Comte's influence on biblical studies is witnessed only occasionally,[19] Weber's is twofold. First, in the final volume of his study on the sociology of religion, *Ancient Judaism*, Weber analyzes the relationship between Bedouin herdsmen and cities, then compares his findings to biblical descriptions of the premonarchical period of Israelite history, asserting that early Israel was a confederacy of twelve tribes connected by its belief in YHWH and the accompanying laws and covenants.[20] Second, Weber lays the groundwork for the development of a taxonomy of cultures, including key variables that characterize and distinguish cultures; the direct influence of Weber's work may be seen explicitly in the works of Bruce Malina and other biblical scholars.[21]

In contrast to the field of sociology, which focuses on developing large-scale theories of inter-human behavior, anthropology is the holistic study of human life and culture in particular times and places. Llobera notes that anthropology is "focused on simple, small-scale, traditional, non-western societies."[22] While sociology and anthropology do, at times, have overlapping interests, "anthropology has generally not shared sociology's interest in overarching theories but has tended to concentrate on the analysis of particular societies and cultural phenomena."[23] Thus, while sociologists work at the macro-level, anthropologists tend to operate at the micro-level.

---

19. Esler, *Ancient Israel*, sees hints of Comte's thought in Wayne A. Meeks, *The First Urban Christians: The Social World of the Apostle Paul* (New Haven, CT: Yale University Press, 1983).

20. Final only because of his sudden death in 1920. Weber had intended to continue with studies of the Psalms, the Book of Jacob, Talmudic Jewry, early Christianity, and Islam (see Reinhard Bendix, *Max Weber: An Intellectual Portrait* [Garden City, NY: Doubleday, 1960], 285).

21. For taxonomy of cultures, see Geert H. Hofstede, *Culture's Consequences: Comparing Values, Behaviors, Institutions, and Organizations across Nations*, 2nd ed. (Thousand Oaks, CA: Sage Publications, 2001). See also Bruce J. Malina, *The New Testament World: Insights from Cultural Anthropology*, 3rd ed. (Louisville, KY: Westminster John Knox, 2001).

22. Llobera, *Invitation to Anthropology*, 13.

23. Wilson, *Sociological Approaches*, 17. Wilson divides anthropology into six categories, including ethnology, social (or cultural) anthropology, ethnography, archaeology, and structural anthropology. For a more detailed discussion of the subfields of anthropology, see Stanley R. Barrett, *The Rebirth of Anthropological Theory* (Toronto: University of Toronto Press, 1984).

In his notable work *Social Anthropology*,[24] British anthropologist E. E. Evans-Pritchard divides anthropology into three distinct periods. The first period, which ran from the eighteenth century to the mid-nineteenth century, was characterized by scholars whose work tended toward the philosophical, without reflecting knowledge of ancient cultures. The second period lasted from the middle of the nineteenth century to the early twentieth century and emphasized gathering data from non-Western cultures for comparative purposes. In this second period biblical scholars began applying social sciences, especially anthropology, to their work. The third period of Evans-Pritchard's history of anthropology ran from the early twentieth century through the mid-twentieth century and is characterized by a focus on fieldwork in one particular culture.

The first biblical scholar to overtly use anthropology in his work was William Robertson Smith. Smith was the chair of OT exegesis and Oriental languages at Aberdeen Free Church College (later Christ College, Aberdeen) beginning in 1870 and became editor of a new edition of the *Encyclopedia Britannica* in 1875. He spent 1880 living with indigenous peoples in various Middle Eastern countries to observe their customs. His findings were published in 1885, making him one of the founders of ethnography and cultural anthropology.[25] His Burnett lectures in Aberdeen in 1888–89, later published as *Lectures on the Religion of the Semites*, established precedent for comparing modern anthropological data with the ancient biblical text.[26]

Following in the steps of Smith, in 1890 James Frazer published the first volumes of his study in comparative religion, which came to be called *The Golden Bough*.[27] In contrast to Smith's fieldwork experience, Frazer relied on surveys sent to people around the globe, which produced a wealth of information about the role of myth and religion among those who returned the survey. In a later publication, *Folk-Lore in the Old Testament*, Frazer

---

24. E. E. Evans-Pritchard, *Social Anthropology* (New York: Free Press, 1951).

25. William Robertson Smith, *Kinship & Marriage in Early Arabia* (Cambridge: Cambridge University Press, 1885).

26. William Robertson Smith, *Lectures on the Religion of the Semites: The Fundamental Institutions*, 3rd ed. (New York: Macmillan, 1927).

27. James G. Frazer, *The Golden Bough: A Study in Magic and Religion*, 3rd ed., 12 vols. (London: Macmillan, 1915).

compared the findings of his survey-research to various narratives in the Hebrew Bible.[28]

These initial endeavors into social-scientific interpretation, however, were limited by the anthropological and sociological methods of that time. Wilson summarizes the innate problem with this early form of the discipline:

> Like the sociologists and anthropologists whose work they used, Old Testament critics often wrenched the comparative material out of its social context and then embedded it in a comprehensive social theory that was frequently dominated by an evolutionary perspective. The theory and its accompanying evidence were then imposed on the Old Testament, which was interpreted so as to produce the desired results.[29]

As this interpretative problem became more evident, biblical scholars began to reject the social sciences and comparison as altogether problematic, thus also rejecting the potential of those methods to contribute to the study of the Bible and religion. However, numerous scholars brought the social sciences back into biblical studies beginning in the 1960s, with a blossoming of research in the 1970s and beyond. Even today, countless scholars utilize social-scientific methods to shape and guide fruitful research projects, as social scientists continuously hone existing interpretive methods and invent new ones.

Of the numerous Hebrew Bible scholars who pioneered the modern use of interpretive tools made available through sociology and anthropology,[30] perhaps the most influential is Norman Gottwald. In his 1979 volume, *The Tribes of Yahweh: A Sociology of the Religion of Liberated Israel, 1250–1050 B.C.E.*, Gottwald used sociological theory drawn from Durkheim, Weber, and Marx to argue that "Israel emerged from a peasants' revolt which was fueled by commitment to an egalitarian social system and a monotheistic

---

28. James G. Frazer, *Folk-Lore in the Old Testament* (London: Macmillan, 1918).

29. Wilson, *Sociological Approaches*, 25.

30. For a thorough treatment of social-scientific interpretations of the Hebrew Bible, see Charles E. Carter and Carol L. Meyers, eds., *Community, Identity, and Ideology: Social Science Approaches to the Hebrew Bible* (Winona Lake, IN: Eisenbrauns, 1996).

faith."[31] Although Gottwald's work has been the subject of intense scrutiny, it demonstrates that a variety of sociological perspectives may be employed in the examination of ancient Israel and that, indeed, no single approach is sufficient.

Such a multifaceted approach to interpretation also appears in NT scholarship. Some of the earliest interest in social-scientific criticism was rooted in the concerns and practices of form criticism, developed by Hermann Gunkel, which related to the social setting of textual traditions.[32] In 1927, Adolf Deissmann contributed to this approach by noting the influence of extracanonical papyri on early Christian literature.[33] The interest in these social dimensions of early Christianity continued, at least in America, in the works of the members of the Chicago school, most prominently Shirley Jackson Case and Shalier Mathews.[34]

This initial interest was followed by a period of decline from the 1920s to the 1970s. Horrell notes that one of the reasons for this shift was the "failure of form criticism ... to explore the social context in which the [biblical] traditions were preserved and developed."[35] Also important was a turn in biblical studies toward existential questions and the dialectical approach to theology, both of which detach the text from its historical/cultural context. This began to shift in the 1970s, when Edwin Judge's *The Social Pattern of the Christian Groups in the First Century* (1960) caught the attention of NT scholars.[36] Judge's work was largely ignored during the 1960s but later was regarded as deserving "a place of honor in the history of modern sociological exegesis."[37] Horrell notes that Judge's work "is often

---

31. Wilson, *Sociological Approaches*, 27. Also see Esler, ed., *Ancient Israel*, 25–26; Norman K. Gottwald, *The Tribes of Yahweh: A Sociology of the Religion of Liberated Israel, 1250–1050 B.C.E* (Maryknoll, NY: Orbis, 1979).

32. See chap. 4 on form criticism.

33. Adolf Deissmann, *Light from the Ancient East: The New Testament Illustrated by Recently Discovered Texts of the Graeco-Roman World* (London: Hodder & Stoughton, 1927).

34. See Leander E. Keck, "On the Ethos of Early Christianity," *JAAR* 42 (1974): 435–52; and Robin Scroggs, "The Sociological Interpretation of the New Testament: The Present State of Research," *NTS* 26 (1980): 164–65.

35. David G. Horrell, *Social-Scientific Approaches to New Testament Interpretation* (Edinburgh: T&T Clark, 1999), 5.

36. Edwin Judge, *The Social Pattern of Christian Groups in the First Century* (London: Tyndale, 1960).

37. Gerd Theissen, *Social Reality and the Early Christians: Theology, Ethics, and the World of the New Testament*, trans. M. Kohl (Edinburgh: T&T Clark, 1993), 19n23.

cited as an important stimulus for the development of the modern interest in the socio-historical aspect of the Pauline communities."[38]

Horrell also believes that the renewed interest in social-scientific criticism is rooted in a dissatisfaction with established methods of exegesis.[39] This is best summarized by Robin Scroggs:

> To some it has seemed that too often the discipline of the theology of the New Testament (the history of *ideas*) operates out of a methodological docetism, as if believers had minds and spirits unconnected with their individual and corporate bodies. Interest in the sociology of early Christianity is no attempt to limit reductionistically the reality of Christianity to social dynamic; rather it should be seen as an effort to guard against a reductionism from the other extreme, a limitation of the reality of Christianity to an inner-spiritual, or objective-cognitive system. In short, sociology of early Christianity wants to put body and soul together again.[40]

This effort to "put body and soul together again" was also situated within a particular social context, one that emphasized doing history "from below" (i.e., from the vantage point of lived experience) rather than "from above" (i.e., from the vantage point of theory) and that saw the rise of feminist and liberation movements.[41]

In the 1970s, several studies were published that highlighted the importance of understanding the social context of the NT writings. For example, Wayne Meeks published an article on John's Gospel, arguing that the Fourth Gospel reflects the situation of a sectarian community that had been alienated and isolated from its neighbors,[42] and Gerd Theissen published a series of essays on topics ranging from the Jesus movement in Palestine to

---

38. Todd D. Still and David G. Horrell, eds., *After the First Urban Christians: The Social-Scientific Study of Pauline Christianity Twenty-Five Years Later* (London: T&T Clark, 2009), 6n1.

39. Horrell, *Social-Scientific Approaches*, 6.

40. Scroggs, "Sociological Interpretation of the New Testament," 165–66.

41. For more on this, see Stephen C. Barton, "The Communal Dimension of Earliest Christianity: A Critical Survey of the Field," *JTS* 43 (1992): 399–406.

42. Wayne A. Meeks, "The Man from Heaven in Johannine Sectarianism," *JBL* 91 (1972): 44–72.

the Pauline church in Corinth.[43] Another important work from this period is John Gager's *Kingdom and Community*, in which he surveys a number of sociological theories and explores their applicability to early Christianity.[44] Several of Gager's examples were expanded on by later scholars.[45]

The 1980s and early 1990s saw an attempt to clarify the purpose and method of social-scientific biblical interpretation, leading to sharp distinctions among those who used social-scientific methods in their work. For example, John Elliott argued, "by no means is every book or article with the term 'social' or 'sociological' in its title an exercise in social-scientific criticism." Moreover, Elliott asserts that studies on "social" matters can be classified into five main categories:

1. investigations of social realities or social facts

2. studies that attempt to construct a social history of a group or a historical period

3. studies in the social organization of ancient Israel, early Judaism, and Christianity

4. studies that focus on the social and cultural scripts evidenced within the Bible

5. studies applying the research, theory, and methods of the social sciences to the analysis of biblical texts[46]

One significant distinction that emerged among social-scientific interpreters was between those who engage primarily in social history, using the methods of traditional historical criticism to describe the cultural and social conditions out of which the biblical texts arose, and those who explicitly use various social-scientific models in their exegetical analysis

---

43. These essays were collected in Gerd Theissen, *Studien zur Soziologie des Urchristentums* (Tübingen: Mohr, 1979).

44. John G. Gager, *Kingdom and Community: The Social World of Early Christianity* (Englewood Cliffs, NJ: Prentice-Hall, 1975).

45. See Bengt Holmberg, ed., *Exploring Early Christian Identity* (Tübingen: Mohr Siebeck, 2008).

46. Adapted from Elliott, *Social-Scientific Criticism*, 18–19.

of biblical texts.[47] While the sharpness of this divide is softening, it illustrates two major traditions within the social-scientific approach.

Perhaps some of the best examples of the use of the social sciences toward a better understanding of the biblical text are found in the works of Bruce Malina and Wayne Meeks. Malina's groundbreaking book, *The New Testament World: Insights from Cultural Anthropology* (1981), is a collection of essays that highlights the systems of values that were operative in the ancient Mediterranean. These cultural values, such as honor/shame, limited good, collectivist personality, and agonism, were deeply embedded in the social reality of the early Christians, and therefore, Malina argues, in the literature they produced. Another example of early scholarship using social-scientific theory to describe the social and cultural contexts of early Christianity is the work of Wayne Meeks. Meeks' most influential work is *The First Urban Christians: The Social World of the Apostle Paul* (1983), in which he examines the social context of the Pauline churches, most notably their presence in urban centers within the Roman Empire.

In the decades between Malina's and Meeks' volumes and today, a wide variety of applications of social-scientific interpretation have emerged as viable lenses through which to examine the biblical text. Issues of ethnicity, ritual, identity, memory, and empire, just to name a few, have all emerged in recent years as important factors for interpreting the Bible. Although the possibilities for how a scholar might engage and apply the social sciences in his or her work are ever expanding, there are a few key areas in which social-scientific means of investigation are particularly helpful for furthering our understanding of Bible-related issues.

7.3 APPLICATIONS OF SOCIAL-SCIENTIFIC CRITICISM

The two social sciences most commonly applied to the study of the Bible are sociology and anthropology, especially the subfield of archaeology,

---

47. Elliott defines this distinction by how explicitly interpreters acknowledge their social-scientific methodology: "Whereas social historians appear to prefer leaving their reading scenarios and models *implicit* so as to appear objective and free of interpretive constraints, social-scientific critics make their theory and models *explicit* so as to allow for assessment and theory confirmation or disconfirmation" (emphasis original; John H. Elliott, "From Social Description to Social-Science Criticism," *BTB* 38 [2008]: 30).

although others have also provided fruitful insights for interpretation. Here we examine three of the broadest issues in biblical studies with a focus on how scholars have used and continue to use social-scientific criticism as a means of understanding the biblical text more deeply. Rather than surveying the vast amount of literature on each topic—the origins of ancient Israel, the social world of ancient Israelite religions, and the social world of early Christianity—we instead offer illustrations of how various social-scientific methods are applied to biblical studies questions, using examples of scholarship that have moved conversations forward within the field in significant ways.

7.3.1 ORIGINS OF ANCIENT ISRAEL

The question of the origins of ancient Israel came to the fore in the mid-1920s, with the publication of Albrecht Alt's essay "The Settlement of the Israelites in Palestine" (first published in German in 1925 as *Die Landnahme der Israeliten in Palästina*).[48] The issue remained a central debate in biblical archaeology until the mid-1990s.[49] In this seventy-year span, various schools of thought offered competing narratives of the process by which ancient Israel came into existence. Scholars argued for a wide variety of theories, such as military conquest, peaceful infiltration, evolution, and peasant revolution, just to name a few of the more popular options that arose during these decades.

In response to the plurality of options presented by scholars working on the issue of the origins of ancient Israel, Norman Gottwald wrote his best-known work, *The Tribes of Yahweh* (1979), a volume that most scholars now consider to be the first major effort to bring the social sciences, primarily sociology, into dialogue with the biblical text. As Gottwald describes the situation, "In the absence of anything that can be firmly known, scholars have grasped at straws and built ingenious theories on the crumbling foundations of possibilities which, while they cannot always be disproved,

---

48. Albrecht Alt, *Die Landnahme der Israeliten in Palästina*, Reformationsprogramm der Universität Leipzig (Leipzig: Druckerei der Werkgemeinschaft, 1925). The essay appeared in English as "The Settlement of the Israelites in Palestine" in a collection of Alt's essays titled *Essays in Old Testament History and Religion*, trans. R. A. Wilson (Oxford: Blackwell, 1966).

49. Avraham Faust, "The Emergence of Israel and Theories of Ethnogenesis," in *The Wiley Blackwell Companion to Ancient Israel*, ed. Susan Niditch (Malden, MA: Wiley-Blackwell, 2016), 155–73, on 155.

have certainly yet to be demonstrated."[50] Drawing primarily on the ideas of Marx, Weber, and Durkheim, Gottwald wrote over seven hundred pages of analysis on the social structures and ideologies evidenced throughout the Hebrew Bible, arguing that the core values and systems operative among those dedicated to Yahweh likely inspired a peasant revolt resulting in the emergence of ancient Israel.

While Gottwald's support of the peasant-revolt model and some of his applications of sociological method have been criticized heavily, his adoption of the critical methods made available through the field of sociology marks a departure from "the encrusted traditions of learning" and theological interpretations that had up until *The Tribes of Yahweh* characterized biblical studies.[51] Gottwald was also the first to use sociology as an explicit element of modern history writing.[52] By illustrating the utility of social-science methods for understanding the social world of ancient Israel, as evidenced in the Hebrew Bible, Gottwald made the case for social-scientific interpretation.

In the mid-1990s, biblical studies witnessed another shift in the question of the origins of ancient Israel, as numerous excavations challenged the notion that those who settled the highlands of Israel in the thirteenth–twelfth centuries BC were indeed Israelite.[53] This shift occurred due to the insights offered by social-scientific criticism, specifically the application of archaeological methods to the study of ancient Israel. As more data became available through excavation, discrepancies emerged between the biblical text and the archaeological record. For example, the borders of these thirteenth–twelfth century settlements are much smaller and more localized than the books of Joshua and Judges describe.

Additionally, excavations in Transjordan—a region mostly outside the boundaries of biblical Israel—yielded material objects fashioned in the same styles that scholars formerly labeled as unique to early Israelites (e.g., four-room houses, collared-rim jars). In challenging both the traditionally accepted boundaries of ancient Israel and the existence of material

---

50. Gottwald, *Tribes of Yahweh*, 5.

51. Gottwald, *Tribes of Yahweh*, 6.

52. Philip R. Davies, *The History of Ancient Israel: A Guide for the Perplexed* (London: Bloomsbury T&T Clark, 2015), 133.

53. Faust, "Emergence of Israel and Theories of Ethnogenesis," 156.

markers that can be used to determine the presence of its people, the question shifted away from *how* Israel became an entity in the Levant to *when* it became a distinct ethnic group known as Israel.[54] These two interrelated questions are still operative in the field of biblical studies and continue to drive scholars from a variety of disciplines.

7.3.2 SOCIAL WORLD OF ANCIENT ISRAELITE RELIGION

Beginning in the 1920s, around the time when archaeology began to blossom as an academic discipline, anthropology as a whole became an increasingly accepted approach to the study of the Bible. While scholars working on the question of the origins of ancient Israel most often draw on sociology and archaeology to produce insight into Israel's society and its collective ideals, those who research the social world of ancient Israelite religion most often draw from the field of anthropology, including the anthropological subfield of archaeology, to further their understanding of the individual systems and ideologies expressed in a given biblical text.

With the first excavation of Ugarit (Tell Ras Shamra in northern Syria) in 1928 and the subsequent translation of the vast archive of Ugaritic and other literature preserved at the site, the ability to understand the social background of ancient Israelite and biblical religions grew exponentially. This was the first time that scholars had any textual or clear iconographic evidence for the worship of local deities mentioned in the Bible, such as Baal and Asherah. Among the most important finds for our understanding of the social background of ancient Israelite religions are epic poems of the gods' adventures, including the famous Baal Epic (i.e., Baal Cycle, Baal Myth); lists of the gods and their roles within the pantheon; and other rare artifacts, including temples, cult statues, and various forms of iconography.

The finds at Ugarit and other archaeological sites excavated throughout the Middle East during the twentieth century fueled an interest in cross-cultural comparison, both between ancient societies and between ancient and modern societies. While most instances of such comparison were (and continue to be) problematic, the field of anthropology offers a few particularly useful examples of how to perform cross-cultural comparison in a fruitful and ethical manner.

---

54. Faust, "Emergence of Israel and Theories of Ethnogenesis," 155.

One classic example of the contributions that anthropology, specifically cultural anthropology, has made to our understanding of the Hebrew Bible is Mary Douglas' *Purity and Danger: An Analysis of Concepts of Pollution and Taboo* (1966). Within *Purity and Danger*, Douglas focuses narrowly on cultural systems of purity, pollution, and taboo, and uses comparison to highlight the underlying concerns that inspire and sustain those systems. Among dozens of case studies from around the globe, Douglas includes the purity system of Leviticus and Numbers.[55]

Douglas' thesis that all systems of purity, pollution, and taboo revolve around deep-seated concerns for orderliness, maintaining natural categories, and eliminating ambiguity illuminates the ways in which the creation theology of Gen 1 informs the entire priestly source to whom scholars attribute the biblical purity system.[56] While this insight is key to understanding the role of the purity system in ancient Israel, Douglas arrived at her analysis through comparative cultural anthropology—not traditional historical-critical methods. Later in her career, Douglas revisited the purity system of Leviticus and Numbers, further developing her ideas and even challenging her earlier assertions numerous times and always through an anthropological lens.[57]

Of course, cultural anthropology is not the only social science that offers great insight into the social world of ancient Israelite religion. In fact, it is often necessary to engage the findings and methods of numerous social sciences in an analysis of the biblical text. Scholars who spend the majority of their careers researching and writing about the social background of Israelite and biblical religions, such as Mark S. Smith, must be able to navigate numerous academic disciplines, including, but not limited to, comparative Semitics, history, archaeology, sociology, religion, and

---

55. Mary Douglas, *Purity and Danger: An Analysis of Concepts of Pollution and Taboo* (London: Routledge, 1966). Douglas discussed the biblical purity system at various places throughout *Purity and Danger* but dedicates an entire chapter to the topic "The Abominations of Leviticus" (42–58).

56. For more on the priestly source in the Pentateuch, see chap. 3 on source criticism, especially §3.1.3 Key Concepts.

57. For example, see Mary Douglas, *In the Wilderness: The Doctrine of Defilement in the Book of Numbers*, 2nd ed. (Oxford: Oxford University Press, 2001); *Leviticus as Literature* (Oxford: Oxford University Press, 1999).

theology; also, they must be able to utilize both traditional historical and social-scientific methods.[58]

7.3.3 SOCIAL WORLD OF EARLY CHRISTIANITY

The social world of early Christianity first emerged as a topic of interest in the 1880s, but scholarship in this area was limited, as the social sciences were still in their infancy and had little to offer biblical scholars in terms of tried-and-tested method. After approximately fifty years, concern over the social environment of early Christianity disappeared from NT studies as scholars turned their attention to other forms of inquiry, such as existential interpretation, redaction criticism, and dialectical theology.[59] For forty years, beginning in the 1930s, few social-scientific interpretations of the NT were published. This dry spell ended in the 1970s, as the social sciences saw a resurgence with new methods, and biblical scholars gradually adopted those methods as viable tools for understanding both ancient texts and their communities.

As previously mentioned, one of the most important social-scientific treatments of the NT to reach publication during this resurgence of social-scientific criticism (1970s–1990s) was *The First Urban Christians*, by Wayne Meeks, published in 1983. Throughout his book, Meeks self-identifies as a "social historian" rather than a social-scientific critic, meaning that he utilizes a variety of tools and data sets borrowed from the social sciences rather than limiting himself to one discipline or theoretical perspective. Meeks calls his application of the social sciences "eclectic" and uses this approach with the understanding that no one method of investigation is capable of addressing all areas of inquiry.[60]

---

58. Smith's best-known volumes include *Gods in Translation: Deities and Cross-Cultural Discourse in the Biblical World* (Grand Rapids: Eerdmans, 2010); *The Origins of Biblical Monotheism: Israel's Polytheistic Background and the Ugaritic Texts* (Oxford: Oxford University Press, 2001); *The Early History of God: Yahweh and the Other Deities in Ancient Israel*, 2nd ed. (Grand Rapids: Eerdmans, 2002). Smith's most recent volume, *Where the Gods Are: Spatial Dimensions of Anthropomorphism in the Bible World* (New Haven, CT: Yale University Press, 2016), brings his historical work into conversation with spatial theory, a relatively new, interdisciplinary branch of the social sciences.

59. Thomas Schmeller, "Sociology and the New Testament," in *Methods of Biblical Interpretation*, ed. John H. Hayes (Nashville: Abingdon, 2004), 290.

60. Meeks, *First Urban Christians*, 6–7.

The one insight from the social sciences that does shape *The First Urban Christians* from start to finish is ethnographer Clifford Geertz's notion that the job of the scholar is to describe culture, which is an inherently interpretive enterprise.[61] Due to the limitations inherent in studying early Christianity, especially as it developed in the latter half of the first century, Meeks holds that it is possible to make suggestions and to redescribe early Christianity in modern terms, but that it is not possible to verify or validate those suggestions. Meeks' eclectic approach enables him to make numerous suggestions about how early Christianity worked and the role that NT texts may have played in shaping early Christian societies.

Due to this newfound appreciation of social-scientific criticism, archaeology of the Graeco-Roman era became an essential topic in the study of the NT.[62] Unlike the archaeology of ancient Israel, which has been central to the study of the Hebrew Bible since the 1920s, Graeco-Roman era archaeology was not brought into conversation with biblical studies until both disciplines began to shift in the 1990s. As the methodologies of both archaeology and NT studies broadened their horizons to include the possibility that one may draw inferences about human thought and action through the study of artifacts and texts, respectively, a rapport was established between these two disciplines.[63] Now, a basic knowledge of the lived experience of ancient Mediterranean communities is considered essential to understanding the NT, even at an introductory level. This is reflected in most publications and university or seminary courses today.

7.4 LIMITATIONS OF SOCIAL-SCIENTIFIC CRITICISM

The degree of familiarity with another culture, whether modern or ancient, that one can achieve is limited by a number of factors, such as language, the element of foreignness, negotiation between insider and outsider understandings, and the sheer amount of time it takes to deeply understand something as complex as a society. These limitations are exponentially more pronounced when it comes to studying the ancient world, mainly

---

61. Meeks, *First Urban Christians*, 5–6.

62. Richard E. DeMaris, "Archaeology and New Testament Interpretation," in *Methods of Biblical Interpretation*, ed. John H. Hayes (Nashville, TN: Abingdon Press, 2004), 9.

63. DeMaris, "Archaeology and New Testament Interpretation," 9–10.

because of our limited resources and the inability to perform fieldwork—to actually observe the participants of ancient societies and to ask questions about their lived experiences and inner worlds. Since there is no society exactly like the ancient Near East and Mediterranean, there will always be a gap in our knowledge.[64]

This is why numerous scholars of the ancient world, including Meeks, are drawn to Geertz's notion of "thick description," which is built on the premise that scholars cannot describe the workings of another culture from that culture's own perspective; what a scholar can do is redescribe that culture using his or her own perspective, thus making the foreign a little more familiar to his or her audience. Some argue that this mode of research and writing is too interpretive, while others argue that, whether scholars like it or not, "thick description" is all we can do. Social-scientific criticism is not designed to prove models or theories as one might in the natural sciences (i.e., the hard sciences), but it does yield interpretations that provide helpful ways of understanding the ancient world and great insight into the biblical texts.[65]

7.5 CONTEMPORARY INFLUENCE

With several decades of social-scientific criticism of the Bible on record, the application of this approach has reached a certain level of maturity and continues to expand in its diversity.[66] Although scholars remain limited by the quantity and quality of data available for understanding the ancient world, social-scientific scholarship continues to expand our understanding of the Bible because new perspectives and questions are brought to that data on a regular basis.[67] In this way, there is a "synergistic relationship between our contemporary reality and the research we do on antiquity. Our reading is nuanced and sometimes changed radically, based on changes in our contemporary world."[68] Of course, additional discoveries of ancient texts and artifacts are extremely helpful in opening new avenues of

---

64. Martin, "Social-Scientific Criticism," 131.

65. Esler, "Social-Scientific Approaches," 339; Martin, "Social-Scientific Criticism," 130–31.

66. Martin, "Social-Scientific Criticism," 138.

67. Martin, "Social-Scientific Criticism," 137.

68. Excerpt from an interview with Andrew Overman, quoted in Martin, "Social-Scientific Criticism," 137.

research and understanding, yet where the text and scholar come together can be just as fruitful, if not more so.

One suggestion that appears frequently in assessments of the role that social-scientific criticism plays in biblical studies is for scholars to integrate the major findings of this approach and to synthesize this material in a way that brings it into conversation with the findings of traditional historical research.[69] With decades of social-scientific scholarship now in publication and more articles, volumes, methods, and perspectives coming out seemingly every day, this is no small feat. However, numerous scholars are slowly but surely undertaking this task of integration and synthesis. By understanding where scholarship is, we can best gauge how to move forward using the tools at our disposal and inventing new ones to accomplish interpretive tasks that have yet to be addressed.

7.6 RESOURCES FOR FURTHER STUDY

Chalcraft, David J., ed. *Social-Scientific Old Testament Criticism*. Sheffield: Sheffield Academic, 1997.

> This book draws together essays originally published in the *Journal for the Study of the Old Testament* that dealt with concepts central to social-scientific investigations, such as identity, social roles and hierarchy, power and leadership roles, gender roles, and religion. Some essays make explicit attempts to apply social-scientific theory and method to an understanding of the subject. The opening essays on theory and methodology provide insightful arguments about the strengths and weaknesses of a social-scientific approach.

Hanson, K. C., and Douglas E. Oakman. *Palestine in the Time of Jesus: Social Structures and Social Conflicts*. Minneapolis: Fortress, 1998.

> This introduction to the social world of first-century Palestine offers a readable and informative overview of the social aspects and institutions of Roman Palestine and the ancient Mediterranean. Hanson and Oakman explore the key topics of social research—kinship, religion, economy, and politics.

---

69. Steinberg, "Social-Scientific Criticism," 278.

Levy, Thomas E., ed. *The Archaeology of Society in the Holy Land*. New York: Facts on File, 1995.

> A collection of thirty-two essays that together provide an overview of the history of Israel and the societies that lived there, from prehistory to the modern era. This volume focuses exclusively on archaeological finds in its analyses of the area's social history.

Malina, Bruce J., and Richard L. Rohrbaugh. *Social Science Commentary on the Synoptic Gospels*. 2nd ed. Minneapolis: Fortress, 2003.

> This commentary is the first of six volumes dedicated to providing social-scientific commentary on the NT, illuminating the first-century cultural background of early Christianity and the relationship of that cultural background to the biblical text. Malina wrote each volume with either Richard Rohrbaugh or John Pilch as coauthors.

Niditch, Susan., ed. *The Wiley Blackwell Companion to Ancient Israel*. Malden, MA: John Wiley, 2016.

> A collection of twenty-eight essays informed by a wide variety of disciplines and methodological perspectives. The book is divided into three sections: (1) Methodology: Questions, Concepts, Approaches, and Tools; (2) Political History; and (3) Themes in Israelite Culture. Many of the essays draw on comparative material and the insights of archaeology or other social sciences in their attempts to explain the world of ancient Israel.

Rohrbaugh, Richard, ed. *The Social Sciences and New Testament Interpretation*. Peabody, MA: Hendrickson, 2003.

> The essays in this collection provide an excellent survey of the main social sciences, many of which are unfamiliar to students and scholars of the Bible. Focusing on the NT, Rohrbaugh provides a basic bibliography and introduction to the application of the social sciences in biblical interpretation. Other essays introduce key social-scientific concepts such as honor/shame, kinship, and hospitality.

Van Seters, John. *The Pentateuch: A Social-Science Commentary*. 2nd ed. London: Bloomsbury T&T Clark, 2015.

> Van Seters' commentary is a guidebook to the modern study of the Pentateuch, tracing the development of historical-critical methods as necessary precursors and companions to social-scientific criticism. He emphasizes the impact of the history of biblical studies on its practice today.

BIBLIOGRAPHY

Adam, A. K. M. *What Is Postmodern Biblical Criticism?* Minneapolis: Fortress, 1995.

Aland, Kurt. *Synopsis of the Four Gospels: Greek-English Edition of the Synopsis Quattuor Evangeliorum.* Stuttgart: German Bible Society, 1993.

Aland, Kurt, and Barbara Aland. *The Text of the New Testament: An Introduction to the Critical Editions and to the Theory and Practice of Modern Textual Criticism.* 2nd ed. Grand Rapids: Eerdmans, 1995.

Allen, Susan Heuck. *Finding the Walls of Troy: Frank Calvert and Heinrich Schliemann at Hisarlík.* Berkeley: University of California Press, 1999.

Alt, Albrecht. *Die Landnahme der Israeliten in Palästina: territorialgeschichtliche Studien.* Reformationsprogramm der Universität Leipzig. Leipzig: Druckerei der Werkgemeinschaft, 1925.

———. *Essays on Old Testament History and Religion.* Translated by R. A. Wilson. Oxford: Blackwell, 1966.

Ansberry, Christopher B., and Christopher M. Hays. "Faithful Criticism and a Critical Faith." In *Evangelical Faith and the Challenge of Historical Criticism,* edited by Christopher M. Hays and Christopher B. Ansberry, 204–22. London: SPCK, 2013.

Aune, David E. "Historical Criticism." In *The Blackwell Companion to the New Testament,* edited by David E. Aune, 101–15. Malden, MA: Wiley-Blackwell, 2010.

Baden, Joel S. *J, E, and the Redaction of the Pentateuch.* Tübingen: Mohr Siebeck, 2009.

Baker, David W. "Source Criticism." In *Dictionary of the Old Testament: Pentateuch*, edited by T. Desmond Alexander and David W. Baker, 798–805. Downers Grove, IL: InterVarsity Press, 2003.

Barker, James W. "Ancient Compositional Practices and the Gospels: A Reassessment." *Journal of Biblical Literature* 135 (2016): 109–21.

Barrett, Stanley R. *The Rebirth of Anthropological Theory*. Toronto: University of Toronto Press, 1984.

Bartlett, Kenneth R. *A Short History of the Italian Renaissance*. Toronto: University of Toronto Press, 2013.

Barton, John. *Reading the Old Testament: Method in Biblical Study*. Rev. and enlarged. Louisville, KY: Westminster John Knox, 1996.

———. *The Nature of Biblical Criticism*. Louisville, KY: Westminster John Knox, 2007.

Barton, Stephen C. "The Communal Dimension of Earliest Christianity: A Critical Survey of the Field." *JTS* 43 (1992): 399–406.

Bateman, Herbert W. IV. *Interpreting the General Letters: An Exegetical Handbook*. Grand Rapids: Kregel Academic, 2013.

Bauckham, Richard. *Jesus and the Eyewitnesses: The Gospels as Eyewitness Testimony*. Grand Rapids: Eerdmans, 2006.

Baum, A. D. "Synoptic Problem." In *Dictionary of Jesus and the Gospels*, 2nd ed., edited by Joel B. Green, Jeannine K. Brown, and Nicholas Perrin, 911–19. Downers Grove, IL: IVP Academic, 2013.

Bendix, Reinhard. *Max Weber: An Intellectual Portrait*. Garden City, NY: Doubleday, 1960.

Bird, Michael F. *The Gospel of the Lord: How the Early Church Wrote the Story of Jesus*. Grand Rapids: Eerdmans, 2014.

Black, David Alan. *New Testament Textual Criticism: A Concise Guide*. Grand Rapids: Baker, 1994.

Black, David Alan, and David S. Dockery, eds. *Interpreting the New Testament: Essays on Methods and Issues*. Nashville: Broadman & Holman, 2001.

Blenkinsopp, Joseph. *The Pentateuch: An Introduction to the First Five Books of the Bible*. New Haven, CT: Yale University Press, 1992.

Bock, Darrell L. "Form Criticism." In *Interpreting the New Testament: Essays on Methods and Issues*, edited by David Alan Black and David S. Dockery, 106–24. Nashville: Broadman & Holman, 2001.

Boynton, Susan, and Diane J. Reilly. *The Practice of the Bible in the Middle Ages: Production, Reception, and Performance in Western Christianity.* New York: Columbia University Press, 2011.

Bright, John. *The Authority of the Old Testament.* London: SCM Press, 1967.

Brown, Francis, Samuel R. Driver, and Charles A. Briggs, eds. *A Hebrew and English Lexicon of the Old Testament, with an Appendix Containing the Biblical Aramaic.* Oxford: Oxford University Press, 1906.

Brown, Jeannine K. *Scripture as Communication: Introducing Biblical Hermeneutics.* Grand Rapids: Baker Academic, 2007.

Brown, Raymond E. *An Introduction to the Gospel of John.* Edited by Francis J. Moloney. New York: Doubleday, 2003.

———. *The Gospel According to John (I–XII).* Anchor Bible 29. Garden City, NY: Doubleday, 1966.

Bultmann, Rudolf. *The History of the Synoptic Tradition.* Translated by John Marsh. New York: Harper & Row, 1963.

———. "The Study of the Synoptic Gospels." In *Form Criticism: Two Essays on New Testament Research,* translated by Frederick C. Grant. New York: Harper & Row, 1962.

Burkett, Delbert. *The Unity or Plurality of Q.* Vol. 2 of *Rethinking the Gospel Sources.* Atlanta: Society of Biblical Literature, 2009.

Buss, Martin J. *Biblical Form Criticism in Its Context.* Sheffield: Sheffield Academic Press, 1999.

Butler, Basil Christopher. *The Originality of St. Matthew: A Critique of the Two-Document Hypothesis.* Cambridge: Cambridge University Press, 1951.

Callaway, Joseph A. "Sir Flinders Petrie, Father of Palestinian Archaeology." *Biblical Archaeology Review* 6, no. 6 (1980): 44–55.

Campbell, Antony F., and Mark A. O'Brien. *Sources of the Pentateuch: Texts, Introductions, Annotations.* Minneapolis: Fortress, 1993.

Campbell, Constantine R. *Basics of Verbal Aspect in Biblical Greek.* Grand Rapids: Zondervan, 2008.

Caragounis, Chrys C. *The Development of Greek and the New Testament: Morphology, Syntax, Phonology, and Textual Transmission.* Grand Rapids: Baker Academic, 2006.

Carlson, Stephen C. "Clement of Alexandria on the 'Order' of the Gospels." *New Testament Studies* 47 (2001): 118–25.

Carson, D. A., and Douglas J. Moo. *An Introduction to the New Testament.* 2nd ed. Grand Rapids: Zondervan, 2005.

Carter, Charles E., and Carol L. Meyers, eds. *Community, Identity, and Ideology: Social Science Approaches to the Hebrew Bible.* Winona Lake, IN: Eisenbrauns, 1996.

Carvalho, Corrine L. *Primer on Biblical Methods.* Winona, MN: Anselm Academic, 2009.

Catchpole, David R. "Source, Form and Redaction Criticism of the New Testament." In *Handbook to Exegesis of the New Testament*, edited by Stanley E. Porter, 167–88. Leiden: Brill, 1997.

———. "Tradition History." In *New Testament Interpretation: Essays on Principles and Methods*, edited by I. Howard Marshall, rev. ed., 165–80. Waynesboro, GA: Paternoster, 1979.

Chalcraft, David J., ed. *Social Scientific Old Testament Criticism.* Sheffield: Sheffield Academic Press, 1997.

Childs, Brevard S. *Myth and Reality in the Old Testament.* London: SCM Press, 1960.

Coats, George W. *Genesis: With an Introduction to Narrative Literature.* Forms of the Old Testament Literature. Grand Rapids: Eerdmans, 1983.

———. *Saga, Legend, Tale, Novella, Fable: Narrative Forms in Old Testament Literature.* Sheffield: JSOT Press, 1989.

Cohen, Mordechai Z. *Three Approaches to Biblical Metaphor: From Abraham Ibn Ezra and Maimonides to David Kimhi.* Leiden: Brill, 2003.

Comte, Auguste. *Auguste Comte and Positivism: The Essential Writings.* Edited by Gertrud Lenzer. New Brunswick, NJ: Transaction Publishers, 1998.

Conzelmann, Hans. *Die Mitte der Zeit: Studien zur Theologie des Lukas.* Tübingen: J. C. B. Mohr, 1954.

Corley, Bruce, Steve Lemke, and Grant Lovejoy, eds. *Biblical Hermeneutics: A Comprehensive Introduction to Interpreting Scripture.* 2nd ed. Nashville: Broadman & Holman, 2002.

Cross, Frank Moore. *Canaanite Myth and Hebrew Epic: Essays in the History of the Religion of Israel.* Cambridge, MA: Harvard University Press, 1973.

Curtius, Georg. *A Grammar of the Greek Language.* Edited by William Smith. New York: Harper & Bros., 1872.

Davids, Peter H. "Authority, Hermeneutics, and Criticism." In *Interpreting the New Testament: Essays on Methods and Issues,* edited by David Alan Black and David S. Dockery, 2–17. Nashville: Broadman & Holman, 2001.

Davies, Philip R. *The History of Ancient Israel: A Guide for the Perplexed.* Guides for the Perplexed. London: Bloomsbury T&T Clark, 2015.

Deissmann, Adolf. *Light from the Ancient East: The New Testament Illustrated by Recently Discovered Texts of the Graeco-Roman World.* Translated by Lionel R. M. Strachan. London: Hodder and Stoughton, 1927.

DeMaris, Richard E. "Archaeology and New Testament Interpretation." In *Methods of Biblical Interpretation,* edited by John H. Hayes, 9–14. Nashville: Abingdon Press, 2004.

Di Vito, Robert A. "Tradition-Historical Criticism." In *To Each Its Own Meaning: An Introduction to Biblical Criticisms and Their Application,* edited by Steven L. McKenzie and Stephen R. Haynes, rev. and expanded, 90–104. Louisville, KY: Westminster John Knox, 1999.

Dibelius, Martin. *From Tradition to Gospel.* Translated by Bertram Lee Woolf. New York: Scribner's Sons, 1965.

Dillmann, August. *Die Bücher Numeri, Deuteronomium und Josua.* Leipzig: S. Hirzel, 1886.

Douglas, Mary. *In the Wilderness: The Doctrine of Defilement in the Book of Numbers.* Oxford: Oxford University Press, 2001.

———. *Leviticus as Literature.* Oxford: Oxford University Press, 1999.

———. *Purity and Danger: An Analysis of Concepts of Pollution and Taboo.* London: Routledge, 1966.

Dozeman, Thomas B., and Konrad Schmid, eds. *A Farewell to the Yahwist?: The Composition of the Pentateuch in Recent European Interpretation.* Atlanta: Society of Biblical Literature, 2006.

Driver, S. R. *An Introduction to the Literature of the Old Testament.* New York: Scribner's Sons, 1914.

Dungan, David Laird. *A History of the Synoptic Problem: The Canon, the Text, the Composition, and the Interpretation of the Gospels*. New Haven: Yale University Press, 1999.

Dunn, James D. G. *Neither Jew nor Greek: A Contested Identity*. Grand Rapids: Eerdmans, 2015.

———. *The Oral Gospel Tradition*. Grand Rapids: Eerdmans, 2013.

———. *A New Perspective on Jesus: What the Quest for the Historical Jesus Missed*. Grand Rapids: Baker Academic, 2005.

———. *Jesus Remembered*. Grand Rapids: Eerdmans, 2003.

Elliott, John H. "From Social Description to Social-Scientific Criticism. The History of a Society of Biblical Literature Section 1973-2005." *Biblical Theology Bulletin* 38, no. 1 (2008): 26-36.

———. *What Is Social-Scientific Criticism?* Edited by Dan O. Via, Jr. Guides to Biblical Scholarship: New Testament Series. Minneapolis: Fortress, 1993.

Engnell, Ivan. *Gamla Testamentet: En Traditionshistorisk Inledning*. Vol. 1. Stockholm: Svenska Kyrkans Diakonistyrelses Bokförlag, 1945.

Erickson, Millard J. *Christian Theology*. 2nd ed. Grand Rapids: Baker Academic, 1998.

Esler, Philip F. *Ancient Israel: The Old Testament in Its Social Context*. Minneapolis: Fortress, 2006.

———. "Social-Scientific Approaches." In *Dictionary of Biblical Criticism and Interpretation*, edited by Stanley E. Porter, 337-40. New York: Routledge, 2007.

Evans, Craig A. "The Two Source Hypothesis." In *The Synoptic Problem: Four Views*, edited by Stanley E. Porter and Bryan R. Dyer, 27-46. Grand Rapids: Baker Academic, 2016.

Evans-Pritchard, E. E. *Social Anthropology*. New York: Free Press, 1951.

Eve, Eric. *Behind the Gospels: Understanding the Oral Tradition*. London: SPCK, 2013.

Farmer, William R. *The Synoptic Problem: A Critical Analysis*. New York: Macmillan, 1964.

Farnell, F. David. "How Views of Inspiration Have Impacted Synoptic Problem Discussions." *The Master's Seminary Journal* 13 (2002): 33-64.

Farrer, A. M. "On Dispensing with Q." In *Studies in the Gospels: Essays in Memory of R. H. Lightfoot*, edited by D. E. Nineham, 55–88. Oxford: Blackwell, 1955.

Faust, Avraham. "The Emergence of Israel and Theories of Ethnogenesis." In *The Wiley Blackwell Companion to Ancient Israel*, edited by Susan Niditch, 155–73. Malden, MA: John Wiley & Sons, 2016.

Fishbane, Michael. *Biblical Interpretation in Ancient Israel*. Oxford: Clarendon, 1985.

Fitzmyer, Joseph A. "Historical Criticism: Its Role in Biblical Interpretation and Church Life." *Theological Studies* 50, no. 2 (1989): 244–59.

Floyd, Michael. *Minor Prophets: Part 2*. Forms of the Old Testament Literature. Grand Rapids: Eerdmans, 2000.

Frazer, James G. *Folk-Lore in the Old Testament: Studies in Comparative Religion, Legend and Law*. London: Macmillan, 1918.

———. *The Golden Bough: A Study in Magic and Religion*. 3rd ed. 12 vols. London: Macmillan, 1915.

Gager, John G. *Kingdom and Community: The Social World of Early Christianity*. Englewood Cliffs, NJ: Prentice-Hall, 1975.

Geisler, Norman L. "Beware of Philosophy: A Warning to Biblical Scholars." *Journal of the Evangelical Theological Society* 42, no. 1 (1999): 3–19.

———. *Introduction/Bible*. Vol. 1 of *Systematic Theology*. Minneapolis: Bethany House, 2002.

Gerstenberger, Erhard S. *Psalms, Part 1: With an Introduction to Cultic Poetry*. Forms of the Old Testament Literature. Grand Rapids: Eerdmans, 1988.

Gesenius, Wilhelm. *Gesenius' Hebrew Grammar*. Edited by E. Kautzsch. Revised and translated by A. E. Cowley. 2nd English ed. Oxford: Clarendon, 1910.

———. *Gesenius' Hebrew-Chaldee Lexicon to the Old Testament Scriptures*. Translated and edited by Samuel Prideaux Tregelles. London: Samuel Bagster and Sons, 1857.

———. *Lexicon Manuale Hebraicum et Chaldaicum in Veteris Testamenti Libros*. Leipzig, 1833.

Gesenius, Wilhelm, and E. Kautzsch. *Gesenius' Hebrew Grammar and the Influence of Gesenius: As Edited and Enlarged by the Late E. Kautzsch.* Piscataway, NJ: Gorgias Press, 2008.

Gilliland, Maegan C. M. "Redaction Criticism, New Testament." In *The Lexham Bible Dictionary.* Edited by John D. Barry et al. Bellingham, WA: Lexham Press, 2016.

Goldsworthy, Graeme. *Gospel-Centered Hermeneutics: Foundations and Principles of Evangelical Biblical Interpretation.* Downers Grove, IL: IVP Academic, 2006.

Goodacre, Mark S. *The Case against Q: Studies in Markan Priority and the Synoptic Problem.* Harrisburg, PA: Trinity Press International, 2002.

———. "The Farrer Hypothesis." In *The Synoptic Problem: Four Views,* edited by Stanley E. Porter and Bryan R. Dyer, 49–58. Grand Rapids: Baker Academic, 2016.

———. "Fatigue in the Synoptics." *New Testament Studies* 44 (1998): 45–58.

———. *The Synoptic Problem: A Way through the Maze.* London: T & T Clark, 2001.

Gottwald, Norman K. *The Tribes of Yahweh: A Sociology of the Religion of Liberated Israel, 1250-1050 B.C.E.* Maryknoll, NY: Orbis Books, 1979.

Goulder, Michael D. *Luke: A New Paradigm.* Sheffield: JSOT Press, 1989.

Greenlee, Jacob Harold. *Introduction to New Testament Textual Criticism.* Rev. ed. Peabody, MA: Hendrickson, 1995.

Gross, Walter. "Is There Really a Compound Nominal Clause in Biblical Hebrew?" In *The Verbless Clause in Biblical Hebrew: Linguistic Approaches,* edited by Cynthia L. Miller, 18–49. Winona Lake, IN: Eisenbrauns, 1999.

Gunkel, Hermann. *Einleitung in Die Psalmen: Die Gattungen Der Religiösen Lyrik Israels.* Completed by Joachim Begrich. Göttingen: Vandenhoeck & Ruprecht, 1933.

———. *Genesis.* Translated by Mark E. Biddle. Macon, GA: Mercer University Press, 1997.

———. *Genesis Übersetzt Und Erklärt.* Göttingen: Vandenhoeck & Ruprecht, 1901.

———. *Introduction to Psalms: The Genres of the Religious Lyric of Israel*. Completed by Joachim Begrich. Translated by James D. Nogalski. Macon, GA: Mercer University Press, 1998.

———. *The Legends of Genesis*. Translated by W. H. Carruth. Chicago: Open Court Publishing, 1901.

———. *The Psalms: A Form-Critical Introduction*. Translated by Thomas M. Horner. Philadelphia: Fortress, 1967.

Habel, Norman C. *Literary Criticism of the Old Testament*. Philadelphia: Fortress, 1971.

Hagner, Donald A. "Interpreting the Gospels: The Landscape and the Quest." *Journal of the Evangelical Theological Society* 24, no. 1 (March 1, 1981): 23–37.

Hallo, William W., ed. *The Context of Scripture*. 3 vols. Leiden: Brill, 1997–2002.

Halpern, Baruch. "Sacred History and Ideology: Chronicles' Thematic Structure: Indications of an Earlier Source." In *The Creation of Sacred Literature: Composition and Redaction of the Biblical Text*, edited by Richard E. Friedman, 35–54. Berkeley: University of California Press, 1981.

Hanson, K. C., and Douglas E. Oakman. *Palestine in the Time of Jesus: Social Structures and Social Conflicts*. Minneapolis: Fortress, 1998.

Haran, Menahem. "The Books of the Chronicles 'of the Kings of Judah' and 'of the Kings of Israel': What Sort of Books Were They?" *Vetus Testamentum* 49, no. 2 (1999): 156–64.

Harris, R. Laird. *Exploring the Basics of the Bible*. Wheaton, IL: Crossway, 2002.

Harris, Robert A. "Medieval Jewish Biblical Exegesis." In *A History of Biblical Interpretation: The Medieval through the Reformation Periods*, edited by Alan J. Hauser and Duane F. Watson, 141–71. Grand Rapids: Eerdmans, 2009.

Hays, Christopher M. "Towards a Faithful Criticism." In *Evangelical Faith and the Challenge of Historical Criticism*, edited by Christopher M. Hays and Christopher B. Ansberry, 1–23. London: SPCK, 2013.

Hays, Christopher M., and Christopher B. Ansberry, eds. *Evangelical Faith and the Challenge of Historical Criticism*. London: SPCK, 2013.

Hemer, Colin J. *The Book of Acts in the Setting of Hellenistic History*. Edited by Conrad H. Gempf. Tübingen: J. C. B. Mohr, 1989. Reprint, Winona Lake, IN: Eisenbrauns, 1990.

Henry, Carl F. H. *God, Revelation, and Authority*. 6 vols. Wheaton, IL: Crossway, 1999.

Herr, Larry G. "W. F. Albright and the History of Pottery in Palestine." *Near Eastern Archaeology* 65, no. 1 (2002): 51–55.

Hirsch, E. D., Jr. *Validity in Interpretation*. New Haven, CT: Yale University Press, 1967.

Hobbes, Thomas. *Leviathan*. London, 1651.

Hofstede, Geert H. *Culture's Consequences: Comparing Values, Behaviors, Institutions, and Organizations across Nations*. 2nd ed. Thousand Oaks, CA: Sage Publications, 2001.

Holmberg, Bengt, ed. *Exploring Early Christian Identity*. Tübingen: Mohr Siebeck, 2008.

Horowitz, Edward. *How the Hebrew Language Grew*. New York: Jewish Educational Committee Press, 1960.

Horrell, David G. "Models and Methods in Social-Scientific Interpretation: A Response to Philip Esler." *JSNT* 78 (2000): 83–105.

———. *Social-Scientific Approaches to New Testament Interpretation*. Edinburgh: T&T Clark, 1999.

Horsley, Richard A., Jonathan A. Draper, and John Miles Foley, eds. *Performing the Gospel: Orality, Memory, and Mark*. Minneapolis: Fortress, 2006.

Johnson, Alan F. "The Historical-Critical Method: Egyptian Gold or Pagan Precipice?" *Journal of the Evangelical Theological Society* 26, no. 1 (1983): 3–15.

Judge, Edwin A. *The Social Pattern of the Christian Groups in the First Century: Some Prolegomena to the Study of New Testament Ideas of Social Obligation*. London: Tyndale Press, 1960.

Kaiser, Walter C., and Moisés Silva. *Introduction to Biblical Hermeneutics: The Search for Meaning*. Rev. and expanded. Grand Rapids: Zondervan, 2007.

Kauppi, Lynn Allan. *Foreign but Familiar Gods: Greco-Romans Read Religion in Acts*. London: T & T Clark, 2006.

Keck, Leander E. "On the Ethos of Early Christianity." *JAAR* 42
    (1974): 435–52.

Keener, Craig S. *Miracles: The Credibility of the New Testament Accounts*. 2
    vols. Grand Rapids: Baker Academic, 2011.

King, Dorothy. *The Elgin Marbles*. London: Hutchinson, 2006.

Klein, William W., Craig L. Blomberg, and Robert L. Hubbard, Jr.
    Introduction to Biblical Interpretation. Nashville: Thomas
    Nelson, 2004.

Kloppenborg, John S. *Excavating Q: The History and Setting of the Sayings
    Gospel*. Minneapolis: Fortress, 2000.

Knierim, Rolf. "Old Testament Form Criticism Reconsidered."
    Interpretation 27, no. 4 (1973): 435–68.

Knierim, Rolf, and George W. Coats. *Numbers*. Forms of the Old
    Testament Literature. Grand Rapids: Eerdmans, 2005.

Knight, Douglas A. *Rediscovering the Traditions of Israel*. 3rd ed. Atlanta:
    Society of Biblical Literature, 2006.

Koch, Klaus. *The Growth of the Biblical Tradition: The Form-Critical Method*.
    Translated by S. M. Cupitt. New York: Scribner's Sons, 1969.

Kraus, Hans-Joachim. *Psalms 1–59: A Continental Commentary*. Translated
    by Hilton C. Oswald. Minneapolis: Fortress, 1993.

Krentz, Edgar. "Historical Criticism and Confessional Commitment."
    Currents in Theology and Mission 15, no. 1 (1988): 128–36.

———. *The Historical-Critical Method*. Philadelphia: Fortress, 1985.

Kugel, James L. "The Bible's Earliest Interpreters." *Prooftexts: A Journal of
    Jewish Literary History* 7 (1987): 269–83.

Lancaster, Irene, and Abraham ben Meïr Ibn Ezra. *Deconstructing
    the Bible: Abraham Ibn Ezra's Introduction to the Torah*. London:
    Routledge, 2003.

Lemmelijn, Bénédicte. "The So-Called 'Priestly' Layer in Exod
    7,14–11,10: 'Source' And/Or/Nor 'Redaction'?" *Revue Biblique* 109
    (2002): 481–511.

Leonard, Jeffery M. "Historical Traditions in Psalm 78." PhD diss.,
    Brandeis University, 2006.

———. "Inner-Biblical Interpretation and Intertextuality." In *Literary
    Approaches to the Bible*, edited by Douglas Mangum and Douglas

Estes. Lexham Methods Series 4. Bellingham, WA: Lexham Press, 2017.

Levin, Christopher. "Das System der zwölf Stämme Israels." In *Congress Volume Paris 1992*, edited by J. A. Emerton, 163–78. Leiden: Brill, 1995.

Levy, Thomas E., ed. *The Archaeology of Society in the Holy Land*. New York: Facts on File, 1995.

Llobera, Josep R. *An Invitation to Anthropology: The Structure, Evolution and Cultural Identity of Human Societies*. New York: Berghahn Books, 2003.

Lohfink, Norbert F. "Was There a Deuteronomistic Movement?" In *Those Elusive Deuteronomists: The Phenomenon of Pan-Deuteronomism*, edited by Linda S. Schearing and Steven L. McKenzie, 36–66. Sheffield: Sheffield Academic Press, 1999.

Lundin, Roger, Clarence Walhout, and Anthony C. Thiselton. *The Promise of Hermeneutics*. Grand Rapids: Eerdmans, 1999.

Maier, Gerhard. *Biblical Hermeneutics*. Translated by Robert W. Yarbrough. Wheaton, IL: Crossway, 1994.

Malina, Bruce J. *The New Testament World: Insights from Cultural Anthropology*. 3rd ed. Louisville, KY: Westminster John Knox, 2001.

Malina, Bruce J., and Richard L. Rohrbaugh. *Social-Science Commentary on the Synoptic Gospels*. 2nd ed. Minneapolis: Fortress, 2003.

Mangum, Douglas, and Douglas Estes, eds. *Literary Approaches to the Bible*. Lexham Methods Series 4. Bellingham, WA: Lexham Press, 2017.

Mangum, Douglas, and Josh Westbury, eds. *Linguistics & Biblical Exegesis*. Lexham Methods Series 2. Bellingham, WA: Lexham Press, 2016.

Martin, Dale. "Social-Scientific Criticism." In *To Each Its Own Meaning: An Introduction to Biblical Criticisms and Their Application*, edited by Steven L. McKenzie and Stephen R. Haynes, rev. and expanded, 125–41. Louisville, KY: Westminster John Knox, 1999.

Marxsen, Willi. *Der Evangelist Markus: Studien zur Redaktionsgeschichte des Evangeliums*. Göttingen: Gütersloh Mohn, 1956.

McKenzie, Steven L. *King David: A Biography*. New York: Oxford University Press, 2000.

———. *The Chronicler's Use of the Deuteronomistic History*. Atlanta, GA: Scholars Press, 1985.

McKenzie, Steven L., and Stephen R. Haynes, eds. *To Each Its Own Meaning: An Introduction to Biblical Criticisms and Their Applications*. Rev. and expanded. Louisville, KY: Westminster John Knox, 1999.

McKnight, Edgar V. *What Is Form Criticism?* Philadelphia: Fortress, 1969.

Meeks, Wayne A. *The First Urban Christians: The Social World of the Apostle Paul*. 2nd ed. New Haven, CT: Yale University Press, 2003.

———. "The Man from Heaven in Johannine Sectarianism." *JBL* 91 (1972): 44–72.

Meier, John P. *Mentor, Message and Miracles*. Vol. 2 of *A Marginal Jew: Rethinking the Historical Jesus*. New York: Doubleday, 1994.

Mesguich, Sophie Kessler. "Early Christian Hebraists." In *Hebrew Bible/Old Testament: The History of Its Interpretation: Volume II: From the Renaissance to the Enlightenment*, edited by Magne Sæbø, 254–75. Göttingen: Vandenhoeck & Ruprecht, 2008.

Metzger, Bruce M. "On the Translation of John i. 1." *Expository Times* 63 (1951–1952): 125–26.

Miller, Edward Frederick. *The Influence of Gesenius on Hebrew Lexicography*. 1927. Reprint, Piscataway, NJ: Gorgias Press, 2009.

Moore-Jumonville, Robert. *The Hermeneutics of Historical Distance: Mapping the Terrain of American Biblical Criticism, 1880–1914*. Lanham, MD: University Press of America, 2002.

Mowinckel, Sigmund. *Psalmenstudien II: Das Thronbesteigungsfest Jahwas Und Der Ursprung Der Eschatologie*. Kristiania: A. W. Brøggers Bogtrykkeri, 1922.

———. *The Psalms in Israel's Worship*. Grand Rapids: Eerdmans, 2004.

Muilenburg, James. "Form Criticism and Beyond." *Journal of Biblical Literature* 88, no. 1 (1969): 1–18.

Nestle, Eberhard, Erwin Nestle, Kurt Aland, Barbara Aland, Johannes Karavidopoulos, Carlo M. Martini, and Bruce M. Metzger, eds. *Novum Testamentum Graece*. 28th rev. ed. Stuttgart: Deutsche Bibelgesellschaft, 2012.

Nicholson, Ernest W. *The Pentateuch in the Twentieth Century: The Legacy of Julius Wellhausen*. Oxford: Clarendon, 1998.

Niditch, Susan. *Oral World and Written Word: Ancient Israelite Literature.*
    Louisville, KY: Westminster John Knox, 1996.

———, ed. *The Wiley Blackwell Companion to Ancient Israel.* Malden, MA:
    John Wiley & Sons, 2016.

Noth, Martin. *A History of Pentateuchal Traditions.* Translated by
    Bernhard W. Anderson. Englewood Cliffs, NJ: Prentice-Hall, 1972.

———. *Das System der zwölf Stämme Israels.* Stuttgart: Kohlhammer, 1930.

———. *The Chronicler's History.* Translated by H. G. M. Williamson.
    Sheffield: JSOT Press, 1987.

———. *The Deuteronomistic History.* 2nd ed. Sheffield: JSOT Press, 1991.

Osborne, Grant R. "Historical Criticism: A Brief Response to Robert
    Thomas's 'Other View.'" *Journal of the Evangelical Theological
    Society* 43, no. 1 (2000): 113–17.

———. "Historical Criticism and the Evangelical." *Journal of the
    Evangelical Theological Society* 42, no. 2 (1999): 193–210.

———. "Round Four : The Redaction Debate Continues." *Journal of the
    Evangelical Theological Society* 28, no. 4 (December 1, 1985): 399–410.

———. *The Hermeneutical Spiral: A Comprehensive Introduction to
    Biblical Interpretation.* 2nd ed. Downers Grove, IL: InterVarsity
    Press, 2006.

Panning, Armin J. "Tischendorf and the History of the Greek New
    Testament Text." *Wisconsin Lutheran Quarterly* 69, no. 1
    (1971): 12–25.

Peabody, David Barrett. "Reading Mark from the Perspectives of
    Different Synoptic Source Hypotheses: Historical, Redactional
    and Theological Implications." In *New Studies in the Synoptic
    Problem: Oxford Conference, April 2008 : Essays in Honour of
    Christopher M. Tuckett,* edited by Paul Foster, Andrew F. Gregory,
    John S. Kloppenborg, and Jozef Verheyden, 159–86. Leuven:
    Peeters, 2011.

———. "The Two Gospel Hypothesis." In *The Synoptic Problem: Four Views,*
    edited by Stanley E. Porter and Bryan R. Dyer, 70–79. Grand
    Rapids: Baker Academic, 2016.

Petersen, David L. *The Prophetic Literature: An Introduction.* Louisville,
    KY: Westminster John Knox, 2002.

Piper, John. "Historical Criticism in the Dock: Recent Developments in Germany." *Journal of the Evangelical Theological Society* 23, no. 4 (1980): 325–34.

Poirier, John C. "Why the Farrer Hypothesis? Why Now?" In *Marcan Priority without Q: Explorations in the Farrer Hypothesis*, edited by John C. Poirier and Jeffrey Peterson, 1–15. London: Bloomsbury, 2015.

Porter, Stanley E. *Handbook to Exegesis of the New Testament*. Leiden: Brill, 1997.

Porter, Stanley E., and Bryan R. Dyer. "What Have We Learned Regarding the Synoptic Problem, and What Do We Still Need to Learn?" In *The Synoptic Problem: Four Views*, edited by Stanley E. Porter and Bryan R. Dyer, 165–78. Grand Rapids: Baker Academic, 2016.

Porter, Stanley E., and Jason C. Robinson. *Hermeneutics: An Introduction to Interpretive Theory*. Grand Rapids: Eerdmans, 2011.

Porter, Stanley E., and David Tombs, eds. *Approaches to New Testament Study*. Sheffield: Sheffield Academic Press, 1995.

Rad, Gerhard von. *The Problem of the Hexateuch and Other Essays*. Translated by E. W. Trueman Dicken. Edinburgh: Oliver & Boyd, 1966.

Rast, Walter E. *Tradition History and the Old Testament*. Philadelphia: Fortress, 1972.

Rendtorff, Rolf. *Das Überlieferungsgeschichtliche Problem Des Pentateuch*. Berlin: Walter de Gruyter, 1977.

———. *The Problem of the Process of Transmission in the Pentateuch*. Translated by John J. Scullion. Sheffield: Sheffield Academic Press, 1990.

Richter, Wolfgang. *Exegese Als Literaturwissenschaft*. Göttingen: Vandenhoeck & Ruprecht, 1971.

Ricœur, Paul. *Interpretation Theory: Discourse and the Surplus of Meaning*. Fort Worth: Texas Christian University Press, 1976.

Riesner, Rainier. "Orality and Memory Hypothesis Response." In *The Synoptic Problem: Four Views*, edited by Stanley E. Porter and Bryan R. Dyer, 157–64. Grand Rapids: Baker Academic, 2016.

———. "The Orality and Memory Hypothesis." In *The Synoptic Problem: Four Views*, edited by Stanley E. Porter and Bryan R. Dyer, 89–111. Grand Rapids: Baker Academic, 2016.

Robertson, A. T. *A Grammar of the Greek New Testament in the Light of Historical Research*. New York: George H. Doran, 1914.

———. *The Minister and His Greek New Testament*. New York: George H. Doran, 1923.

Robinson, James M., Paul Hoffmann, and John S. Kloppenborg, eds. *The Critical Edition of Q: Synopsis Including the Gospels of Matthew and Luke, Mark and Thomas with English, German, and French Translations of Q and Thomas*. Minneapolis: Fortress, 2000.

Rodríguez, Rafael. *Oral Tradition and the New Testament: A Guide for the Perplexed*. London: Bloomsbury, 2014.

Rohrbaugh, Richard L., ed. *The Social Sciences and New Testament Interpretation*. Peabody, MA: Hendrickson, 2003.

Rollston, Christopher A. Review of *Evangelical Faith and the Challenge of Historical Criticism*, edited by Christopher M. Hays and Christopher B. Ansberry. *Review of Biblical Literature*, 2016. http://www.bookreviews.org.

Römer, Thomas, and Albert de Pury. "Deuteronomistic Historiography (DH): History of Research and Debated Issues." In *Israel Constructs Its History: Deuteronomistic Historiography in Recent Research*, edited by Albert de Pury, Thomas Römer, and Jean-Daniel Macchi, 24–141. Sheffield: Sheffield Academic Press, 2000.

Rosenthal, Franz. *A Grammar of Biblical Aramaic: With an Index of Biblical Citations*. 7th ed. Wiesbaden: Harrassowitz, 2006.

Rost, Leonhard. *The Succession to the Throne of David*. Sheffield: Almond, 1982.

Rummel, Erika. *Erasmus as a Translator of the Classics*. Toronto: University of Toronto Press, 1985.

Sæbø, Magne. *On the Way to Canon: Creative Tradition History in the Old Testament*. Sheffield: Sheffield Academic Press, 1998.

———. *Sacharja 9–14: Untersuchungen von Text und Form*. Neukirchen-Vluyn: Neukirchener Verlag, 1969.

Sailhamer, John H. *Introduction to Old Testament Theology: A Canonical Approach*. Grand Rapids: Zondervan, 1999.

Sanday, William, ed. *Studies in the Synoptic Problem, by Members of the University of Oxford.* Oxford: Clarendon, 1911.

Sayce, A. H. *The "Higher Criticism" and the Verdict of the Monuments.* London: SPCK, 1894.

Schmeller, Thomas. "Sociology and the New Testament." In *Methods of Biblical Interpretation*, edited by John H. Hayes, 289–96. Nashville: Abingdon, 2004.

Schmidt, Karl Ludwig. *The Place of the Gospels in the General History of Literature.* Translated by Byron R. McCane. Columbia, SC: University of South Carolina Press, 2002.

Schweitzer, Albert. *The Quest of the Historical Jesus: A Critical Study of Its Progress from Reimarus to Wrede.* Translated by W. Montgomery. 2nd English ed. London: Adam and Charles Black, 1911.

Scroggs, Robin. "The Sociological Interpretation of the New Testament: The Present State of Research." *NTS* 26 (1980): 164–79.

Silva, Moisés, Tremper Longman III, V. Philips Long, Vern S. Poythress, and Richard A. Muller. *Foundations of Contemporary Interpretation: Six Volumes In One.* Grand Rapids: Zondervan, 1996.

Simon, Richard. *Histoire Critique Du Vieux Testament.* Paris, 1678.

Simon, Uriel. "Ibn Ezra between Medievalism and Modernism: The Case of Isaiah xl–lxvi." In *Congress Volume: Salamanca 1983*, edited by J. A. Emerton, 257–71. Leiden: Brill, 1995.

Ska, Jean-Louis. *Introduction to Reading the Pentateuch.* Translated by Pascale Dominique. Winona Lake, IN: Eisenbrauns, 2006.

———. "A Plea on Behalf of the Biblical Redactors." *Studia Theologica* 59 (2005): 4–18.

Smalley, Beryl. *The Study of the Bible in the Middle Ages.* New York: Philosophical Library, 1952.

Smith, Mark S. *The Early History of God: Yahweh and the Other Deities in Ancient Israel.* Grand Rapids: Eerdmans, 2002.

———. *God in Translation: Deities in Cross-Cultural Discourse in the Biblical World.* Grand Rapids: Eerdmans, 2010.

———. *The Origins of Biblical Monotheism: Israel's Polytheistic Background and the Ugaritic Texts.* Oxford: Oxford University Press, 2001.

———. *Where the Gods Are.* New Haven, CT: Yale University Press, 2016.

Smith, William Robertson. *Kinship and Marriage in Early Arabia.*
Cambridge: Cambridge University Press, 1885.
———. *Lectures on the Religion of the Semites: The Fundamental Institutions.*
3rd ed. New York: Macmillan, 1927.
Spinoza, Benedict. *Tractatus Theologico-Politicus.* Amsterdam, 1670.
Stanton, Graham N. "Presuppositions in New Testament Criticism."
Pages 57–70 in *New Testament Interpretation.* Edited by I. Howard
Marshall. Milton Keynes, UK; Waynesboro, GA: Paternoster, 1977.
———. "Q." In *Dictionary of Jesus and the Gospels*, edited by Joel B. Green,
Scot McKnight, and I. Howard Marshall, 644–50. Downers Grove,
IL: InterVarsity Press, 1992.
Stein, Robert H. *Studying the Synoptic Gospels: Origin and Interpretation.*
Grand Rapids: Baker Academic, 2001.
Steinberg, Naomi. "Social-Scientific Criticism." In *Methods of Biblical
Interpretation*, edited by John H. Hayes, 275–80. Nashville:
Abingdon, 2004.
Steiner, Richard C. *A Biblical Translation in the Making: The Evolution
and Impact of Saadia Gaon's Tafsīr.* Cambridge, MA: Harvard
University Press, 2010.
Still, Todd D., and David G. Horrell, eds. *After the First Urban Christians:
The Social-Scientific Study of Pauline Christianity Twenty-Five Years
Later.* London: T & T Clark, 2009.
Streeter, Burnett Hillman. *The Four Gospels: A Study of Origins.* New York:
Macmillan, 1925.
Styler, G. M. "The Priority of Mark." In *The Birth of the New Testament*, by
C. F. D. Moule, 223–32. New York: Harper & Row, 1962.
Sweeney, Marvin A. "Form Criticism." In *To Each Its Own Meaning: An
Introduction to Biblical Criticisms and Their Application*, edited by
Steven L. McKenzie and Stephen R. Haynes, rev. and expanded
ed., 58–89. Louisville, KY: Westminster John Knox, 1999.
———. *Form and Intertextuality in Prophetic and Apocalyptic Literature.*
Tübingen: Mohr Siebeck, 2005.
———. *Isaiah 1-39: With an Introduction to Prophetic Literature.* Forms of
the Old Testament Literature. Grand Rapids: Eerdmans, 1996.
———. *Isaiah 40-66.* Forms of the Old Testament Literature. Grand
Rapids: Eerdmans, 2016.

———. "The Latter Prophets: Isaiah, Jeremiah, Ezekiel." In *The Hebrew Bible Today: An Introduction to Critical Issues*, edited by Steven L. McKenzie and M. Patrick Graham, 69–94. Louisville, KY: Westminster John Knox, 1998.

———. *The Prophetic Literature*. Nashville: Abingdon, 2005.

———. *The Twelve Prophets*. 2 vols. Berit Olam. Collegeville, MN: Liturgical Press, 2000.

———. *Zephaniah: A Commentary*. Minneapolis: Fortress, 2003.

Terry, Milton S. *Biblical Hermeneutics: A Treatise on the Interpretation of the Old and New Testaments*. New York: Phillips & Hunt, 1883.

Theissen, Gerd. *Social Reality and the Early Christians: Theology, Ethics and the World of the New Testament*. Edinburgh: T & T Clark, 1993.

———. *Studien zur Soziologie des Urchristentums*. Tübingen: Mohr, 1979.

Thiselton, Anthony C. *Hermeneutics: An Introduction*. Grand Rapids: Eerdmans, 2009.

Thomas, Robert L. "Current Hermeneutical Trends: Toward Explanation or Obfuscation?" *Journal of the Evangelical Theological Society* 39, no. 2 (1996): 241–56.

———. *Evangelical Hermeneutics: The New versus the Old*. Grand Rapids: Kregel, 2002.

———. "Historical Criticism and the Evangelical: Another View." *Journal of the Evangelical Theological Society* 43, no. 1 (2000): 97–111.

Thomas, Robert L., and F. David Farnell, eds. *The Jesus Crisis: The Inroads of Historical Criticism into Evangelical Scholarship*. Grand Rapids: Kregel, 1998.

Tischendorf, Constantin von, ed. *Novum Testamentum Graece*. Editio octava critica maior. 2 vols. Leipzig: Giesecke & Devrient, 1869.

Tolar, William B. "The Grammatical-Historical Method." In *Biblical Hermeneutics: A Comprehensive Introduction to Interpreting Scripture*, edited by Bruce Corley, Steve W. Lemke, and Grant I. Lovejoy, 21–38. Nashville: Broadman & Holman, 1996.

Toorn, Karel van der. *Scribal Culture and the Making of the Hebrew Bible*. Cambridge, MA: Harvard University Press, 2007.

Torrey, R. A., A. C. Dixon, and Louis Meyer, eds. *The Fundamentals: A Testimony to the Truth*. 4 vols. Los Angeles: Bible Institute of Los Angeles, 1917.

Travis, Stephen H. "Form Criticism." In *New Testament Interpretation: Essays on Principles and Methods,* edited by I. Howard Marshall, rev. ed., 153–62. Waynesboro, GA: Paternoster, 1979.

Tucker, Gene M. *Form Criticism of the Old Testament.* Philadelphia: Fortress, 1971.

Tuckett, Christopher M. "The Current State of the Synoptic Problem." In *New Studies in the Synoptic Problem: Oxford Conference, April 2008: Essays in Honour of Christopher M. Tuckett,* edited by Paul Foster, Andrew F. Gregory, John S. Kloppenborg, and Jozef Verheyden, 9–50. Leuven: Peeters, 2011.

Van Seters, John. *The Edited Bible: The Curious History of The "Editor" in Biblical Criticism.* Winona Lake, IN: Eisenbrauns, 2006.

———. "An Ironic Circle: Wellhausen and the Rise of Redaction Criticism." *Zeitschrift Für Die Alttestamentliche Wissenschaf* 115 (2003): 487–500.

———. "The Pentateuch." In *The Hebrew Bible Today: An Introduction to Critical Issues,* edited by Steven L. McKenzie and M. Patrick Graham, 3–49. Louisville, KY: Westminster John Knox, 1998.

———. *The Pentateuch: A Social-Science Commentary.* 2nd ed. London: Bloomsbury T&T Clark, 2015.

———. "The Redactor in Biblical Studies." *Journal of Northwest Semitic Languages* 29 (2003): 1–19.

———. "The Role of the Scribe in the Making of the Hebrew Bible." *Journal of Ancient Near Eastern Religions* 8 (2008): 99–129.

Wallace, Daniel B. *Greek Grammar Beyond the Basics: An Exegetical Syntax of the New Testament.* Grand Rapids: Zondervan, 1996.

Watson, Francis. *Gospel Writing: A Canonical Perspective.* Grand Rapids: Eerdmans, 2013.

Weber, Max. *Ancient Judaism.* Translated by Hans H. Gerth and Don Martindale. New York: Free Press, 1952.

———. *The Religion of China: Confucianism and Taoism.* Translated by Hans H. Gerth. New York: Free Press, 1951.

———. *The Religion of India: The Sociology of Hinduism and Buddhism.* Translated by Hans H. Gerth and Don Martindale. New York: Free Press, 1958.

———. *The Sociology of Religion.* Translated by Ephraim Fischoff. Boston: Beacon, 1963.

———. *The Theory of Social and Economic Organization.* Translated by A.M. Henderson and Talcott Parsons. New York: Free Press, 1964.

Weinfeld, Moshe. *The Place of the Law in the Religion of Ancient Israel.* Leiden: Brill, 2004.

Wellhausen, Julius. *Prolegomena to the History of Israel.* Translated by J. Sutherland Black and Allan Menzies. Edinburgh: Adam & Charles Black, 1885.

———. *Prolegomena zur Geschichte Israels.* Berlin: G. Reimer, 1883.

Westcott, Brooke Foss, and Fenton John Anthony Hort, eds. *The New Testament in the Original Greek.* Cambridge: Macmillan, 1881.

Westermann, Claus. *Basic Forms of Prophetic Speech.* Translated by Hugh C. White. Louisville, KY: Westminster John Knox, 1991.

———. *Genesis 12–36: A Continental Commentary.* Translated by John J. Scullion. Minneapolis: Fortress, 1995.

Whybray, R. N. *The Making of the Pentateuch: A Methodological Study.* Sheffield: Sheffield Academic Press, 1987.

Widder, Wendy. *Textual Criticism of the Bible.* Edited by Douglas Mangum. Lexham Methods Series 1. Bellingham, WA: Lexham Press, 2013.

Williamson, H. G. M. "Isaiah: Book of." In *Dictionary of the Old Testament: Prophets*, edited by Mark J. Boda and J. Gordon McConville, 364–78. Downers Grove, IL: InterVarsity Press, 2012.

———. *The Book Called Isaiah: Deutero-Isaiah's Role in Composition and Redaction.* Oxford: Clarendon Press, 1994.

Wilson, Robert R. *Sociological Approaches to the Old Testament.* Philadelphia: Fortress, 1984.

Yarbrough, Robert W. "Should Evangelicals Embrace Historical Criticism? The Hays-Ansberry Proposal." *Themelios* 39, no. 1 (2014): 37–52.

Young, Edward J. *An Introduction to the Old Testament.* Grand Rapids: Eerdmans, 1977.

SUBJECT INDEX

SCRIPTURE INDEX

Old Testament

Apocrypha